Direct Democracy
and International Politics

DIRECT DEMOCRACY AND INTERNATIONAL POLITICS

Deciding International Issues Through Referendums

John T. Rourke
Richard P. Hiskes
Cyrus Ernesto Zirakzadeh

Lynne Rienner Publishers ▪ Boulder & London

Published in the United States of America in 1992 by
Lynne Rienner Publishers, Inc.
1800 30th Street, Boulder, Colorado 80301

and in the United Kingdom by
Lynne Rienner Publishers, Inc.
3 Henrietta Street, Covent Garden, London WC2E 8LU

Library of Congress Cataloging-in-Publication Data
Rourke, John T., 1945-
  Direct democracy and international politics : deciding
international issues through referendums / by John T. Rourke,
Richard P. Hiskes, and Cyrus Ernesto Zirakzadeh.
        p.   cm.
  Includes bibliographical references and index.
  ISBN 1-55587-263-8

  1. Referendum. 2. Democracy. 3. International relations.
4. World Politics—1945-   I. Hiskes, Richard P., 1951- .
II. Zirakzadeh, Cyrus Ernesto, 1951- . III. Title.
JF491.R68   1992
328.2—dc20   92-8773
                                                                CIP

British Cataloguing in Publication Data
A Cataloguing in Publication record for this book
is available from the British Library.

Printed and bound in the United States of America

The paper used in this publication meets the requirements
of the American National Standard for Permanence of
Paper for Printed Library Materials Z39.48-1984.

Contents

1

Democracy and History: The End or New Direction?

Democracy is on the upsurge throughout the world. Both a simple reading of the daily newspapers and scholarly research tell us that authoritarian governments were falling and being replaced by more democratic versions as the 1980s closed and the 1990s began.[1] Not only that, some observers assure us that democracy stands on the threshold of global triumph. Indeed, we are at "the end of history," according to Francis Fukuyama's provocative essay in *The National Interest*.[2] He proposes that "we may be witnessing ... the end of mankind's ideological evolution and the universalization of Western liberal democracy as the final form of human government." In the foreseeable future, he predicts, political evolution will settle on a political system that is "liberal insofar as it recognizes and protects through a system of law man's universal right to freedom, and democratic insofar as it exists only with the consent of the governed."

Fukuyama's discussion is less cavalier than some critics suggest. He concedes, for example, that religious fundamentalism has a resurgent, often powerful appeal and could lead to full or quasi-theocratic political systems, such as Khomeini's Iran, and that persistent nationalism is fertile ground for all sorts of potentially dark political impulses—and Fukuyama does not dismiss the development of new, yet unforeseeable, political movements.

Even with these caveats, Fukuyama's assertion justifiably has evoked considerable discussion and criticism. The new democracies in many countries in Latin America, Africa, and Asia are still in their infancy and thus fragile. As for Europe, conservative critics fault Fukuyama, a Sovietologist, for being too optimistic in assuming the demise of totalitarian Communism as a political system under the impact of Gorbachev's glasnost and perestroika rhetoric and the democratic rumblings of Tiananmen Square. The failure of the 1991 coup attempt by Communist traditionalists, then the atomization of the USSR itself into fifteen independent countries seemingly proved the conservative critics wrong, but there are new predictions that Soviet communist totalitarianism will be replaced by Russian chauvinist authoritarianism and similarly repressive regimes in some of the other erstwhile Soviet republics. It is ironic that while the plotters did not succeed in replacing Mikhail Gorbachev with themselves,

1

they did (unwittingly) help to replace him with Boris Yeltsin. The Russian president is certainly charismatic and has preached democratic reform, but he has also sometimes been erratic, and as his strength has grown his governance of Russia has not always fully met democratic standards.

From the other end of the spectrum, some of Fukuyama's liberal critics doubt that democracy, which has been unable to cure societies of poverty, drugs, racism, and other social ills, can confidently be described as the wave of the future. Other liberal critics argue that democratic theory is too state-oriented and is not likely to result in a truly liberal world regime. What is needed, they suggest, is a globalization of democratic thinking that will promote substantive, egalitarian democracy as well as procedural democracy in a global context.[3]

There is another line of criticism, important to this work, that looks to the evolution of democracy rather than to the competition of democracy with other political systems or to the test of whether it betters social conditions. Fukuyama takes the view that the principles and practice of democracy have not changed significantly in nearly two centuries, that "the present world seems to confirm that the fundamental principles of sociopolitical organization have not advanced terribly far since 1806."[4]

We are skeptical that democracy's need to compete with other political ideologies is over. More important for this study, we do not even believe that democracy's own internal dialectical evolution has achieved its ultimate form of being. The liberal democracies that Fukuyama argues are the epitome of political development are all republics, representative democracies. Are such republican systems the "end of democratic history?" The answer may well be no.

Whether or not Fukuyama is correct in the long run, the political changes that sparked his essay have also urged many other scholars to examine the relationship between peace and democracy. Questions about the coming of democracy and its policy impacts have indeed occupied entire issues of some leading academic journals in recent years.[5] It is also important to note that the debate over the future of democracy in the world is not simply an abstract issue to challenge intellectuals. There is a strong argument that democracy is an agent for peace. This contention has, of course, been pondered by political philosophers for centuries. In 1795, Immanuel Kant argued in *Perpetual Peace* that the spread of democracy would change the world by eliminating war, because "if the consent of the citizens is required in order to decide that war should be declared . . . , nothing is more natural than [that] they would be very cautious in commencing such a poor game, decreeing for themselves all the calamities of war."

Some scholars have reached the Kantian conclusion that democracies are more peaceful than authoritarian political systems.[6] Most others have been more cautious. There is evidence, for example, that overall democracies and authoritarian systems are equally likely to be at war.[7] But what is truly enticing is the finding of several recent studies that democracies are both more likely to align themselves and less likely to go to war with each other because of similar political cultures and that in democracies popular pressure does seem to restrain bellicose leaders at least some.[8] Also, the long-standing and prevailing view among political scientists that the public is largely inert, ignorant, and impotent in foreign policy matters has undergone significant revision. The quality of mass involvement in such issues will be a major topic here, but suffice it to say that numerous recent studies have painted a much more optimistic picture of public interest and input in foreign and defense policymaking.[9]

If there is validity, as there seems to be, in the correlation between democracy and peaceful state behavior, then the spread of democracy makes it arguable that the expansion of popular government will bring greater freedom from the oppression of international war as well as from oppression by domestic regimes. It is also plausible that strengthening the role of citizens in their country's decisionmaking will further increase the restraints on leaders that some studies have found. Popular participation can be enhanced through a variety of techniques.

Although generally neglected in scholarship and even less present in the popular mind, there is a slow evolution of direct democracy techniques. These involve a process whereby voters, not representatives, directly decide whether or not to adopt specific statutory or constitutional proposals. There are several types of direct democracy procedures, and they will be addressed presently. The point here is that they are not only becoming more common but are also a possible evolutionary direction for human governance. It would be rash to suggest that representative government as the current, basic democratic form is threatened. But it would be equally inappropriate to ignore the growth of direct democracy as a method of democratic decisionmaking.

The growth of direct democracy is evident in Figure 1.1, which looks solely at national referendums. There are thousands of additional subnational referendums each year. Two trends can be particularly noted in Figure 1.1. One is basic growth. The first national referendums in the post-Greco-Roman world occurred about 500 years ago. They were rarities, however, and even during the nineteenth century, national referendums were held at an annual rate of less than one (0.74). The global spread of representative democracy in the twentieth century, either in practice or as a caricatured standard of legitimacy, was accompanied by a collateral growth of direct democracy. During the century's first decade, referendums were held at an annual rate of 1.9; by mid-century (the 1950s), the frequency stood at 8.1; and in the 1980s (through 1986), an average of 16.8 national referendums were held each year.

Fig. 1.1 Average Annual Referendums, 1800-1986

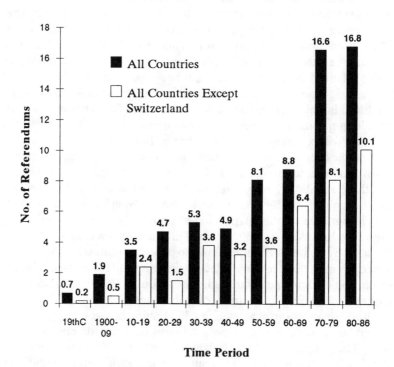

This figure is based on data from David Butler and Austin Ranney, eds., *Referendums: A Comparative Study of Practice and Theory* (Washington, D.C.: American Enterprise Institute, 1978) and John Austin, David Butler, and Austin Ranney, "Referendums, 1978–1986," *Electoral Studies* 6/2 (1987): 139–142.

The second notable phenomenon is the geographic spread of direct democracy. The Swiss pioneered national direct democracy, and during the eighteenth century, 74 percent of the world's seventy-four national referendums occurred in Switzerland. By the mid-twentieth century, however, Switzerland's share had dropped to 56 percent of eighty-one national referendums, and it further ebbed to 40 percent of 118 national referendums from 1980 through 1986.

This spread of direct democracy initially occurred in Europe and areas dominated by European immigrants, but in more recent years, referendums have also become more common in Third World countries. As Figure 1.2 shows, the average annual referendum rate in the Third World has increased from a mere 0.1 during 1900–1909, to 2.8 at mid-century, to 4.3 from 1980 through 1986. This is certainly no tidal wave, but it does indicate a steady, if slow, flood tide.

Fig. 1.2 Average Annual 1st & 3rd World Referendums, 1800-1986

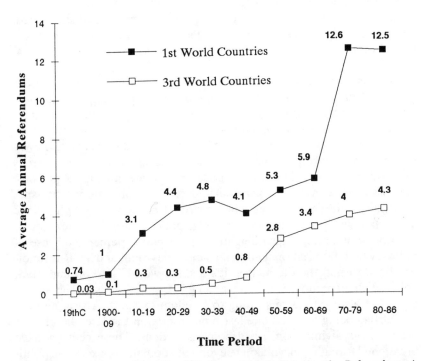

This figure is based on data from David Butler and Austin Ranney, eds., *Referendums: A Comparative Study of Practice and Theory* (Washington, D.C.: American Enterprise Institute, 1978) and John Austin, David Butler, and Austin Ranney, "Referendums, 1978–1986," *Electoral Studies* 6/2 (1987): 139–142.

The increase in the national referendum rate from less than one a year in the nineteenth century to a point where, by 1980-1986, an average 1.4 national referendums were being held each month, persuades us that direct democratic decisionmaking warrants further research.

This study addresses direct democracy with a particular focus on its use to decide issues related to international relations.[10] There are several reasons to believe that the use of direct democracy in general and the use of direct democracy to decide international issues in particular may grow. Two of these reasons are domestically focused: the general spread of democratic systems; and the persistent, and in some cases growing, distrust of government by its citizens. These may augur greater demand for national referendums, particularly as citizens become accustomed to the process, see it used in other countries, and/or participate in it at subnational levels in their own countries. Numerous studies in the United States, for example, have documented the upsurge in the incidence of direct democracy there. Furthermore, U.S. opinion surveys over the last decade or so indicate that, depending on timing and how the question is worded, between 54 and 69 percent of respondents with an opinion favor using referendums or some other form of direct democracy at the national level.[11]

Changes in the world political environment will also enhance the growth of direct democracy decisionmaking. Burgeoning international interdependence is blurring the lines between foreign affairs—the traditional preserve of the leadership—and domestic affairs, in which self-interested groups and citizens are more interested and more active. Fewer issues are now purely *inter*national or do*mestic*, as such; instead, there is a growing number of "intermestic" issues. People are more apt to perceive these issues in terms of their personal impact. Therefore, intermestic issues are, like their domestic cousins, more often subject to pluralistic decisionmaking processes than are foreign policy decisions.[12] The communications revolution is also heightening the public perceptual sense of intimacy with international affairs. Radio, television, and VCR technology have turned the old adage "it's a small world" into an important political phenomenon. Students standing in front of tanks in Tiananmen Square, Nelson Mandela striding to freedom in South Africa, and the Soviet flag being lowered one last time from atop the Kremlin all now occur in our living rooms, bedrooms, and dens. These changes have broadened foreign policymaking beyond the domains of executive political leadership and the bureaucracy to include increased pluralistic participation by the mass, interest groups, and legislatures. This, in turn, will promote a concomitant rise of direct democracy decisionmaking on international issues.

Before outlining our approach to this study, it would be wise to define several key terms. These include *national referendums, international issue,* and *referendums*.

We use *national referendums* in a fairly broad sense, including votes by existing countries, votes in what were countries at the time of the vote, and votes in what later did or might have become countries. This third group especially includes votes on political status—mostly independence. It should be noted that this criterion was used to compile the statistics in Figures 1.1 and 1.2, but the study itself will also include subnational referendums on international issues.

International issue is a trickier term. The dividing line between what is an international issue and what is a domestic issue was never precise; increased international interdependence has rendered the distinction even less clear today. Therefore, we will use the term broadly. Some issues, such as Spain's decision to remain in NATO, are obvious. Others are less so, and we include as international-issue referendums those that, immediately or potentially, involved possible sovereignty (or presovereign autonomy) for a dependent territory or the shift of national association for a dependent territory from one country to another; votes that significantly and directly affected a country's military structure, resources, or utilization; and votes on matters involving foreign commerce.

The plural *referendums* merits brief etymological and conceptual discussion. We have chosen to pluralize *referendum* as *referendums* instead of *referenda* because we are persuaded by Butler and Ranney's rationale for preferring *referendums*,[13] by the preference of most dictionaries for that form, and by the (somewhat reluctant) need to bow to modernity.

We use *referendum* to designate all procedures whereby voters directly cast ballots on issues. This includes classic referendums, in which an issue is referred to the voters either after the legislature has voted on it or in lieu of legislative decision. There are also advisory referendums that come before but are not binding on or even prefatory to legislative action. Whatever their exact form, they all rely on the agreement of the government to refer an issue to the voters before popular action is possible. Beyond these, we use *referendums* to include initiatives, an even more direct form of democracy. An initiative is begun by popular action, usually in the form of a petition, to place an issue on the ballot for voter decision. In some cases, the legislature may have an opportunity to adopt the legislation before the popular decision or to place an alternative proposal before the voters. At root, though, the placement of the issue on the ballot comes from the citizenry, not the government. To avoid rather clumsy construction, we will use *referendum* to include all referendums and initiatives, and we further intend to include both starting points (government and citizens) and both outcomes (binding and advisory) in our definition of *referendum*. The various procedural forms receive further attention in Chapter 3 and in the subsequent discussion of specific referendums.

The following discussion of international-issue referendums is both philosophical and empirical. In the first chapter we explore the conceptual relationship between referendums and democratic theory. We ask three fundamental questions relating to democracy, referendums, and international politics. First, is there a necessary connection between the use of referendums and the meaning of democracy? Second, even if there is a good democratic argument for using referendums, do the realities of international politics suggest that referendums might be an inappropriate method of making foreign policy decisions? Third, do the special requirements of diplomacy, such as continuity, expertise, and secrecy, presume that in the relations between states too much democracy is a dangerous thing?

Chapter 3 then surveys the history of direct democracy, with an emphasis on international-issue referendums. Chapter 3 also briefly discusses the technical procedures for initiating and holding referendums. Chapter 4 lays the groundwork for the ensuing study of international-issue referendums. We begin that chapter by building on the work done by David Magleby, Thomas Cronin, and other scholars on direct democracy in the United States and by David Butler and Austin Ranney and by others on general comparative direct democracy. These studies combine with the discussion of democratic theory in Chapter 2 and the historical survey of international-issue referendums in Chapter 3 to provide the basis for a series of questions about the nature of referendums. The resultant questions, in turn, help structure the examination of specific types of international-issue referendums in Chapters 5 through 7 and our conclusions and recommendations in Chapter 8.

Referendums relating to relations between countries and international organizations are the subject of Chapter 5. These include votes by Norway, Great Britain, Ireland, Denmark, and France on the European Economic Community; Spain's decision on NATO membership; and Switzerland's referendum on United Nations membership.

Chapter 6 focuses on independence succession, devolution, and other such issues of national status and territorial jurisdiction. This includes votes in Quebec, Scotland, Wales, and several Spanish regions about their future relations with the countries in which they are located. Several recent national-status referendums in the former Soviet Union and its constituent republics are also discussed.

Chapter 7 examines a series of nonbinding referendums held in U.S. states on the international issues of implementing a nuclear freeze and ending U.S. participation in the war in Vietnam. The study of voter interest and participation in these exercises and their impact provides insights into the role of opinion, especially when electorally expressed, on policy.

Chapter 8 concludes the study. In it we bring together the comparative evidence on the propositions formulated in Chapter 4. We also address the issues of democratic theory raised in Chapter 2, and, last, make some suggestions about the path of future research.

NOTES

1. On the growth of democracy, see Harvey Starr, "Democratic Dominoes," *Journal of Conflict Resolution* 35/2 (June 1991), pp. 356–381.

2. Francis Fukuyama, "The End of History?" *The National Interest* No. 16 (Summer 1989), pp. 3, 5. Along with Fukuyama's essay, *National Interest* printed comments by Allan Bloom, Pierre Hassner, Gertrude Himmilfarb, Irving Kristol, Daniel Patrick Moynihan, and Stephen Stanovich. Other comments can be found

in an editorial, probably by literary editor Leon Wiesteltier, "It's a Small World After All," *New Republic* 3/596–597 (September 18–25, 1989), pp. 7–9; and in Samuel P. Huntington, "No Exit: The Errors of Endism," *National Interest* 17 (Fall 1989), pp. 3–10.

3. Examples include David Held, "Democracy, the Nation-State and the Global System," *Economy and Society* 20/2 (May 1991), pp. 138–172; and Yoshikazu Sakamoto, "Introduction: The Global Context of Democratization," *Alternatives* 16/2 (Spring 1991), pp. 119–128.

4. Fukuyama, "End of History?" p. 15. Fukuyama's choice of 1806 is a reference to Georg W. F. Hegel's contention in *Phenomenology of Mind* (1807) that the dialectic of political ideology came to an end in 1806 when the French defeated the Prussians at Jenna, thereby (Hegel supposed) signaling the triumph of the French Revolution's liberal democratic ideals over the autocratic foundation of the Prussian crown.

5. For example, see the symposium in *Journal of Conflict Resolution* 35/2 (June 1991).

6. For example, R. J. Rummel, "The Politics of Cold Blood," *Society* (November/December 1989), pp. 32–40.

7. Melvin Small and J. David Singer, "The War-Proneness of Democratic Regimes, 1816-1965," *Jerusalem Journal of International Relations* 1 (1976), pp. 50–69.

8. Zeev Maoz and Nasrin Abdolali, "Regime Type and International Conflict, 1816–1976, *Journal of Conflict Resolution* 33/1 (1989), pp. 3–35; Michael Doyle, "Liberalism and World Politics," *American Political Science Review* 80 (1986), pp. 1151–1169; T. Clifton Morgan and Sally Howard Campbell, "Domestic Structure, Decisional Constraints, and War," *Journal of Conflict Resolution* 35/2 (1991), pp. 187–211. Morgan and Campbell find only a small relationship between regime type and bellicosity, but their indicators, while weak, point in that direction.

9. An excellent multinational study that finds public opinion not as unstable as earlier assumed is Bruce M. Russett, *Controlling the Sword* (Cambridge: Harvard University Press, 1990). A study of Denmark can be found in Hans-Henrik Holm, "A Democratic Revolt? Stability and Change in Danish Security Policy 1979–1987," *Cooperation and Conflict* 24 (1989), pp. 179–197; for Finland, see Krister Stålberg, "Public Opinion in Finnish Foreign Policy," *Yearbook of Finnish Foreign Policy*, 1987 (Helsinki: Finnish Political Science Association, 1987), pp. 15-25; and for the United States, Robert T. Shapiro and Benjamin I. Page, "Foreign Policy and the Rational Public," *Journal of Conflict Resolution* 32 (1988), pp. 211–247.

10. Most of the work on direct democracy has concentrated on domestic issues, which are the most common subject of referendums. The most extensive work has been done on the United States, with the work of David Magelby (1984) standing out as a comparative (among states), general study. A recent work by Cronin (1989) adds to this U.S.-focused literature. Less has been done with the international-issue referendums. The majority of studies have examined a particular referendum. Two edited volumes, one by Butler and Ranney (1978), the other by Ranney (1981), pioneered the cross-national study of referendums. Both these works made valuable contributions, but they are generally compendiums

of national experiences, and there is a need to be more systematically comparative.

11. Thomas E. Cronin, *Direct Democracy: The Politics of Initiative, Referendum, and Recall.* (Cambridge: Harvard University Press, 1989), pp. 174–176.

12. Bayless Manning, "The Congress, the Executive, and Intermestic Affairs," *Foreign Affairs* 57 (1979), pp. 308–324.

13. David Butler and Austin Ranney, *Referendums: A Comparative Study of Practice and Theory* (Washington, D.C.: American Enterprise Institute, 1978), p. 4.

2

Referendums and the Theory of Democracy

Democracy is often considered akin to Gertrude Stein's "Rose is a rose is a rose is a rose." But we know that all roses are not alike; nor are all democracies. Democracies differ both politically in terms of the processes they encompass and economically in terms of the notions of distributive justice they embrace. Democracies also vary according to the degree of citizen participation they presume, with "direct" democracies requiring a great deal of input by citizens and indirect democracies relying primarily on the decisions of elected representatives.

These aspects of democracy are explored within democratic theory, a domain that traditionally has not been central to the scholarly discourse about the nature and conduct of international relations. The long-dominant and still powerful realist school of international relations theory discounts the possibility that the type of domestic regime might be an independent variable that affects the conduct of state behavior in the international sphere. As Francis Fukuyama correctly observes, "Realism maintains that the struggle for power among nations is universal in both time and space, and that is only the [polar] shape of the international system . . . that determines the likelihood of war or peace."[1]

The gap between international relations theory and democratic theory is rapidly narrowing, however. The reason for the enhanced interest in democracy among many international relations scholars is, as we noted in Chapter 1, the surge of democratization that has occurred and continues globally. By Fukuyama's count, "there were three democracies in 1790; 13 in 1900, 27 in 1919, and 62" in 1991.[2] What particularly intrigues international relations theorists is the "unrealpolitik" possibility that type of domestic-regime does affect foreign policy. Is it true, as Immanuel Kant believed, that democracies are more peaceful? If so, and if democratization continues, then world politics should become steadily less combative. This topic has been addressed by symposiums in leading international relations publications such as the *Journal of Conflict Resolution* (June 1991). Even more recently, the American Political Science Association's journal *PS* (December 1991) chose the issue of democracy and foreign policy for its "In focus" symposium.

The bulk of the research to date finds that, indeed, democracies and

11

nondemocracies do behave differently. Detailing the growing body of literature on this subject is beyond our needs here, but its general trend is worth noting. R. J. Rummel argues strongly for a connection between democracy and relative pacifism. He contends that "theoretical and empirical research establishes that democratic civil liberties and political rights promote nonviolence and lay a path to a warless world."[3] It must be said that most other scholars are much less categorical and that a great deal of debate continues on why and how often democracies fight.[4] Still, there is a general finding that amongst themselves democracies are less aggressive than are authoritarian governments.[5] Democracies are also more likely to form alliances with one another than they are to ally themselves with nondemocracies.[6]

Even more central to this study is the finding that the *degree* of democracy may be related to relative peaceableness. Rummel, for one, observes that his research leads him to believe that "the more democratic the political system of two states, the less violence between them."[7] Other studies by T. Clifton Morgan and Valerie Schwebach and by T. Clifton Morgan and Sally Howard Campbell tend to confirm Rummel.[8] Morgan and Schwebach consider the degree to which democracies are "constrained," that is, their competitiveness in selecting political leaders and their diversity of decisionmaking structures. The scholars conclude that "constrained democracies seem to be the least war-prone type of state. . . . This can be interpreted as further support for the . . . argument . . . that the 'most democratic' of the democracies are the most peace loving."[9]

These studies serve to bring democratic theory into the mainstream of international relations theorizing, as do other studies that explore such topics as the degree of elite reliance on public opinion when making foreign policy, and differences between elites and masses in their opinions on foreign policy options.[10] Yet these studies do not venture far into the realm of democratic theory. This hesitance is understandable given the purpose of the studies, but it is regrettable nevertheless for two reasons. First, if one wants to argue that degrees of democracy are relevant to international relations because *more* democratic governments act differently than *less* democratic governments, then one must have some idea of what constitutes more or less democracy. Usually these degrees are defined within the context of representative government by asking and answering such questions as "Are elections contested?" or "Is there decisionmaking competition among governmental institutions?"

It may be, however, that a truer measure of degree of democracy has to do with increased citizen participation that is not related to representative institutions. That is, a higher level of democracy is evidenced not merely by higher voter turnout in elections, but in the use of direct democratic procedures to make final decisions. For our purposes, the measure of democracy will be utilization of international-issue referendums. To make use of this measure, we need to spend some time exploring its relevance to the theory of democracy.

The second reason to consider democratic theory rests on its ability to help us reach well-reasoned, normative proposals. It is easy to give lip service to the desirability of democracy, but we need to ask more penetrating questions about the worth of heightened democratic procedures in the making of foreign policy. Doing so puts us in sharp contrast with the realist position that the threatening thicket of world politics is singularly unsuited for popular decisionmaking. If democracy is good *and* the realists are right, then how should we make foreign policy? Should we sacrifice one good (democracy) for another good (foreign policy expediency), or is the reverse choice the better one? What if we find that the direct democratic process is neither better nor worse than the representative democratic process in terms of policy wisdom. Do we accept the status quo because changing it gains no policy advantage? Or do we change the process because we lose no policy advantage by doing so while we gain more democracy? Questions such as these require that we probe democratic theory more deeply, which we will now do.

All definitions of democracy include some notions of popular self-government or control over political elites. In the United States, these ideas exist within the context of representative government, wherein the people supposedly rule by electing those who make and enforce law. This is held to be democracy, but of a particular type—"indirect democracy." Indirect, or representative, democracy dates to the eighteenth-century ideas of John Locke and James Madison, among others, and encompasses within it a fear of excessive popular interference with the process of government. Interference here would be like citizens making their own laws or insisting on the right to ratify or reject legislation passed by their representatives. This type of interference defines what is known as "direct democracy" and its best-known instrument: the citizen referendum. Direct democracy sometimes goes by the name "participatory democracy" to highlight the demands of its nature (and its advocates), and it has a history that dates to the practices of the ancient Greeks and to the arguments of Rousseau. Those who have provided the philosophical arguments for direct democracy have often been considered visionaries, utopians, or the like. They were certainly far-sighted, but they were not woolly dreamers because, as noted earlier, the use of referendum politics has greatly increased in recent decades. Furthermore, referendums are increasingly used to decide international as well as domestic issues. Therefore, in this chapter we will explore the relationship between democracy, referendums, and international politics.

Any such relationship, if indeed one exists, will be complex and not immediately apparent within the vicissitudes of contemporary international relations or democratic theories. The habits of representation in politics and secrecy in international affairs are difficult to break, and doing so will require changes in both political thinking and behavior. Direct democracy requires habits of participation and openness, characteristics not always or automatically assumed pertinent to the practice of foreign or domestic policy in representative governments. Our examination of the connections among democracy, referendums, and international relations will focus on three questions. First, are referendums an essential part of democratic politics due to their requirement of public participation? Second, even if participation in referendums is necessary for democratic politics, do the hard realities of international politics require that we temper any democratic urges for popular decisionmaking? Third, does the traditional baggage of diplomacy, including secrecy, expertise, and an assumption of required continuity amid the flux of democratic politics, presume that decisions must be left to those well trained in the language and history of foreign relations?

DEMOCRACY AND PARTICIPATION

Democracy is easier to define using prepositions than verbs. We say that democracy is distinctive as government "by" and "of" the people, not merely "for" them. But this does not tell us what either democratic citizens or their governments are supposed to "do." Furthermore, in a sense democracy includes what citizens and governments "may not do," in that it restricts actions on the part of both citizens and government as much as it requires them to act. Citizens must respect the freedom and rights of others, and this often presumes restraint. Similarly, governments must not encroach unnecessarily onto the citizen's private realm of individual autonomy and freedom of choice. These are all democratic sentiments in one way or another about what citizens and government must not do, but they tell us little about the actual practice of politics in democratic societies.

Politics is about "doing," but what democratic citizenry should do has been the subject of debate in political theory for 2,000 years. The ancient Greeks determined that democracy meant that all citizens play an active role in the day-to-day affairs of government. Thus, each citizen was available for selection to the Senate (or Boule), as chosen annually by lot. Also, an assembly of all citizens made final decisions on all legislation (based on a quorum of 6,000 for important decisions) and provided citizen judges and juries for criminal trials, such as the one that convicted Socrates of impiety and condemned him to death. This is clearly democracy of a thoroughly direct sort, and it is distinct from the sentiments of Joseph Schumpeter, who defined democratic practice as nothing more than the "competitive struggle for the people's vote."[11]

Schumpeter's idea of democracy as a "method" rather than an "end in itself" clearly specifies the activity of democracy, but for the citizen that activity is limited to voting periodically for individuals who will make policy and law.[12] This is a very restrictive view of the role of participation in a democracy, but one that has more adherents today than the ancient Greek view. One of the reasons for this preference for the Schumpeterian image of democracy is reflected in the opinion of James Madison, who held that

> if men were angels, no government would be necessary.... In framing a government which is to be administered by men over men, the great difficulty lies in this: you must first enable the government to control the governed; and in the next place oblige it to control itself. A dependence on the people is, no doubt, the primary control on the government; but experience has taught mankind the necessity of auxiliary precautions.[13]

Here Madison defends representative democracy as a more stable and workable alternative to monarchy than was the Greek model. But that defense incorporates a suspicion that common citizens are unable to make complex political decisions themselves. Therefore, Madison allows only a restricted realm of political action open to citizens in indirect democracy.

Disagreements about the degree of participation required for democracy fill the pages of journals and books, and this is an important dispute. Widespread use of referendums would increase the opportunities for participation a great deal, thereby at least potentially surpassing the Madisonian and Schumpeterian strictures on citizen action. These disputes raise two issues about democracy and participation. First, what activities count as actual political participation? Second, how much participation should democracy require?

These two questions frequently merge into a question concerning what individuals must do to protect their freedom, a value at the center of all definitions of democracy. Democratic politics by any definition is always about political freedom in some sense. But if not all life's activities can be called political, then democratic freedom may have little to do with how much one participates in political activity. For instance, is one doing political things when at work, at church, in the kitchen, studying for exams, or playing soccer? If not, then political freedom may refer to a small part of one's life. But if everything one does is political in some sense, then democracy and the struggle to protect freedom permeates one's daily life. Similarly, the second issue of democracy and participation also elicits questions about the nature and protection of individual freedom. If one is required to spend a great deal of time in political activity, such as attending meetings, is one's freedom enhanced or lessened? It might be argued that the less participation is required, the more freedom exists from such imposition on one's time. Conversely, it could be said that the more time one spends making political decisions, the freer that person is. This reasoning is based on the Rousseauian assumption that real freedom means obedience to laws that one has made oneself—even if this means one has to be "forced to be free."

Reducing questions about the degree and nature of participation required in democracy to questions about individual freedom may not immediately seem very helpful. Even if democratic theorists who disagree about the need for participation do agree on the priority of liberty in democracy, what good does that do if they disagree on the meaning of liberty? Yet, it does help in light of Sir Isaiah Berlin's famous dichotomy between kinds of liberty, which directly relates to the direct and indirect models of democracy we are discussing and to the degree and kinds of participation the two models embody.

In his essay "Two Concepts of Liberty," Berlin distinguishes between what he calls "negative" and "positive" liberty.[14] This distinction is well known among political theorists, but here we will add to the dichotomy by applying what Berlin says about liberty to participation and kinds of democracy as well. Thus, we will extend the metaphor to include "negative and positive participation" as well as "negative and positive democracy," the latter being roughly equivalent to indirect or representative democracy and direct or participatory democracy.

Berlin characterizes negative liberty as "simply the area within which a man can act unobstructed by others."[15] Negative liberty refers to the relative degree of coercion exercised against the individual. It does not concern the source of coercion as much as simply the amount. Thus, a person is considered free to the extent that the individual is exempt from outside interference when attempting to do or be what he or she wishes. Full negative liberty then would be the total absence of coercion. Negative liberty, as Berlin rightly admits, does not necessarily (or at least logically) presume democratic politics or government. It may turn out for other reasons that the political system that best protects negative liberty is democratic, but this is because of other ideas such as rights, equality, or the definition of what things are political that have come to be affiliated with the idea of pluralism in the defense of the individual. As strictly a provider or protector of negative liberty, no form of government presents itself as a uniquely superior form.

Nor does negative liberty by itself recommend any particular kinds or degree of participation as necessary to protect the negative liberty of the individual. Indeed, some forms of participation may seem, if not actually coercive, at least intrusive and therefore to be avoided. Face-to-face political meetings of the New England town meeting type, for instance, present clear moments of coercion to many participants.[16] Similarly, political advertisements affiliated with either elections or, conceivably, referendums might contain intrusiveness or even deception, and thus participation in them would actually violate the principle of negative liberty. Also, negative liberty places no intrinsic value on increasing the degree of participation. From an individual's standpoint, participation might seem onerous, and therefore an increase in it may be invasive or coercive. Whether an individual is correct in this assumption is, of course, open to question; but negative liberty allows no appeal beyond the individual as the best judge of his or her own interests.

Positive liberty is both a fuller and potentially more dangerous view of liberty, according to Berlin. The focus of positive liberty is the source, rather than the extent, of coercion and "derives from the wish on the part of the individual to be his own master."[17] This aspect of liberty takes as its goal the self-actualization of the individual as an autonomous being to realize his or her full potential. Here it is not enough to avoid external coercion to be truly free; one must take charge of one's life and be truly able to choose goals and values by oneself. The individual, in short, must be rationally self-directed and a full participant in everything that affects individual direction and choice.

The difference between negative and positive freedom is a subtle one, but Berlin realizes that its impact is potentially huge.[18] Since positive liberty, unlike negative liberty, does not assume that the individual is the best judge of his or her own interests, positive liberty opens the door both for democracy with its emphasis on self-government and participation and for authoritarian systems that promise discovery of the true self. Positive liberty also stretches the political realm to include every aspect of life where power is exercised—at work, home, school, church, everywhere. If power is exercised, politics is present. If politics is present, it must be democratic politics, and I must participate in it to ensure that I am part of the decision.

Positive liberty is a democratic notion in a way that negative liberty is not. The former demands activity by the individual as a self-actualizing, rational actor in the political process. In so doing, positive liberty requires participation both to a fuller degree and of a different kind than does negative liberty. More participation is needed to make the individual better educated in the political process and to ensure that he is author of political decisions that affect him. A different kind of participation is also required in that the definition of politics is broadened to include not just governmental activities but all potential sources of coercion over the individual. Thus, participation is for individual development as a whole person, not just for the protection of negative liberty as a citizen defined as voter. Carole Pateman offers a classic presentation of the argument for "positive participation":

> The theory of participatory democracy is built around the central asser-
> tion that individuals and their institutions cannot be considered in isola-

tion from one another. The existence of representative institutions at the national level is not sufficient for democracy; for maximum participation by all the people at that level of socialization, or "social training," for democracy must take place in other spheres in order that the necessary individual attitudes and psychological qualities can be developed. This development takes place through the process of participation itself. The major function of participation in the theory of participatory democracy is therefore an educative one, educative in the very widest sense, including both the psychological aspect and the gaining of practice in democratic skills and procedures.[19]

The strongest arguments in favor of citizen referendums can be made within this theoretical context of positive liberty, participation, and democracy. Several scholars have debated the merits of referendums, and we will look briefly at their reasons for and against. In the last analysis, however, the argument about referendums is essentially about participation and whether or not democracy requires this type of citizen input. Political theorist Benjamin Barber testified before a U.S. congressional subcommittee considering a constitutional amendment allowing the use of a national referendum. Barber held that democracy and referendums are inseparable, contending that

in the end, in fact, the real issue at stake in [this proposed amendment] is whether or not America believes in democracy, and believes it can afford the risks that go with democratic life. All of the objections to it are so many different ways of saying "the people are not to be trusted"—a skepticism which, it is perfectly true, can be traced back to the "realism" and cynical elitism of a significant group of constitutional fathers. But there is really no democratic alternative to such trust: if the American people are not capable of self-government, our democracy will perish— whether or not elites keep them from initiating legislation.[20]

Barber's view of democracy is one that presumes positive liberty and participation. For him this presents a clear argument in favor of referendums.[21] Others argue in favor of referendums on the grounds that they are useful in "checking" government, but this line of reasoning is less important to Barber based on his view that these reasons invoke negative liberty as the standard of democratic freedom. Also, arguments against referendums based on citizen ignorance, laziness, and lack of expertise fail to impress Barber, since the political quality of the citizenry is not really the issue of democracy. Instead, he argues that it is more important to realize that

[even] if Americans sometimes seem unfit to legislate, it may be because they have for so long been passive observers of government. The remedy is not to continue to exclude them from governing, but to provide practical and active forms of civic education that will make them more

fit than they were. Initiative and referendum processes are ideal instruments of civic education; paradoxically, the more truth there is to the charge that the people are not fit to govern, the greater is the need to involve them in government.[22]

For Barber then, powerful arguments for referendums derive from his view of positive liberty as the basis of democracy. He defends referendums as means of participation that educate citizens about how to take control of their own lives and develop as human beings. As such, referendums are part of a larger notion of democracy—"strong" democracy—that encompasses all of individual life and subsumes it under the title *politics*.

Not all democratic theorists agree with Barber's view of democracy or with the arguments for referendums that his view entails. Some of those who disagree with Barber respond that the widespread use of referendums will lessen the power of political parties and interest groups in electoral politics while simultaneously reinforcing the power of special interests in the more important function of agenda setting.[23] Organized groups with money therefore might easily dominate referendums both because of their abilities to organize signature-gathering efforts and their capacity to mount slick advertising campaigns to sway votes.[24]

Other criticisms of referendums include the belief that direct legislation will result in excessively complex and lengthy ballots that will discourage voting, thereby losing all educative effect on voters. Furthermore, referendum opponents often argue that expanding the role of referendums will lead to frivolous legislation or, even worse, to "hate" legislation focusing on hot emotional issues that stir up temporary demands for changes that, if adopted, would violate precious constitutional guarantees. At best, critics charge, such referendums would stimulate eventual judicial determination on the constitutionality of the legislation approved by the vote and thereby violate the populist spirit of both direct and representative models of democracy.[25] Finally, some critics argue that citizens are simply not equipped intellectually to understand the complicated process of legislation or the compromises frequently necessary to complete it.

These are serious challenges to the idea of participatory democracy and its reliance on referendums. They are not, however, necessarily damning criticisms. Though there certainly have been some cases where referendums have been abused and have resulted in badly worded ballot propositions or even bad law when approved, there is also evidence supporting the efficiency and propriety of many referendums. Besides, many of these criticisms apply equally well to legislatures and the traditional process of lawmaking.[26]

To some extent Barber is correct in asserting that behind the case against referendums there lurks an essentially antidemocratic distrust of the public. But we should be careful not to belittle the risks of direct legislation out of a misguided faith in the educative effects of referendums. It is true that in the act of legislation a society is not necessarily seeking the truth but merely the common good or the public interest. In this function, citizens have as legitimate a role as any would-be (and full-time) legislative "expert." It is also at least plausible that increased opportunities for participation in the legislative process would make citizens more civilly aware and virtuous and in some sense freer. But the case for referendums does presume either a different kind of politics or a different kind of citizen than that required for representative, indirect democracy. Politics would no longer be defined merely by elections, and responsible citizens would have to do more than accept the role of passive voters. How easy this transformation would be is difficult to gauge, and on some issues—those of international politics—we must also ask how dangerous.

Arguments for referendums—or, broadly, for direct democracy—are almost never based on international political issues. This is curious, in a way, since in the United States and elsewhere, many referendums have been held to determine issues as diverse as declaring U.S. cities "nuclear-free zones" to Britain's decision to remain in the European Economic Community, or Common Market. Bizarre decisions were not forthcoming, and disaster did not result. On the other hand, even those who favor referendums on domestic issues might make a case for not holding referendums on international issues. These issues are often very complex, involve a variety of different kinds and degrees of expertise, and, as von Clausewitz observed, the possibility of war always hovers somewhere in the background. Furthermore, the classic realist school of international political analysis contends that international politics is based on power, not rights, justice, or other moralistic ideas that motivate everyday citizens. Given these complexities and dangers, the argument goes, it is more reasonable to leave international politics to the experts. This line of reasoning cannot be ignored before we examine, in the following chapters, the possibility of using referendums to resolve issues of foreign policy and international relations.

Therefore, we must confront some special arguments against direct democracy that allegedly arise from the nature of international politics. This nature includes four aspects that do not seem amenable to direct legislation: the requirement of "realism" in useful international relations theory and the accompanying necessities of expertise, secrecy, and continuity in the practice of foreign policy. Of course, some might argue that these are necessary attributes of politics at any level and that therefore direct democracy is always a bad idea. This argument seems extreme, but at the international level it has a certain plausibility—at least traditionally so. Thus, to explore the place of direct democracy in this context is to test the strength of its appeal and the applicability of its transforming politics.

DEMOCRACY AND INTERNATIONAL POLITICS

Only with difficulty can the world of international affairs be compared with the direct democracy advocates' favorite images of a New England town meeting or the deliberations of the Athenian Boule. International politics is not carried out by neighbors in any meaningful sense. It is characterized by a cultural relativism of principle and a heterogeneity of institutions that make agreement difficult on the simplest of matters. International politics incorporates a plethora of languages and speaks its own patois of diplomacy; it carries its own sense of history amid the rewriting of the past by those who survive; and it presumes to practice the political craft behind closed doors in the shadow of war. According to the realist school, international politics is not about rights, justice, freedom, or morality by any but the victor's definitions. To quote some of the first to expound this essence, international politics is the realm of necessity and power, wherein "the strong do what they can and the weak suffer what they must."[27]

So reads the theory of realism as it pertains to international relations. Realism begins with the assumption that domestic politics and international politics are fundamentally different, that unlike citizens in the modern state, nations exist in a Hobbesian state of nature because of the absence of a supreme authority over them. In the words of contemporary theoretician Kenneth Waltz, while domestic politics "is the realm of authority, of administration, and of law, international politics is the realm of power, struggle and accommodation."[28] Realism asserts that, as is the case in Hobbes's state of nature, relations between states are based almost exclusively on considerations of national interest and power, not on issues of morality, because in the absence of supreme authority there exists no consensus on morality's dictates. As noted U.S. diplomat and writer George F. Kennan asks, "If our government should set out to pursue moral purposes in foreign policy, on what would it base itself? Whose outlooks, philosophy, religious concepts would it choose to express?"[29] Similarly, Hans Morganthau delivers the realist catechism: "The purpose of [U.S.] foreign policy is not to bring [moral] enlightenment or happiness to the rest of the world but to take care of the life, liberty and happiness of the American people."[30]

We should see immediately why the doctrine of realism challenges the usage of referendums on international issues. First, realists are apt to conclude that because citizens have a regrettable tendency to moralize about issues, including those of international politics, prudence dictates that foreign policy should be left to the experts. Realism downplays the moralistic aspects of international politics as distracting, or even dangerous to the national interest. Realists are therefore suspicious of referendums, which even their defenders acknowledge could be a tool of emotional hate groups or others seeking to legislate their own moral agenda.[31] And even if the referendum process were altered to prevent such occurrences, the theory of participation that stands behind referendums seems, to the advocates of realism, somehow out of place or "unrealistic" in the realm of foreign affairs.

Referendums and the Theory of International Relations

We cannot evaluate all of the theory of realism here, but two points should be made about how it relates both to democracy and to the "real" world.[32] First, it has been argued that realism is fundamentally antidemocratic, particularly in its most current application in nuclear deterrence theory. Nuclear deterrence is realism in its purest—and most secretive—manifestation. Thus, to show that deterrence theory is flawed due to its antidemocratic stance is to strike at the heart of realism in general. Second, because it ignores the deeply felt moral impulses of real people, as well as the need for greater humanitarian cooperation between states, it can also be argued that realism is fundamentally unrealistic as a guide for action or decisionmaking.

Nuclear deterrence theory is full of ironic acronyms such as MAD (Mutual Assured Destruction) that obscure its place as the centerpiece of contemporary realist thought. Deterrence theory prescribes mutual assured destruction, that is, virtually simultaneous mass incineration, as the primary defense strategy among nuclear superpowers and a main deterrent to war between nuclear-armed states. MAD requires a willingness on the part of one nation utterly to obliterate another, and it presumes that this response would in some sense be acceptable to its citizens. If the strategy is to work, the target nation must *believe* that retaliatory mass annihilation is supported by the other side's citizens. Therefore, at least to a significant degree, public opposition to massive retaliation will decrease this credibility, without which MAD is empty and the strategy flawed. In the United States, the recent nuclear freeze movement, which is examined in Chapter 7, illustrated that MAD is indeed not an acceptable defense posture in the minds of many U.S. citizens. Furthermore, as we will see, the success of that movement was itself a product of forty-five years of U.S. ambivalence about nuclear weapons and the strategies that rely on them.

For this reason, Richard Falk argues that if the threat of MAD is unacceptable to the citizens of a democratic nation such as the United States, then the strategy clearly cannot work and is "unrealistic." MAD is absurd, he contends, because it poses an ethical dilemma that is unresolvable: the threat of nuclear destruction is itself heinous to any rational human being, because it would never be moral to carry it out. Thus, Falk contends, the United States could pursue this strategy only in secrecy, thereby making its fundamental foreign policy one unaccountable to the public. This makes deterrence basically antidemocratic, and also potentially destabilizing in the domestic politics of a democratic society that would not accept such levels of unaccountability in any other policy area. Accepting a destabilizing defense policy is clearly moronic, since the point of defense is stability. Thus, because it negates its own foreign policy goal by contradicting the requirements of domestic policy, MAD is truly mad, or at least not worthy of the name "realist" in a democratic society.[33]

Falk's argument is clever, but perhaps merely so. For as Michael Walzer points out, weapons systems are seldom chosen democratically in the modern state, and when compared to other means of destruction, there is nothing intrinsically undemocratic in nuclear weapons themselves. Thus, as policy, MAD may indeed be undemocratic, but not necessarily unrealistic given the history of defense policies in democratic nations.[34] Walzer suggests that democracies can remain stable domestically while pursuing nuclear deterrence if they have a variety of what he calls "normal" and "abnormal" avenues of political participation. Abnormal avenues include demonstrations, civil disobedience, nonparty social movements, and the like, which can restrain political leaders without threatening the political system as a whole.

Walzer's argument essentially tries to retrieve nuclear deterrence by providing other forms of political restraint on leaders who ultimately must make any nuclear initiation or response decision. These forms of restraint try to provide both democratic and moral controls on foreign policy in order to make it achievable in a democratic society. That is, they are attempts to render foreign policy realistic in democratic political terms. However, an interesting possibility here is that the use of referendums relating to defense strategy (or to those who carry it out) might provide the same "reality check" on deterrence theory and thereby make this hallmark of realist foreign policy truly realistic. Referendums that asked for advisory opinions from the public on the development of new, or the discontinuation of old, weapons systems and strategies would give clear signals to leaders and provide needed legitimacy for eventual policies. At the same time, while referendums might today be considered "abnormal" politics in the area of defense policy, they are certainly less threatening to the political system as a whole than are Walzer's other abnormal measures. If democracies in fact require special measures for the acceptance of defense policy as democratic, moral, and therefore realistic, then perhaps referendums should become part of the realist's strategy.

Referendums and the Practice of International Relations

There seems, then, to be room in the theory of international relations for the argument in favor of referendums. But can the same be said for the actual practice of international politics? Does not the world of foreign affairs require decision by technical experts and discretion by those schooled in the history of policy and the art of silver-tongued communication known as diplomacy? And does not foreign policy require a continuity and constancy unsuitable to the unpredictable nature of popular opinion? These are serious challenges to the case for referendums, and their ready acceptance show us how accustomed we have become to the idea that the world of foreign affairs is a rarified realm where common citizens have little place.

Expertise is required in international affairs both in the formulation of policy and its articulation abroad. This is why, for instance, the State Department plays both an advisory role in the making of foreign policy and a representative one in the provision of diplomats and ambassadors. These are distinct functions, however, and they offer separate arguments against the use of referendums in foreign policymaking. The two also come together, in theory at least, to provide a third aspect of foreign policy—continuity in foreign affairs. A persistent theme of the arguments against referendums is that they open the way for inconsistency and vacillation in policy areas where they are employed to make decisions.[35] The practice of international politics then demands three functions of policymaking that referendums must fulfill if they are to be utilized: formulation, articulation, and continuity.

Two arguments can be made for why the formulation of international affairs policy need not be under the exclusive purview of policy elites. First is the general contention concerning the need for and benefits of increased democratic participation. Democracy under any definition presumes that citizens have some say over decisions that affect their lives in significant ways, and certainly this applies to foreign as well as domestic affairs. It should be remembered that foreign policy and domestic legislation share one essential feature: they are at best approximations of the public interest, not necessarily of revealed truth. Regularly, as numerous diplomatic case studies show us, foreign policy decisions are also driven by a number of factors that have little to do with public interest. These include the likes of a leader's personality quirks, mental and physical health, ego, political ambitions, and personal belief system. Other studies demonstrate that while the public is normally willing to follow the policy advocated by national leaders, sometimes mass and elite opinion differ on issues, sometimes the public disagrees with leadership policy, and sometimes following the public's preference would have been the wiser course. Thus, though the public interest does require some expertise for its articulation, it is a fundamental belief of any democratic theory that citizens should, at some level, always be called upon to render an opinion on what that interest is or who can best serve it. Calling upon the citizens in this way requires trust in their ability to perceive the interests they share in common, but this is no more or less than trust in democracy in general.

There is a second, stronger argument for giving citizens a voice in foreign policy formulation via the referendum process. At least in liberal democracies like the United States, it is a basic political premise that individual freedom demands protecting the right of individuals to make moral decisions. In other words, individual moral autonomy constitutes a basic political goal of liberal democratic theory and politics.[36] Obviously, this means that much of what passes for politics in liberal societies involves decisions about whether issues are primarily moral in nature and thus a matter of private freedom to choose, or primarily political and therefore a matter of public policy. Many domestic policy issues, such as abortion rights and the location of dumps and other types of unwanted public facilities, turn on the question of which is the proper context for decision. In international affairs, such questions as the ethics of intervention or the general morality of war frequently take on, or are invested with, obvious moral overtones. This is not to say that all foreign policy issues are essentially moral in nature and therefore properly in the domain of private decisionmaking by democratic citizens. It does argue, though, that among all political issues those of foreign policy often clearly present moral choices and dilemmas. Thus, from the standpoint of liberal democracy, they present even a stronger argument for citizen input than do many domestic issues, due to the liberal rubric that on issues of morality, there are no experts.

The second function of international politics—that of articulation and representation of national interests abroad, or simply diplomacy—presents more straightforward arguments for referendum use. Viewed cynically, a diplomat "is an honest man who is sent to lie abroad for the good of his country."[37] Viewed charitably, he is "a man of experience, integrity, and intelligence, a man, above all who is not swayed by emotion or prejudice, who is profoundly modest in all his dealings, who is guided only by a sense of public duty, and who understands the perils of cleverness and the virtues of reason, moderation, discretion and tact." Under either view, "mere clerks are not expected to exhibit all these difficult tasks at once."[38]

The argument for using referendums in international affairs requires neither the abolition of the diplomatic corps nor its recruitment of an army of mere clerks from the ranks of citizens. It does require, however, that diplomacy no longer be open to its cynical characterization as lying in the national interest. Using referendums in even an advisory capacity in foreign affairs will certainly make the diplomat's task a more open, less secret one, since representatives from all countries will be able to refer to the vote of citizens in those plebiscites. Also, citizens will be able to judge better if their opinion of the national interest is being represented abroad by their ambassadors. This may indeed tie the hands of diplomats to a degree, but the argument for not doing so, we contend, invokes the cynical view of diplomacy and of public intelligence—a view difficult to defend on democratic grounds.

Finally, the practice of international politics requires some continuity in policy. This seems a troublesome requirement for referendums, since the image of referendum politics is often that of the institutionalization of whim and passing fancy. This image is sometimes deserved, as we see in the next two chapters, since many referendum results have been subsequently reversed or overturned by popular, legislative, or even court decision. Nevertheless, it would be unfair to assume either that referendums are unique among decision procedures in their lack of a sense of history, or that they cannot be designed to place greater emphasis on considerations of continuity. Furthermore, just like policy made by leaders, decisions made by referendums justifiably are changed because of altered circumstances, reordered priorities, or the undesirable outcome of existing policy. Democratic politics in general is messy and tumultuous and frequently has a short attention span. This is true in electoral politics as well, and there is never a guarantee that one administration will carry on the foreign policies of its predecessors. Continuity is a problem then in electoral as well as referendum politics, and the only way to ensure foreign policy continuity is to give all diplomatic power to a permanent, non-elected bureaucracy that would be empowered to appoint its own experts and institute is own decisions. This would surely be an extreme and undemocratic response to the need for continuity, and the fact that it has never been seriously suggested shows that policy continuity ranks lower on the scale of democratic virtues than other political virtues. If one of these virtues is, as we propose, increased citizen participation in the name of positive liberty, then the use of referendums in deciding foreign policy cannot be ruled out.

CONCLUSION

The use of referendums in the practice of international politics will certainly change the way democracies make foreign policy. Mainly it will make the policy process more open to public view and to public action. This carries risks, of course, as every enlargement of the domain of public access invites the dangers of misuse and abuse of power. Particularly in international affairs, democracies have been hesitant to take these risks, and the result has been a policy process shrouded in secrecy. As citizens, we have come to accept and even expect this, as if international politics must by its very nature be populated by shadowy spies and whispering diplomats playing games of hide-and-seek and speaking words that do not mean what they seem.

Democracy deserves better than this so-called "real" world of international affairs. Two thousand years ago the great Athenian leader

Pericles argued that the greatness of democracy lay in its confidence in shouldering the burden of openness. Athens was a city open to the world—its debates on any issue of peace or war were conducted publicly for citizens and visitors to hear. It feared neither new ideas nor strategies from abroad nor the dissemination of its own. And its demise, the historian Thucydides tells us, resulted not from exposing state secrets but from losing the virtue of openness. As Berlin concedes, politics based on positive liberty runs the risk of totalitarianism. But democracy is always a risky proposition, and its only defense is to remain true to its own nature. This is the authenticity of which Pericles spoke and which democracy must still exhibit if it is to be secure. Democracy encompasses in its nature the ideas of openness and empowerment of individuals over the course of their own lives. This nature is not merely the domestic one that stops at the water's edge. Foreign and domestic policies are both presumably the products of one democratic system. If that system is truly democratic, both policies must exhibit the same democratic faith and confidence. It is at least worth exploring, then, the proposition that foreign policy can successfully be made through an open democratic process. Referendums represent a start in the attempt to make international politics more democratic by offering to each citizen a "way in" to this political realm. How well they have functioned in this regard in many countries and how referendums might be further used will be discussed in the following chapters.

NOTES

1. Francis Fukuyama, "Liberal Democracy as a Global Phenomenon," *PS: Political Science and Politics* 34/4 (December 1991), p. 663.
2. Fukuyama, "Liberal Democracy," p. 659.
3. R. J. Rummel, "The Politics of Cold Blood," *Society* (November/December, 1989), p. 40.
4. A balanced, not too convinced, or skeptical review is D. Marc Kilgour, "Domestic Political Structure and War Behavior," *Journal of Conflict Resolution* 35/2 (June 1991), pp. 266–284.
5. Michael Doyle, "Liberalism and World Politics," *American Political Science Review* 80 (1986), pp. 1151–1169; Zeev Moaz and Nasrin Abdulali, "Regime Type and International Conflict, 1816–1976," *Journal of Conflict Resolution* 33/1 (1989), pp. 3–35; Bruce M. Russett, *Controlling the Sword* (Cambridge: Harvard University Press). The realists, of course, have not been silent on this issue. For one article that both disputes Fukuyama's "End of History?" article and the idea of moving toward a democratic, warless world, see Samuel P. Huntington, "No Exit: The Errors of Endism," *National Interest* 17 (Fall 1989), pp. 3–10.
6. Randolph M. Siverson and Juliann Emmons, "Birds of a Feather: Democratic Political Systems and Alliance Choices in the Twentieth Century," *Journal*

of Conflict Resolution 35/2 (June 1991), pp. 285–306.

7. Rummel, "The Politics of Cold Blood," p. 33.

8. T. Clifton Morgan and Valerie L. Schwebach, "Take Two Democracies and Call Me in the Morning: A Prescription for Peace?" paper presented at the American Political Science Association convention, August 1991, Washington, D.C.; T. Clifton Morgan and Sally Howard Campbell, "Domestic Structure, Decisional Constraints, and War: So Why Kant Democracies Fight?" *Journal of Conflict Resolution* 35/2 (June 1991), pp. 187–211.

9. Morgan and Schwebach, "Take Two Democracies," p. 8.

10. There is evidence that the role of public opinion is affected by differing domestic political processes and institutional arrangements in democracies. Thomas Risse-Kappen has examined the interaction of public opinion, domestic structure, and security policy in France, Japan, West Germany, and the United States in "Public Opinion, Domestic Structure, and Security Policy in Liberal Democracies: France, Japan, West Germany, and the United States," paper presented at the International Studies Association convention, April 1990, Washington, D.C. This study was later published as "Public Opinion, Domestic Structure, and Security Policy in Liberal Democracies," *World Politics* 43 (July 1991), pp. 479–512. He argues that "the centralization of the political system and its autonomy from societal forces" (that is, the degree of democracy) within the four democracies "appear to determine whether the public has an impact." In sum, he continues, "the stronger the state institutions and the greater its control of the policy network, the less influential public opinion." This is important because the degree of public opinion input affects policy choice. Leaders and the public do not always have the policy preferences. There is a considerable gap in the United States, for instance, on some issues. These differences are evident in the quadrennial poll done by the Chicago Council on Foreign Relations and analyzed by John Rielly, most recently in his "Public Opinion: The Pulse of the '90s," *Foreign Policy* 82 (1991), pp. 79–96. Rielly found, for instance, that the American public was a good deal less interventionist than its leaders.

11. Joseph Schumpeter, *Capitalism, Socialism, and Democracy* (London: Allen & Unwin, 1943), p. 269.

12. Schumpeter, *Capitalism, Socialism, and Democracy*, p. 241.

13. *The Federalist Papers*, edited by Clinton Rossiter (New York: New American Library, 1951), p. 322.

14. Isaiah Berlin, "Two Concepts of Liberty," in his *Four Essays on Liberty* (London: Oxford University Press, 1969).

15. Berlin, "Two Concepts of Liberty," p. 122.

16. See Jane Mansbridge's discussion of just such meetings in *Beyond Adversary Democracy* (New York: Basic, 1980).

17. Berlin, "Two Concepts of Liberty," p. 131.

18. Some disagree that the difference between negative and positive liberty is real. See Gerald MacCallum, "Negative and Positive Freedom," *Philosophical Review* (July 1967), pp. 312–334.

19. Carole Pateman, *Participation and Democratic Theory* (Cambridge: Cambridge University Press, 1970), p. 42.

20. U.S. Congress, Senate Committee on the Judiciary, *Voter Initiative Constitutional Amendment*, hearings before the Subcommittee on the Constitution on

S.J. Res. 67, 95th Cong., 1st sess. (1977), p. 195.

21. Barber's arguments for referendums are part of a larger description of democratic life he terms "strong democracy," and which encompasses many other participatory measures as well. See Benjamin R. Barber, *Strong Democracy* (Berkeley: University of California Press, 1984), pp. 281–289.

22. U.S. Congress, *Voter Initiative*, p. 195.

23. See David B. Magleby, *Direct Legislation* (Baltimore: Johns Hopkins University Press, 1984), chapters 1 and 2, for a general summary of the arguments for and against referendums.

24. In addition to Magleby's *Direct Legislation* on this point, see the discussion of the use of paid signature-collecting firms in states with referendums, as put forth in Daniel Hays Lowenstein and Robert M. Stern, "The First Amendment and Paid Initiative Petition Circulators," paper presented at the American Political Science Association convention, Atlanta, August 1989.

25. See the testimony of noted participatory democratic theorist Peter Bachrach on these possibilities in U.S. Congress, *Voter Initiative*.

26. On the latter score, see, for instance, Eli M. Noam, "The Efficiency of Direct Democracy," *Journal of Political Economy* 88/4 (1980), pp. 803–809; Harlan Hahn, "Correlates of Public Sentiments About War: Local Referenda on the Vietnam Issue," *American Political Science Review* 64 (1970), pp. 1189–1198.

27. Thucydides, *The History of the Peloponessian War*, edited by John H. Findley (New York: Modern Library, 1951), p. 331. Contemporary realist thinker Robert Gilpin echoes this ancient description of international politics, which, he says, "can still be characterized as it was by Thucydides: the interplay of impersonal forces and great leaders. . . . World politics is still characterized by the struggle of political entities for power, prestige, and wealth in a coalition of global anarchy." *War and Change in World Politics* (New York: Cambridge University Press, 1981), p. 230.

28. Kenneth N. Waltz, *Theory of International Relations* (Reading, Mass.: Addison-Wesley, 1979), p. 113, as quoted in Avner Cohen, "Reflections on Realism in the Nuclear Age," in *Political Realism and International Morality*, edited by Kenneth Kipnis and Diana T. Meyers (Boulder: Westview Press, 1987), p. 221. Waltz is most accurately classified as a "neorealist," but the distinction between neorealism and realism is, for our purposes here, not pivotal, with the exception that neorealists are more prone than realists to consider perceptions and values (and therefore sometimes morality) as a source of international behavior. James E. Dougherty and Robert L. Pfalzgraff, Jr., *Contending Theories of International Relations*, 3d ed. (New York: Harper & Row, 1990), discuss realism (pp. 81–119) and neorealism (pp. 119–123).

29. Unpublished paper delivered at the conference "Morality and Foreign Policy" held in Charlottesville, Virginia, in June 1977, as quoted in Kenneth W. Thompson, "The Ethical Dimensions of Diplomacy," *Review of Politics* 46/3 (July 1984), p. 376.

30. Unpublished paper delivered at the conference "Morality and Foreign Policy" held in Charlottesville, Virginia, June 1977, as quoted in Thompson, "The Ethical Dimensions of Diplomacy," p. 380.

31. See testimony of Barber and Bachrach in U.S. Congress, *Voter Initiative*.

32. For a recent discussion of democratic theory and international realism,

see Alan Gilbert, "Must Global Politics Constrain Democracy? Realism, Regimes, and Democratic Internationalism," *Political Theory* 20/1 (1992), pp. 8–37.

33. Richard Falk, "The Anatomy of Nuclearism," in *Indefensible Weapons*, edited by Robert J. Lifton and Richard Falk (New York: Basic, 1982).

34. Michael Walzer, "Deterrence and Democracy," *New Republic* (July 2, 1984), as discussed in Stephen J. Rosow, "Nuclear Deterrence, State Legitimation, and Liberal Democracy," *Polity* 21/3, (Spring 1989), pp. 346–367.

35. Magleby, *Direct Legislation*, chapter 2.

36. Amy Gutmann, *Democratic Education* (Princeton: Princeton University Press, 1987), pp. 59–63.

37. Attributed to Sir Henry Wotton; quoted in Thompson, "Ethical Dimensions," p. 373.

38. Sir Harold Nicolson, quoted in Thompson, "Ethical Dimensions," p. 374.

3

A Historical
Overview of Referendums

Direct democracy extends far back into political history. Popular voting on public issues occurred in the Greek city-states, and plebiscites were held in Rome. Then, after a lapse of a millennium and a half, the practice reappeared in Europe. The growth of popular voting on issues has grown quite slowly since then, but there is evidence that it, along with general democratic practice, is on the upswing worldwide.

PRE-TWENTIETH-CENTURY REFERENDUMS

Many of the earliest referendums were held to decide questions of foreign relations and defense. The international-issue focus of these pre-twentieth century referendums occurred partly because such issues comprised a large part of the state's legitimate functions before the beginning of popular nationalism and social welfare policy in the late eighteenth century.[1]

As early as 1552, the cities of Metz, Toul, and Verdun decided by unrecorded votes to remain a part of France. There were also several referendums in the 1790s and two in 1860 by which various cities or regions voted to merge into France. Another early example of self-determination occurred in the papal territory of Avignon in 1791. Leaders in the neighboring French department proposed incorporating Avignon, but the Assembly in Paris rejected the plan because there was insufficient evidence about the desires of Avignon's residents. The Assembly sent three commissioners to determine popular sentiment. They conducted a series of "town meetings" in which all males who were twenty-five or older, who were not domestic servants, and who paid at least ten pence in annual taxes were eligible to vote. Of the ninety-eight districts in Avignon, fifty-two voted to join France, nineteen wanted to remain with the pope, and twenty-seven refused to vote at all. Of this third group, seventeen districts reasoned that they had already voted for France once, and, it being harvest time, they could not spare the time to vote again. Based on this crude procedure, and after a spirited debate, the Assembly enacted legislation absorbing Avignon in September 1791.[2]

Italy similarly held a series of votes in the 1860s in which various

31

provinces decided their future national identity. British analyst Philip Goodhart argues that "it is fair to say that the modern state of Italy was built by a series of referendums" and quotes Italian statesman Conte di Cavour's characterization of the Italian "Dukes, Archdukes, and Grand Dukes" as having "been buried under the pile of ballots deposited in the electoral urns."[3]

Foreign issues also have been occasionally subject to popular votes for over five centuries in Switzerland.[4] The first Swiss referendum was held in 1449 when the government of Berne (then an independent Swiss state) asked its citizens to approve a special tax to pay off debts from an earlier war. The government agreed in 1513 not to enter alliances without the consent of the *landsgemeinde* (the canton's active, enfranchised citizens), and in 1531 it further agreed not to go to war prior to obtaining the people's permission by referendum. During the following two and a half centuries, there were seventy-seven similar issues, which, according to Belgian scholar Simon Deploige, were mostly "of a military character—such as the undertaking of an expedition, the conclusion of peace, the making of treaties and alliances, the expediency of prohibiting the enlistment of citizens as mercenaries, [and] the imposition of a war tax."[5] Similar, if less frequent, referendums were held in Zurich as early as 1489. It even appears that in some cases the army constituted itself as a limited and self-interested *landsgemeinde* to decide important military questions. By the early 1600s, the referendum device began to weaken as the various Swiss political units came under control of powerful oligarchies. Swiss democracy and the use of referendums fell victim to tyranny and temporarily disappeared in the 1700s.

Alpine direct democracy had not died, however. The Swiss renewed their use of referendums in the aftermath of the French Revolution, which spread its democratic ideals to Switzerland by dint of both pen and sword. Switzerland's post-Napoleonic restructuring was governed by the Federal Agreement of August 1815, and several cantons used their renewed autonomy to reintroduce referendums. Valais, for instance, decided that among other things, "military capitulations" had to be referred to the voters. By the 1830s, the use of referendums had spread throughout virtually all of the cantons. Soon thereafter, the process of popular initiative also came into use. From this point on, direct democracy persisted, and while its episodic evolution during most of the nineteenth century is beyond the scope of this book, it is appropriate to comment that the practice of holding referendums was well established by the time of the 1874 federal constitution.

The resurgence of direct democracy in Switzerland was marked by forty-one national referendums between 1875 and 1898. Only five of these votes had international implications, and in each case the citizens rejected federal laws adopted by the national legislature. The first of the five referendums occurred in July 1876. In it, 54.2 percent of Swiss voters rejected the government's imposition of a tax on eligible citizens who did not perform military service.[6] Opposition was motivated by several concerns, including resistance to new taxes, the fact that several cantons already had such a tax, and the income-based formula on which the tax was based. In a rarity in the annals of referendums, however, the Federal Assembly persisted, and another, similar law was adopted in June 1878. Surprisingly it was not challenged—an outcome, in the estimate of one analyst, that "was due not so much to the modifications introduced into the original bill as to the indifference of the people who felt that the matter must be settled."[7]

The Swiss could be as reluctant to spend as they were to be taxed. In May 1884, they rejected by a 61.5 margin a special legislative appropriation of 10,000 francs to the Swiss legation in Washington, D.C. Economic considerations also prompted 58.1 percent of the Swiss voters in October 1891 to favor a tariff designed to provide leverage in the renewal of several commercial treaties between Switzerland and its neighbors.

February 1895 again saw the Swiss react against the costs of diplomatic representation. This time, 58.8 percent rejected a federal law that eliminated the possibility of having a referendum to challenge the Federal Council diplomatic appointments and costs associated with maintaining representation abroad. Opposition sprang from two concerns. One was that diplomatic representatives were not popular in Switzerland, where they were regarded as being paid too much for doing too little. This was especially true in cantons that had few relations with foreign lands and that objected to the law on the ground that it would involve additional expense. Democracy was the other concern, and even international-oriented citizens refused to diminish the sphere of referendums.[8]

The fate of several of these votes reflected the Swiss reluctance to grant greater power to the central government, and that sentiment accounted for the rejection of two measures in the middle part of the decade that involved the status of the military. The first, in November 1895, was a compulsory referendum because it involved a constitutional amendment. Except in times of war, control of the army was divided between the cantons and the Federation, and the proposed amendment would have virtually ended cantonal control. Fifty-eight percent of the voters and almost all of the cantons rejected this perceived power grab by the central government. The issue arose again the next year when the Assembly passed a law making military discipline in peace as well as war subject to federal law. This second attempt was rejected even more resoundingly by 81.5 percent of Swiss voters.

The turnout for the international referendums in Switzerland ranged from 44 percent for the February 1895 vote on diplomatic representation to 67.6 percent for the November 1895 constitutional question of military control. As a general rule, the international referendums seemed to spark somewhat less interest than the domestic referendums. Of the eight referendums held during the years 1875 through 1879, the military tax exemption vote (1877) had the second lowest vote total and was 6.8 percent lower than the average referendum turnout during that period. Three other domestic referendums were held on the same day as the 1884 vote on the appropriation for the legation in Washington; of the four, the international referendum had the smallest vote total, although only marginally so. The only international referendum to spark an exceptionally large voter turnout was the constitutional amendment on control of the army. Of eight referendums held from 1894 through 1896, it received both the second largest vote total and 35.5 percent more votes than the average referendum during the period. The second vote on military control also received more votes, in this case 13 percent, than the average referendum during this period. By contrast, the 1895 vote on diplomatic representation received much less attention. Its 11.9 percent below-average-turnout was the worst during the period.

It should also be noted that the outcome of the voting largely depended on the questions' domestic ramifications rather than their international implications. Domestic concerns such as the power of the federal government versus the power of the cantons and the people, costs and taxes, and narrow economic interests were the deciding factors, with Swiss voters regularly rejecting federal laws that seemed to encroach on their sense of popular sovereignty and parochial self-interest.

TWENTIETH-CENTURY
REFERENDUMS IN INDUSTRIALIZED COUNTRIES

The use of referendums has spread during this century, both geographically and in frequency of use. By far the greatest number of referendums have occurred in Europe, North America, Australia, and New Zealand, where, generally speaking, industrial prosperity and democratic practice have existed the longest.

Referendums in Europe

From 1900 through 1986, European countries conducted 365 national referendums, but only a small fraction of these were related to world politics. There were also approximately a dozen international-issue referendums (self-determination, devolution, autonomy) held in provinces, states, regions, or other subnational units. Since 1986, there have been several other international-issue referendums in Europe, involving self-determination issues in Eastern Europe and the former Soviet Union.

In pre–World War II Scandinavia, Iceland voted (92%) in 1918 for union with Denmark, only to reverse itself (100%) in 1944 and opt for independence. Norwegians in 1905 approved (100%) separation from Sweden. The voters in the Aaland Isles also rejected (46%) in 1919 union with Sweden, choosing to stay with Finland. The Danes agreed (64%) to cede the Virgin Islands to the United States in 1916 and also voted (97%) to incorporate North Schleswig into their territory in 1920. At the same time, in a League of Nations plebiscite, the people of that territory approved (75%) their incorporation into Denmark, while the voters of South Schleswig chose (80%) to join Germany. Other League plebiscites during 1920–1921 saw the people of Allenstein (98%), Marienwerder (92%), and Upper Silesia (60%) choose incorporation into Germany rather than Poland. It is worth noting that the national status of regions that opted for or against Germany remained uncontentious during the interwar years, while areas such as Danzig and the Polish corridor and the ethnic German areas of Czechoslovakia, which were refused the referendum option because of the objection of the Poles and Czechs, were subject to revisionist claims by Germany in the late 1930s. Also during 1920–1921, voters in Klagenfurt picked (59%) annexation to Austria rather than Yugoslavia, and those of Sopron preferred (65%) becoming part of Hungary rather than Austria. Somewhat later (1935), the residents of the Saar selected (90%) Germany over France. The people of Luxembourg in 1919 were more favorable to France, choosing (73%) to join it, rather than Belgium, in an economic union. Germans repudiated (95%) war guilt and reparations in 1929, but because of the mere 15 percent turnout, the issue failed to get a majority of the eligible electorate and failed. Germans (99%) and Austrians (100%) agreed to Anschluss in 1938.

Since World War II, the greatest number of national referendums on international issues have been held on relations with the European Economic Community (EEC). In 1972, French voters approved (68%) an expansion of the EEC, and that year Denmark (63%) and Ireland (83%) approved joining the EEC, while Norwegian voters rejected (47%) membership. Three years later, the British electorate voted (67%) to continue membership in the EEC, and in 1986 Danish voters did (56%) the same by approving changes in EEC rules. The self-governing Danish territory of Greenland, however, chose (53%) in 1982 to withdraw from the EEC. Finally, the people of Malta in 1956 approved (77%) integration with Great Britain, then reversed themselves in 1964 and voted by a narrow margin (50.7%) for independence. Another international-issue referendum decided (57%) in 1986 that Spain would remain in NATO.

There were also several referendums involving France and Algeria's relations. In January 1961, simultaneous votes were held in France and Algeria on Algerian self-determination. French voters (75%) and Algerian voters (70%) agreed that Algerians should determine their own future. After negotiations, a new round of referendums was held in 1972, with both French (91%) and Algerian (100%) voters agreeing to the negotiated terms.

Also, at the subnational or territorial level, a 1946 independence movement in the Faroes (islands) failed. A bare 50.1 percent of the vote favored separation from Denmark, but with only a 66.4 percent turnout, the percentage of the total electorate favoring independence was only 33 percent, and the measure was defeated.

Spain had a series of provincial referendums in Andalusia, Basque, Catalonia, and Galacia during 1979-1981, and voters in each favored increased autonomy by at least 77 percent. Voters in Gibraltar chose (100%) in 1963 to maintain the "Rock's" links with Great Britain. In 1973, voters in Northern Ireland also chose (99%) to stay in the United Kingdom, although a widespread Catholic boycott resulted in an only 59 percent turnout and an absolute majority of a narrower 58 percent. Six years later, Wales and Scotland held separate referendums to approve devolution. The proposal garnered only 21 percent of the Welsh vote and was defeated. Scottish voters favored (52%) greater autonomy, but a turnout of only 64 percent meant that only a third of the overall electorate voted for the proposal, which needed an absolute 40 percent to prevail.

The travails of the dying Soviet Union and the profound shifts in Eastern Europe in the late 1980s and early 1990s sparked the most recent round of self-determination referendums on the continent. Yugoslavia was doomed, in the estimate of many, to potential violent disintegration when two of its constituent republics, Croatia and Slovenia, voted by respective margins of 88.2 and 94 percent for sovereignty. The Serbian-dominated central government and army rejected those decisions, and by late 1991 there was bloody fighting between Serbs and Croates.

It is ironic that the Soviet Union was the scene of some of the widest use of referendums. The votes involved the future of the Soviet state and its relations with its constituent republics. Several of these will receive detailed examination in Chapter 6. The Baltic republics of Latvia, Lithuania, and Estonia led the way in February and March 1991 when more than 75 percent of the voters responded yes to referendum questions asking whether they supported independent statehood. The republics of Georgia and the Ukraine followed suit in March, as did Armenia in September, with similarly strong votes for some level of independence or autonomy. The Soviet central government weighed in with its own March 1991 referendum. Soviet president Mikhail Gorbachev attempted to demonstrate popular support for a continuation of the USSR as a unified state in this first and, as it turned out, only nationwide referendum in Soviet history. With nationalist sentiments running high in most republics, the central government cleverly worded the question to read: "Do you consider it necessary to preserve the Union of the Soviet Socialist Republics as a renewed federation of equal, sovereign republics in which human rights and freedoms of a person of any nationality will be fully guaranteed?" Inasmuch as voting against such wording could be construed as favoring the old, oppressive order, the referendum was approved by a large majority of those that voted. The impact was diluted, however, by the fact that six of the republics refused to participate in the vote, and this abstention dropped the referendum majority to 61 percent of all registered voters.[9] Also, the Ukraine submitted two separate questions to its people on the same day relating to greater freedom from Moscow's control, and each received a higher percentage of the vote than did the referendum sponsored by Moscow.[10]

Even given these limits, Gorbachev gained at least temporary relief from centrifugal forces. The turnout was 72.3 percent, rising to about 80 percent if the six abstaining republics are factored out. The overall yes vote was 76.4 percent, which also equates to 61 percent of all registered voters and 56 percent of all Soviet adults. The yes vote in the various republics, ranged from a low of 70.2 percent in the Ukraine and 71.3 percent in Russia to the mid–90 percent range in several of the south-central republics such as the Turkmen SSR.

The erstwhile USSR also held or pondered referendums on other issues. On the same day as the republics were voting on the continuation of the USSR, voters in southern Sakhalin and the Kurile Islands were asked whether the territory should be returned to Japan, from which it had been taken after World War II. Predictably, a scant 11 percent of the Soviets in the area voted yes. Gorbachev proposed in May 1990 to stage a national referendum on his economic reform proposals, although the idea was eventually dropped. Among others, one of the top Kremlin economic planners, Stanislav Shatalin, opposed the idea of a national referendum on economic reform as an attempt by the government to pass the crisis on to the people rather than make a decision. Shatalin also displayed little confidence in the wisdom of the masses, scoffing that "if all progress was subject to a referendum, we would all be still up in the trees throwing coconuts and stones at each other."[11]

The referendum device was also used by the president of the Russian republic, Boris Yeltsin, who maneuvered to improve his bargaining position with Gorbachev by threatening to hold a Russian referendum on the increasing authority that the Soviet parliament was giving to Gorbachev. A final irony of the latter-day use of referendums in the moribund USSR is that a December 2, 1991, referendum in the Ukraine was the death knell of the Soviet Union. Gorbachev had been struggling to preserve the country in a new, decentralized form, but the approximately 90 percent Ukrainian vote for complete independence ended Gorbachev's plan. With only some hyperbole, the republic's new president, Leonid M. Kravchuk, declared that "a new Ukraine has been born. A great historical event has occurred which will not only change the history of the Ukraine, but the history of the world."[12]

There was even a Soviet proposal to hold the first multinational, international-issue referendum. Moscow first reacted to possible German reunification by trying to slow it down, and one gambit was a proposal by Foreign Minister Eduard Shevardnadze that all countries that had gone to war with Nazi Germany should hold national referendums on the issue of German reunification. Not surprisingly, the Germans did not favor the idea. Then West German chancellor Helmut Kohl rejected the international referendum on unification on the grounds that "we don't need a midwife."[13]

Switzerland continued during the twentieth century to be the leading referendum laboratory, holding 243 national referendums, or 67 percent of the European total. The Swiss, appropriately by referendum, reserved the right for themselves to approve or reject treaties signed by their government. A strong majority of 71.4 percent decided in 1921 that all treaties that bound the country for more than fifteen years (or for an unspecified time) would be submitted to referendum if 30,000 citizens or eight cantons demanded a vote. The provision has been little used, however. In 1923, a treaty with France relating to the customs-free zone of Savoy and Gax was rejected. Similarly, a 1975 agreement with the International Development Association (IDA) that would have granted new loans to the IDA was handled as a treaty and was successfully challenged by a slim majority of 51.1 percent of Swiss voters.[14]

Two international-issue referendums in 1977 dealt with the process of ratifying treaties. The Swiss executive (Federal Council) ratifies international treaties but generally only after approval by the Federal Assembly, and prior to 1977 this was not subject to challenge. Under rules established by referendum in 1977, this legislative approval is subject to challenge by petition in limited cases. A popular initiative was proposed allowing all treaties to be challenged by popular initiative, but it failed, receiving only 22 percent of the popular vote and carrying no cantons. Part of the referendum's aim was achieved, however, because the parliament put forth a counterproposal that, by contrast, was adopted, carrying 61 percent of the popular vote and winning a strong majority of the cantons.[15] Under the adopted counterproposal, if a treaty involves becoming a member in a collective security organization, such as the United Nations, or joining a supranational organization (and thus surrendering sovereignty), such as the European Communities, then it is construed as a constitutional change and therefore requires final approval by a majority of both the popular and cantonal votes. Joining an international organization that does not involve military commitments or the subordination of sovereignty or subscribing to multilateral, international lawmaking treaties requires only majority popular vote if challenged, but the successful counterproposal increased the number of needed challenge signatures from 30,000 to 50,000.[16]

Some other international questions have been treated as constitutional questions because they represented a loss of sovereignty. Switzerland's decision to join the League of Nations was one of these. The 56.4 percent majority was carried by strong pro-League voting in French-speaking cantons and was opposed by German-speaking cantons. In the French-speaking canton of Vaud, for example, the vote for joining the League was 63,300, with the vote against a mere 4,800.

The question of becoming an associate member of the European Economic Community was put to Swiss citizens in 1972, and 72.5 percent of them voted yes. More recently, an international-issue referendum was conducted in March 1986 to decide if Switzerland would join the United Nations. The move, which is discussed further in Chapter 4, was favored by only 24.3 percent of the Swiss and was thus rejected. Yet another recent Swiss referendum with important potential international ramifications was a December 1989 vote on completely disbanding the Swiss army. The move was placed on the ballot through an initiative petition sponsored by a coalition of disarmament and leftist groups. Most of Switzerland's political elite condemned the move, with Federal Council president Jean-Pascal Delamuraz characterizing the idea as "an idiocy as big as the Matterhorn."[17] Analysts predicted a low turnout and a 75 percent or more rejection of the proposal, but they were wrong. Almost 70 percent of the eligible voters went to the polls in the largest turnout in nearly twenty years, and 35.6 percent pulled the yes lever. Surveys showed that only about 15 percent really wanted to get rid of the army, but there was widespread support for lessening defense expenditures, the perceived autocratic attitude to the army, and the long obligation virtually all Swiss men have to militia duty. That led many Swiss to vote yes, and the referendum served, in one observer's estimate, as "a slap in the face for the establishment" that would ease the move to reform the military and the rules of military service.[18]

Referendums in Australia and New Zealand

The Oceania countries have regularly held referendums, with Australia conducting forty-one and New Zealand nine national referendums during this century through 1986. New Zealand held no international-issue referendums, although the country's 1949 vote (78%) to continue conscription arguably was related to foreign affairs.

Only four of Australia's referendums involved international issues. Two were partly related to foreign trade. A referendum in 1913 proposing a constitutional amendment to increase the federal government's authority in the areas of domestic and foreign trade and commerce was narrowly defeated when it was favored by only 49 percent of the voters and carried only three states. Thus, the amendment received neither the needed majority of the popular vote nor the majority of state votes. And, a 1946 constitutional amendment referendum on giving the federal government power over the organized marketing of primary products was approved (50.6%) by a majority of the national vote but carried only three states and was lost. There were also two nonbinding referendums held during World War I on the issue of conscription for foreign military service. These pitted Australia's "establishment" against its lower classes. Conscription was supported by wealthier people, Protestants, and Australians of English stock who wished to support London and the economic bene-fits of a strong British Empire. All the major newspapers favored the draft, as did the Anglican churches. The opposition was centered among Catholics, especially Irish Catholics who were more concerned with London's treatment of Ireland than they were about England's war with Germany. Labor unions were also staunchly opposed to a military draft, but union power was quite limited during this period. Given the political dominance of the elite forces that favored conscrip-tion, the referendum results were a surprise. The first in 1916 was narrowly defeated (49%), and another attempt the following year also went down (48%).

Australia has also conducted thirty-four state-level referendums. One of these, Western Australia's 1933 vote on secession from the Common-wealth, is relevant to our discussion. After more than a quarter century of local discontent with federal power and policy, Western Australia held a referendum in April 1933 on the question of secession. Almost 90 percent of the voters went to the polls, where secession carried a strong 66 percent of the vote and 92 percent of the electoral districts. The federal govern-ment was not willing to concede the issue, however, so the state govern-ment appealed to the British "Imperial Parliament" in London. There a joint committee of the House of Lords and the House of Commons rejected the petition, arguing that the people and states of Australia had "agreed to unite in one indissoluble Federal Commonwealth," and that "according to constitutional usage" the Australian union could not be dissolved unless "invoked by the voice of the people of Australia."[19]

Referendums in Canada

Canada has had only two national referendums, the second of which, in 1942, approved (64%) conscription. There also have been a number of provincial or territorial referendums, three of which involved the question of self-determination. The first two occurred in 1948, when Newfoundland voters decided their future relations with Canada.[20] Newfoundland had been a separate dependency of Great Britain and had enjoyed considerable domestic self-governance. Then, in 1933, Newfoundland the territory experienced severe economic difficulties and lost considerable autonomy when it was placed under a "Commission" government controlled by London. The moderate return of prosperity by the end of World War II rekindled the question of Newfoundland's political status. An elected convention of Newfoundlanders pondered several options, including economic union with the United States or confederation with Canada. The convention decided, however, to offer voters only two choices: continuation of the Commission form of government for five years or a return to a "Responsible Government" system of local autonomy. Strong protests over the omission of the Canadian confederation option, however, persuaded the British government to include that third possibility on the ballot. London also decided that in order to win, an option would have to receive a majority vote. A first round of balloting failed to resolve the issue, but the Commission option was eliminated because it trailed (14%) far behind Responsible Government (45%) and confederation (41%). The second vote six weeks later resulted in a slim majority (52%) for confederation, and in 1949 Newfoundland became Canada's tenth province.

A second international-issue referendum concerning the future national and perhaps international status of one of Canada's subnational units occurred in 1980. This time an existing province, Quebec, considered greatly loosening confederation ties, and there were some in the predominantly French-culture province who advocated independence from the balance of predominantly English-culture Canada. An upsurge of Québécois nationalism in the 1960s and 1970s culminated with the separatist-leaning Parti Québécois led by René Lévesque gaining control of the provincial parliament in 1976. This was followed in 1980 by a referendum on whether the province should seek "sovereignty-association," an undefined separate status with the rest of the confederation. In a triumph of Canadian (instead of regional) nationalism, the proposal was defeated (40%) amid a strong (84%) turnout.

That did not end the controversy, however. The 1990 failure of Canada's provinces to ratify the so-called Meech Lake accord, which was designed to ensure Quebec a degree of cultural uniqueness, sparked renewed unrest in the province. Even before the rejection, surveys showed almost two-thirds of French-speaking Québécois favoring some degree of autonomy from Canada, and in the aftermath even Quebec's pro-unity premier, Robert Bourassa, was moved to warn that "English Canada must clearly understand that Quebec is today and forever a distinct society, capable of ensuring its own development and its destiny."[21] That sentiment, backed by an act by the province's parliament that called for a referendum to be held no later than October 1992, helped spur the national government of Prime Minister Brian Mulroney in September

1991 to propose new constitutional language aimed at conciliating Quebec's French-speaking majority. It remains to be seen, but increasingly strong sentiments in both Quebec and the other provinces may even end the chance of an autonomous, but still associated, Quebec. In November 1991, an angry Mulroney rejected the idea that Quebec could have both political independence and the benefits of continued economic association with Canada. "Well the hell with you," Mulroney expostulated. "If Canada is unacceptable, it's unacceptable completely. You can't be a part-time Canadian. You don't get it both ways. You can't walk about like a cafeteria, taking the best part of Canada saying, 'I'm going to take these, and I'm going to leave you with the rest.'"[22]

Referendums in the United States

The United States holds the ironic twin distinctions of being the world leader in number of direct democracy decisions (by referendum, initiative, recall) while, at the same time, being one of the few long-term democratic countries that has never held a national referendum.[23]

Referendums in the United States are as old as the republic. The first exercise in direct democracy was held by Massachusetts in 1778 on adoption of the new state constitution. The proposed document lacked a bill of rights and was therefore rejected by a five-to-one margin. A redrafted constitution received public approval two years later. Through the 1800s, referendums were only sporadically used, but they did resolve such issues as the site of the Texas capital (1845), voting rights in Colorado (1848), and whether to create a Michigan state bank (1850).[24]

The spirit of the populist movement and the progressive era sparked a dramatic growth in the establishment of direct democracy after more than a century of sporadic use. In 1892, the People's party became the first national party to call for direct democracy in its presidential platform. South Dakota became the first state to adopt the procedure for statutory law in 1898, and eighteen other states followed suit by the end of World War I. Interest in initiative and referendum faded with the progressive movement's decline, and for the next forty years no new states added the procedure. Then, in tandem with its entering the union as a state, Alaska adopted the procedure in 1959, and a new pattern of growth began. Now all U.S. states except Delaware have some form of initiative, referendum, or recall. There are a few states, such as Connecticut, where referendums are limited to constitutional amendment proposals, but in about 75 percent of the states, initiatives or referendums can decide statutory as well as constitutional proposals.

There is no precise compilation of all statewide referendums in U.S. history, but there have been over 3,000 such votes, including approximately 1,500 initiatives.[25] There has also been a host of local referendums, numbering 16,000 in 1968 alone.[26] Most of these measures have been on state and local issues, but there has been a smattering of votes relevant to world affairs. During the war in Vietnam, for instance, there were votes on the issue of continued U.S. participation, and in the early 1980s there were a number of votes on the nuclear freeze issue.

Contrary to the widespread use of referendums and initiatives at the state and local levels, popular voting on issues has never been possible at the national level. Pragmatic and philosophical reasons persuaded the delegates to the 1787 constitutional convention to establish a representative form of government. There is no record indicating that referendums were considered in Philadelphia. Pragmatically, geographic distance and transportation difficulties in the fledgling country dictated a republican form of government because, as James Wilson noted, "it is impossible for the people to act collectively."[27] Philosophically, the framers were influenced by Montesquieu, David Hume, and others who argued that the divergent interests and social inequalities that characterize large states would spark clashes leading to civil disruptions. Many delegates were thus skeptical about the ability of the people to exercise restraint and wisdom while directly governing themselves. Massachusetts delegate Elbridge Gerry commented that "the evils we experience flow from the excess of democracy. The people . . . are the dupes of pretended patriots." And Roger Sherman of Connecticut similarly proclaimed that he was operating under the premise that the common people should have as little as possible to do with the direction of government.[28] As a result of these views, the Constitution provides that "all legislative Powers herein granted shall be vested in a Congress of the United States."

It is important to note that, contrary to a widely held assumption, the legislative authority placed in Congress does not constitutionally deny that power to the people. Congress can allow legislative issues to be decided by referendum and on one occasion did so. In 1846, Congress voted to return part of the original land ceded by Virginia for the federal district of Washington if the people of what became Alexandria County agreed to the retrocession by referendum. The voters chose to rejoin Virginia, and the state began to exercise jurisdiction without further congressional action. More than two decades later, an unhappy Alexandria taxpayer challenged his obligation to pay Virginia taxes claiming that the referendum was unconstitutional on several grounds. The matter was finally settled by the U.S. Supreme Court. It ruled in *Phillips v. Payne* (1876) that Virginia's reannexation of Alexandria and, by inference, the referendum were legal.[29] The opinion for the majority written by Justice Noah Swayne did not rest primarily on the referendum issue, but he did note that "under certain circumstances, a constitutional provision may . . . be waived by a party entitled to insist upon it." The court has become even more precise in its support of the possibility of a national referendum without the need for a constitutional amendment, a development that we will explore more extensively in Chapter 6.

The first strong movement for holding a national referendum occurred just prior to the Civil War when the Senate defeated by a single vote a proposal to hold a national vote on the abolition of slavery. As the crisis that culminated in World War II grew, the Ludlow amendment calling for a public vote before a declaration of war renewed interest in a national referendum.[30] This idea of requiring popular consent before going to war first emerged during World War I. Progressive Republicans unsuccessfully tried to persuade the 1916 Republican convention to endorse such a referendum; earlier Democratic presidential candidate and secretary of state William Jennings Bryan supported it; the Senate twice (1915, 1917) voted in favor of it; and the 1924 Democratic national platform included it. In 1935, Indiana Democratic representative Louis Ludlow revived the controversy when he proposed a constitutional amendment that read in part, "Except in the event of an invasion of the United States or its Territorial possessions and attack upon its citizens residing therein, the authority of Congress to declare war shall not become effective until confirmed by a majority of all votes cast thereon in a Nationwide referendum."

Public opinion strongly favored the amendment. Two polls taken in late 1937 found three-quarters and two-thirds of the respondents supporting Ludlow's proposal. Nevertheless, the amendment was defeated in both houses of Congress. The House of Representatives voted it down 209 to 188 in January 1938, and the Senate rejected the proposal 73 to 17 in October 1939. Despite the strong public support for the proposal, its rejection posed no political liability to members of Congress. Of those who ran again, 76 percent who had voted for the amendment were reelected; 82 percent who had voted against it were reelected. Thus, public support was wide but not deep.

The idea of a national direct democracy procedure also received some attention in the mid-1970s as a reaction to the twin traumas of Vietnam and Watergate. Several joint resolutions were introduced in the House and in the Senate that would have amended the Constitution to establish a national initiative procedure. Polls indicated that 73 percent of the public with an opinion supported the proposal; yet, the joint resolutions languished after hearings and never came to a floor vote.[31]

The aborted attempt to move legislation to establish national direct democracy through Congress in the mid-1970s does not mean that the movement is dead. Certainly it is dormant, but direct democracy remains vigorous at the state and local levels in the United States, there is continued interest at the academic level, and there are renewed calls by political activists to give U.S. citizens a greater and more direct say in their country's policy.[32]

TWENTIETH-CENTURY REFERENDUMS IN LESS DEVELOPED COUNTRIES

Although little has been written about them, referendums in African, Asian, and Latin American countries are not infrequent.[33] Virtually all of the referendums in these countries have addressed domestic issues, especially constitutional changes and expressions of support for the government or its policies. But there have been a few international-issue referendums, mostly on sovereignty and similar political status questions. The first in an independent country occurred in 1917 when Uruguay held a referendum to approve its constitution. Since then, more than 100 other referendums have been held. With few exceptions, the voting has not been held under Western-style democratic conditions, and the results have been lopsided and predictably have favored the government position.

Referendums in Asia

Sixteen Asian countries or their territories held forty-four referendums between World War II and 1986. They mostly involved domestic issues, although a 1947 referendum in the Philippines granted special concessions to U.S. multinational corporations. There were also several international-issue referendums related to such self-determination issues as territorial jurisdiction, autonomy, and sovereignty. These included Turkish Cypriots approving (70%) a separatist constitution in 1985, several border regions voting to join either India or Pakistan in 1948, and Sikkim's voters deciding (no data available) to join India in 1975.

A similar referendum was held in Singapore. There, in September 1962, 71.1 percent of the voters approved a plan to merge their city-state with Malaya, Sarawak, and Sabah in order to establish the Federation of Malaysia. There was no legal obligation for Singapore, which was autonomous within the British Commonwealth, to hold the referendum, but Prime Minister Lee Kwan Yew sought the vote as a legitimization of his plan to merge with Malaya and the other provinces. The voters did not truly have a democratic choice, however. There was no provision on the ballot to vote against merger. Rather, voters could select among three plans: the negotiated pact with Malaya or the terms of either of the other two pacts (with Sarawak or Sabah) creating the federation. Lee justified this tactic by declaring that all Singapore's political parties supported federation, but this was not the case, and one opposition party urged voters to reject merger by casting a blank ballot.

The inability to vote against merger and an intense government campaign for the negotiated settlement ensured overwhelming support. The size of the majority was the only real question. By that measure, Lee's ability to gain only 71 percent of the vote, while 3 percent voted for one of the other two plans and nearly 26 percent inferentially voted no by casting blank ballots, indicated substantial resistance by the populace. It is even reasonable to speculate that the voters might have rejected the merger if they had been given more balanced information and a more democratic choice. Ironically, the blank-ballot voters may have been wiser. After only three years, predominantly Chinese Singapore withdrew from the predominantly Malay federation because of ethnic tensions.

Referendums in Africa

Countries and territories in Africa had held eighty-eight referendums through 1986, the first of which was a 58 percent decision by Natal to merge with South Africa in 1909. Southern Rhodesian voters in 1922 gave 59 percent approval to self-government rather than joining South Africa. The rest of the African referendums have occurred since 1945.

Many African referendums were on independence or some other question of political association, with understandably huge majorities favoring freedom. Several nascent African countries voted on whether to stay in the French Community, with most opting by large majorities to do so. The only exception was Guinea, which chose immediate independence by 97 percent in 1958. Egypt's president, Gamal Abdul Nasser, led a movement to merge his country along with Syria into the United Arab Republic, a plan that was approved in 1958 by 99 percent of the voters in the two countries. There was a related movement to establish the Federation of Arab Republics in 1971, and this was also overwhelmingly supported by voters in Egypt (99%), Syria (96%), and Libya (99%). In the end, however, all of these plans failed, as did a similar gesture by Moroccan voters, who in August 1984 approved (99%) an abortive federation with Libya.

There were a few other referendums that had vote margins narrow enough to characterize as a contest. Fifty-seven percent of Equatorial Guinea's citizens in 1963 chose autonomous government under Spain over independence, but five years later they reversed themselves and chose independence by a 63 percent vote. In 1964, Malta's voters approved independence from Great Britain by a narrow 50.7 percent majority. British Togoland, in a UN-sponsored referendum, voted by 58 to 42 percent in 1956 to join Ghana rather than French Togoland, and in 1959 the voters in the northern section of British Cameroon decided (62 percent) to delay a decision on whether to join with Nigeria. Two years later, under UN auspices, they chose (60%) to merge with Nigeria, while the voters in the southern section opted (70%) to merge with French Cameroon in the newly independent county of Cameroon.

The only African international-issue referendum on a question other than self-determination issues was held by Egypt. President Anwar Sadat sought a show of public support in 1979 for his peace treaty with Israel to offset the nearly universal condemnation from other Arab countries. Peace, but not democracy, was served when a virtual 100 percent turnout approved the treaty by 90 percent.

Referendums in Latin America and the Caribbean

Seventeen countries or territories in Latin America and the Caribbean held thirty-four referendums in the twentieth century to 1986. The vast majority of these occurred after 1945. Only a few of these referendums were related to international policy, however. Seventy-seven percent of Puerto Rican voters agreed to commonwealth status with the United States in June 1951; in July 1967, voters reaffirmed that stand, with 60.5 percent voting for continued commonwealth status, 38.9 percent preferring statehood, and only 0.6 percent wishing independence. The British sponsored a West Indies Federation in the late 1950s, comprising several of their Caribbean possessions, but in 1961 Jamaicans rejected (46%) continued association, and the island became independent in 1962. Aruba voters chose (82%) to differentiate their island from the rest of the Netherlands Antilles in March 1977, and that led to their independence in 1986.

Panamanians approved the Panama Canal treaty with the United States by 67 percent in October 1977. What was remarkable about this vote was not the outcome, but its relatively narrow margin. The treaty had been negotiated by Panamanian strongman General Omar Torrijos, and he had staked considerable political capital on the treaty and a strong show of support. Voting against the treaty, he told Panamanians, "means committing a crime against the country."[34] For Panamanians, the most controversial issue of the treaty was the continued U.S. right of intervention if the canal's operation was threatened. A combination of political pressure, pride at regaining sovereignty over the Canal Zone (even with conditions), and the treaty's economic benefits persuaded business and most other organizations in Panama to support Torrijos and the treaty. Both left- and right-wing nationalists remained opposed, however. The resulting drumfire of criticism against the treaty's acceptance because it allegedly permitted possible "Yankee imperialism" and because voting was monitored by UN officials and by representatives from two dozen North and South American universities kept the winning margin well below the

90 percent Torrijos had desired.

In 1979, voters in the Virgin Islands rejected (44%) autonomy from the United States in a very low (38%) turnout. The most recent international-issue referendum was held in Argentina in November 1984, with 81 percent of the vote approving the Beagle Channel treaty with Chile.

The Pacific

Nationalist stirrings and accompanying political changes have led in recent years to the first referendums in the Pacific region. All were held in U.S. dependencies. Citizens of Guam faced six choices about their future in January 1982, and a strong plurality (49%) favored commonwealth status. During 1983, three other territories made choices about their political future. Voters in the Federated States of Micronesia approved (79%) a Free Association Compact with the United States, and Marshall Islanders voted (58%) for a similar agreement. A majority (56%) of voters on the islands of Palau opted for a Free Association Compact with the United States. The vote required 75 percent approval, however, and the compact was therefore defeated. This was reversed in September 1984, when the compact was approved (67%) under new rules.

REFERENDUM PROCEDURES

There have been hundreds of referendums in this century, but they have hardly been identical. Instead, the technical procedures that govern the holding and conduct of referendums are as diverse as the different countries that hold them. The rules that govern the initiation, conduct, and impact of referendums are of more than just technical interest. They also often have an important impact on the outcome and impact of the referendum.

One way of classifying referendums is by their legal status. The constitutions of some countries establish referendums, in some countries there is statutory authority only, and in other countries referendums are extralegal. Another way to categorize referendums is by the specific mechanisms by which referendums are initiated. These include referendums mandated by the constitution, initiated by the legislature, proclaimed by the executive, and begun by popular petition. Referendums can also be distinguished by their impact: some are binding, others are not. Then there are differentiations according to degree of government regulation of and intervention in the campaign. Voting procedures are, of course, established by the government. But beyond this, some governments take a passive or limited role, while other governments are active in regulating the campaign and participating in it. There are also decision criteria. Most referendums are a yes/no vote decided by a simple majority. A minority have special rules requiring extraordinary majorities of a specified percentage of all eligible voters. Furthermore, many referendums are not democratic at all. Democracy is, of course, a matter of spirit as well as process, and in some countries referendum procedures and voters are oppressively manipulated. The resulting votes then are not true examples of direct democracy; they merely serve as government-controlled exercises to acquire the patina of popular support for despotic decisions.

The following sections will illustrate some of the diversity of the rules and circumstances of referendums, and subsequent chapters will further discuss technical procedures and political activity as they affect the outcomes of the various referendums. It is impossible to catalog all the complexities of referendums, however. What is perhaps most important to understand is that there are diverse possibilities to construct and conduct referendums. Sometimes, when they fail to meet full democratic ideals, it is because the referendum process has been abused by politicians bent on achieving a particular outcome rather than determining the people's wishes. This condemns those politicians, not the referendums. Furthermore, the diversity of process provides us with examples of even-handed governments and informed and active voters, and these are models for reform and the future.

* Legal Status: Constitutional change frequently requires a referendum. Ireland's move to join the EEC is an example, in that joining the supranational organization required some surrender of legislative authority. Forty-nine of fifty U.S. states require popular approval of constitutional changes. About half the states have procedures for constitutional or statutory change that can be begun by the voters by signing petitions. Arizona has the most difficult qualifying formula, requiring the signatures of 10 percent of the electorate. The easiest standard, found in Massachusetts, requires signatures equal to 2 percent of the vote in the last general election. Given the 1988 turnout, this would require fewer than 30,000 signatures in a state with a population of 5.9 million (or 0.5 percent of the population).

* Initiation: Swiss referendums are sometimes mandated by the constitution and are sometimes initiated by popular petition.[35] Constitutional changes require referendums. Optional referendums can be initiated only by a petition of the people. This contrasts with most countries, where referendums are begun by the government and where the people have no similar authority. In Switzerland, any legislative act can be put to referendum if within ninety days of publication 50,000 citizens sign a petition calling for a referendum. Referendums can also be activated by popular initiative requiring the signatures of 100,000 citizens. This procedure is usually used for constitutional change. The Federal Assembly cannot change the wording of the proposed change, but it can put forth a

counterproposal.

In some countries, the legislature may initiate a referendum. According to the Danish constitution, bills passed by parliament may be put to referendum at the request of one-third of parliament's members. Some bills, including those that discharge treaty obligations, are exempt. Furthermore, legislation involving the transfer of power to an international organization, such as the UN or the EC, must be submitted to a referendum unless the legislation authorizing transfer is supported by five-sixths of the Folketing's members.

The 1948 referendums in Newfoundland illustrate extralegal procedures. They were neither constitutionally mandated nor legislatively proscribed. Instead, a popularly elected special convention decided to put two choices (continued rule by London or autonomy) before the people, and the British secretary of state for Commonwealth relations decided to add confederation with Canada as a third option.

While referendums are allowed under the French constitution, the votes of 1961, 1962, and 1972 all violated constitutional requirements in one or more ways and therefore were extralegal and executive initiated. The constitution provides that the president may propose referendums only if a proposal is sent to him or her by the government (premier) and the legislature. In the case of referendums on constitutional change, the proposal can go forward only after both chambers of the legislature have passed the amendment. The 1961 vote on Algeria was announced by President Charles de Gaulle on November 16, 1960, and the government's proposal was not made until December 8. Furthermore, since the freeing of Algeria (which was legally an integral part of France) violated the constitutional provision guaranteeing inviolability of French territory, action by both chambers was necessary but not taken. The 1972 vote on expanding the EEC contravened constitutional requirements much as the 1961 vote had done, with President Georges Pompidou announcing the vote three weeks before the government proposal was received.

• Impact: Swiss referendums are always binding. Norway's and Ireland's votes on joining the EEC were binding. Denmark's was not, although the Danish government pledged that it would honor the people's decision. Similarly, the British vote on the EEC was not binding, but the government was committed to carrying out the popular mandate. There was speculation, however, that if the referendum had resulted in a slim majority for withdrawal, a substantial number of pro-EEC majority party (Labour) members might have joined with Conservative and Liberal party members to block legislation to withdraw Great Britain from the EEC. In the Spanish NATO referendum, Prime Minister Felipe González initially indicated that the referendum was not binding, but his party later conceded that it would be morally bound to abide by the results.

Referendum results, whether binding or not, are normally put into effect by the government, but not always. After World War I, Upper Silesia was claimed by both Poland and Germany. A vote was held on a community-by-community basis. A majority of these, as well as a majority (60%) of the popular vote, opted for inclusion in Germany. The Allies decided, however, to partition the region, with roughly 60 percent going to Germany and 40 percent going to Poland.

• Regulation and Intervention: Beyond establishing basic voting procedures, the degree of government regulation of referendums varies considerably. Most countries, for example, do not try to limit expenditures on referendum campaigning, although some countries and U.S. states provide for campaign finance reporting. A few countries, such as the United Kingdom in 1975, have provided limited funds for conducting the campaign.

In countries with publicly owned broadcast media, the degree of equal access to the airwaves is a critical issue that we will return to in later chapters. Sometimes media time is allocated equitably; often it is not. During some referendum campaigns, the government has also printed and distributed not only its own information (sometimes biased, sometimes not), but also statements and background by opposing sides.

The degree of participation in the campaign by the government on behalf of one side or the other of the issue also varies. In the 1972 Irish EEC election, the government was technically neutral, but it informally campaigned vigorously for membership. Civil servants produced pro-membership literature and helped prepare promembership speakers. The cost of these and other government activities far exceeded the limited official funds given to the pro- and antimembership movements, resulting in a lopsided advantage for those who favored joining the EEC.

This favoritism contrasts sharply with the Danish and Norwegian EEC campaigns, which were administered more evenhandedly. In Norway, funds were given to each of the country's political parties in proportion to its legislative strength, and equal funds were given to pro- and antimembership organizations. The government also spent considerable funds in a generally neutral effort to inform voters, and the public broadcast media were analyzed to ensure fair coverage.

The United Kingdom did not attempt to regulate contributions in its EEC referendum campaign. It did, however, legislatively recognize two ad hoc umbrella organizations that had sprung up to respectively favor and oppose continued EEC membership. The two organizations had literature distributed free by the government, were allowed access to the BBC, and received equal public funds. The government favored continued membership, and there were some changes of bias; but public manifestations of this pro-EEC position were not egregious, and official publications and the government-controlled media were generally evenhanded.

The 1980 Quebec referendum was also waged under the aegis of two opposing umbrella organizations sanctioned by the parliament and controlled by the two major parties. Only the established organizations could spend significant sums on the campaign or receive access to public broadcasting time. The object was to avoid the influence of money; the drawback was that those with independent views or arguments not in accord with the legislative parties were effectively shut out of the contest. One analyst does conclude, however, that "when it was tested in 1980, the Quebec law . . . proved less draconian than many had feared."[36]

Sometimes the government takes a very strong stand. Beginning the 1972 EEC referendum campaign in France, President Pompidou told his country by radio and television:

> The question asked of you is clear and concise. Each of you can understand it easily. Since you want a France which is strong, prosperous and free, and since here destiny can only be accomplished within a powerful Europe, mistress of herself, you will respond massively to my appeal . . . , you will go to the polls and accomplish your duty as a citizen, you will say "Yes" to the future of your children, "Yes" to France, "Yes" to Europe.[37]

• Decision criteria: Majority rule is the most common standard, but there are variations and exceptions. Swiss constitutional amendment referendums, for example, must be agreed to by both a national overall popular majority and a popular majority in a majority of the cantons. Other referendums are decided by simple national majorities.

Referendums usually are conducted with only two choices: accepting or rejecting the proposal on the ballot. Where there are more than two options, it is common to require a majority, with a runoff referendum if a majority is not received on the first round of voting. The 1948 Newfoundland referendums are an example, and confederation, which finished second to autonomy on the first ballot, gained a majority on the second.

According to the Danish constitution, rejecting a referendum proposal requires a negative vote by both a majority of those voting and at least 30 percent of the entire electorate. This provision had no effect in the high-turnout (90%) EEC referendum.

Against the government's recommendation, the British Parliament decided that the Scottish devolution vote would be authoritative only if supported by 40 percent of the entire electorate as well as a majority of those voting. Scottish voters opted for devolution by a narrow 51.6 percent, but the turnout was less than 63 percent. This meant that less than a third of the entire electorate voted for devolution, and the measure was defeated. To have passed the measure would have required an approximate 63 percent yes vote given the turnout.

On constitutional amendments, almost all U.S. states require simple majorities. One state requires three-fifths approval, another two-thirds, and three states require approval by a plurality equal to a majority of those voting in the electoral contest or referendum with the highest participation on election day. In all other types of initiative and referendum, only a simple majority of the popular vote is required.

The method of counting can sometimes be important, especially on votes involving territorial status. The British decision to count the 1973 Northern Ireland vote on a provincewide, instead of a county-by-county, basis virtually ensured that the result would overwhelmingly be for continued union with Great Britain. Not only did Protestants outnumber Catholics two to one, but, recognizing the sure outcome, most Catholics boycotted the referendum. One MP proposed to count votes on a county-by-county basis, and that might have had a very different impact. Of the six counties, Fermanagh and Tyrone had Catholic majorities, and a separatist vote in those counties would have substantially increased the pressure on London to allow the two counties to join the Irish Republic.

• Wording: The wording of a referendum is sometimes a controversial issue. At times, the wording is purposely vague to try to minimize opposition or even to avoid the defeat of a proposal. The Parti Québécois won power in 1976 in part on its pledge to hold a referendum prior to any declaration of independence. That attracted some voters who, while opposed to the governing Liberal party, were also opposed to or doubtful about independence. When it structured the 1980 vote, the Parti Québécois, knowing it would be routed on a straight independence referendum, chose to ask the voters for authority to negotiate *sovereignty-association*, an uncertain term. The strategy failed, the referendum was lost, and the Parti Québécois was soon also defeated.

The word *devolution* used in the Scottish and Welsh referendums to describe their possible future status was similarly opaque. Vernon Bognador comments that "devolution is, after all, a rather peculiar constitutional category; ... lying as it does somewhere along the spectrum between the unitary and the federal states." In his estimation, the concept was "meaningless" to most of the electorate, and it was "not surprising, therefore, that there was considerable confusion among the yes and no camps in the referendum campaign."[38]

Wording may have also contributed to the defeat of the World War I Australian referendums on overseas use of military conscripts. Don Aitkin argues that both referendums "were strangely worded indeed," and this may have helped prompt their defeat.[39] The 1916 ballot, for example, asked Australians:

> Are you in favour of the Commonwealth having, in this grave emergency, the same compulsory powers over citizens in regard to the requiring of their military service for the terms of this war, outside the Common-

wealth, as it now has in regard to military service within the Common-wealth?

At other times, long and specific wording may be a key to adoption. In the general election that brought him to power, Spanish prime minister Felipe González campaigned against continued Spanish membership in NATO. Once in power, though, he changed his view, but the prime minister was faced with splits within his party, many of whose members remained strongly opposed to staying in NATO. To ensure a pro-NATO vote, to ease the difficulty of explaining his switch, and to avoid splitting his party, González needed to word the question with "all of the political shrewdness that . . . [he] and his aides could muster."[40] The result was a question that, among other things, stipulated that Spain's military would not integrate with the NATO command structure; thus the outcome of the vote left Spain in NATO—just.

There are two main points to be taken from this brief overview of the technical aspects of the referendum process. The first is that it is difficult to make general statements about the conduct of referendums. Their authority, initiation, impact, level of government involvement and regulation, decisional criteria, and wording are highly variegated. Yet, these technical aspects are important, and the second point to draw is that the way in which referendums are held can affect their outcome. Since a referendum is, after all, a political process, if and how such exercises in direct democracy should be conducted is often the field of considerable controversy as a proposal's proponents and opponents maneuver for advantage.

NOTES

1. This chapter relies heavily on David Butler and Austin Ranney, *Referendums: A Comparative Study of Practice and Theory* (Washington, D.C.: American Enterprise Institute, 1978); and John Austen, David Butler, and Austin Ranney, "Referendums, 1978–1986," *Electoral Studies* 6 (August 1987), pp. 139–147. Also on the development of referendums, see A. Chunkath, "Referendum: Its Genesis, Growth and Raison d'Etre," *Journal of Constitutional and Parliamentary Studies* 11 (December 1979), pp. 86–100.
2. Philip Goodhart, "Referendums and Separatism I," in *The Referendum Device,* edited by Austin Ranney (Washington, D.C.: American Enterprise Institute, 1981).
3. Goodhart, "Referendums and Separatism," p. 139.
4. This section relies heavily on Simon Deploige, *The Referendum in Switzerland* (London: Longmans, Green, 1898).
5. Deploige, *The Referendum in Switzerland,* p. 46.
6. As an example of the number of votes during this period, the 1876

referendum was rejected by 156,157 yes (45.8%) to 184,894 no (54.2%).

7. Quoted in Deploige, *The Referendum in Switzerland*, p. 219.

8. Deploige, *Referendums in Switzerland*, p. 240.

9. The six were Armenia, Estonia, Georgia, Latvia, Lithuania, and Moldavia.

10. Moscow's question received a 70.2 percent yes vote in the Ukraine. One of the two other questions, which was asked in the mixed ethnic area of eastern Ukraine and which asked whether people wanted to be part of the "Union of the Soviet Sovereign States," received an 80.2 percent yes vote. The other question, asked in the strongly ethnic Ukrainian western area of the republic, asked whether voters favored an independent Ukraine. The yes vote was 90.2 percent.

11. *New York Times*, September 21, 1990, p. A1.

12. *Hartford Courant*, December 3, 1991, p. A1.

13. *Hartford Courant*, February 2, 1990, p. A9.

14. George A. Codding, Jr., "The Swiss Political System and the Management of Diversity," in *Switzerland at the Polls: The National Elections of 1979*, edited by Howard R. Penniman (Washington, D.C.: American Enterprise Institute, 1979), p. 21.

15. In addition to twenty full cantons, there are six cantons that because of their small populations count as a half canton for voting purposes.

16. Codding, "The Swiss Political System."

17. *Time*, December 11, 1989, p. 70.

18. *New York Times*, November 29, 1989, p. A6.

19. Canadian Unity Information Office, *Understanding Referenda: Six Histories: Australia, Newfoundland, Ireland, Norway, Denmark, United Kingdom* (Ottawa: Minister of Supply and Services, 1978), p. 6.

20. Canadian Unity Information Office, *Understanding Referenda*, pp. 8–14.

21. *Time*, July 2, 1990, p. 30.

22. *New York Times*, November 21, 1991, p. A3.

23. Other countries that have been continuously democratic since 1945 and that have not held national referenda include the Netherlands, Japan, Costa Rica, Israel, India, and Mexico during their years as democracies. Other democratic countries that have not held referenda since World War II include Austria and Finland. Germany held referenda prior to the war but has held none since.

24. Penelope J. Gazey, "Direct Democracy—A Study of the American Referendum," *Parliamentary Affairs* 29 (Spring 1971), pp. 123–139.

25. The reader is reminded that to avoid clumsy wording we are using *referendum* to cover all the various techniques of direct democracy, including initiatives and recalls, as discussed in Chapter 1.

26. Eugene C. Lee, "The American Experience, 1778–1978," in Ranney, *The Referendum Device*.

27. James Madison, *Notes on the Debates in the Federal Convention of 1787*, June 6, 1787.

28. Madison, *Notes*, May 31, 1787.

29. *Phillips v. Payne*, 92 U.S. 130 (1876).

30. Ernest C. Bolt, Jr., *Ballots before Bullets: The War Referendum Approach to Peace in America, 1914–1941* (Charlottesville: University of Virginia Press, 1977); Richard Dean Burns and W. Addams Dixon, "Foreign Policy and

the 'Democratic Myth': The Debate on the Ludlow Amendment," *Mid-America* 47 (October 1965), pp. 288–306.

31. A Gallup poll in 1978, as reproduced in U.S. Congress, Senate Committee on the Judiciary, *Voter Initiative Constitutional Amendment*, hearings before the Subcommittee on the Constitution (on S.J. Res. 67), 95th Cong., 1st sess. (1977), p. 646, found that 57 percent favored a national initiative procedure, 21 percent opposed it, and 22 percent were uncertain.

32. A recent, somewhat skeptical, view of the referendum process and the possibilities for a national system in the United States is presented by Thomas E. Cronin, *Direct Democracy: The Politics of Initiative, Referendum, and Recall* (Cambridge: Harvard University Press, 1989). For a recent book advocating more direct democracy, see David S. Schmidt, *Citizen Lawmakers: The Ballot Initiative Revolution* (Philadelphia: Temple University Press, 1989).

33. See Thomas B. Smith, "Referendum Politics in Asia," *Asian Survey* 26 (July 1986), pp. 793–814; Alvaro Marques and Thomas B. Smith, "Referendums in the Third World," *Electoral Studies* 4 (April 1984), pp. 85–105. *The South* refers to those countries that usually share a history of colonization and lagging economic development. These factors are also often accompanied by sporadic democracy.

34. *Facts on File*, September 9, 1977, p. 698.

35. Jean-François Aubert, "Switzerland," in *Referendums: A Comparative Study of Practice and Theory*, edited by David Butler and Austin Ranney (Washington, D.C.: American Enterprise Institute, 1978).

36. Ranney, *The Referendum Device*, p. 183.

37. Claude Leleu, "The French Referendum of April 23, 1972," *European Journal of Political Research* 4 (1976), p 26.

38. Vernon Bogdanor, "Referendums and Separatism II," in Ranney, *The Referendum Device*, p. 45.

39. Don Aitkin, "Australia," in Butler and Ranney, *Referendums: A Comparative Study of Practice and Theory*, p. 131.

40. Gary Prevost, "Spain's NATO Choice," *World Today* 49 (August-September 1986), p. 131.

4

Realists' Fears, Democrats' Hopes, and Questions for Research

We have thus far emphasized the growing, worldwide use of referendums to decide national and international policy issues. We have also examined the possible significance of this trend in light of theories about strong democracy and about the need for realism in foreign policy. To recapitulate, realists tend to oppose using referendums in foreign policy. They fear that if foreign policy is partially removed from the hands of seasoned diplomats and government experts, decisions will be made cavalierly, without the benefits of dispassionate knowledge and first-hand experience. Either popular ignorance or sentimental moralism will prevail.

Advocates of participatory or strong democracy tend to be divided about the use of referendums. Many, but—as we shall emphasize in this chapter—not all, celebrate referendums and view them as leading to greater citizen awareness and activism. The admirers believe that referendums increase citizens' political participation, interest, and understanding and that they buttress the legitimacy of the political order.[1]

A few advocates of participatory democracy, however, fear that under current social conditions referendums can easily be distorted into a tool that shrewd elites can use to manipulate politically inexperienced masses. Referendums, according to such wary democratic theorists as Peter Bachrach, are desirable only if they take place in a wider environment of constant participation in workplace councils, neighborhood assemblies, and other places where decisions that affect one's life can be made.[2] This environment arguably will nurture in voters the political knowledge, empathetic attitudes, and compromising skills required for thoughtful participation in international-issue referendums. Without this environment, Bachrach and others believe, referendums can easily lead to harmful, often xenophobic policies; most voters, living in a largely nonparticipatory society, lack the preparation to act as mature, morally responsible citizens.

The realist and the two strong-democratic views of referendums—one optimistic, the other wary—differ considerably. As we discussed earlier, the theoretical traditions have different relationships to the moral principle of positive liberty. Each tradition also rests on different perceptions about how people typically act during referendums and, correspondingly, predicts dire or wonderful consequences.

These different perceptions evoke questions for empirical research. For example, when and why are referendums used in foreign policy? By what methods and to what degree are citizens educated about the relevant issues and presented with appropriate information? Do people vote with little information or no basic understanding of the issues, or are voters informed and aware? Which political and social groups—the incumbent elite, oppositional demagogues, the rich, the poor, or others—win in the short run through the use of referendums? Do referendums frequently produce reckless discontinuities in nations' foreign policy? Or is the impact of international-issue referendums on a nation's overall foreign policy limited or, at other times, salutary?

In this chapter, the different empirical propositions implicit in strong-democratic and realist theories will be identified and briefly elaborated. This effort will allow us to explore in later chapters what recent international-issue referendums can teach us about the benefits and dangers of a more democratic foreign policy.

TIMING OF REFERENDUMS

In terms of the timing of referendums—why referendums sometimes occur and sometimes do not—at least three testable propositions come to mind. One theory, advanced by Vernon Bogdanor, is that referendums frequently appear in liberal democracies when factions within a ruling party so intensely disagree over a major policy question that the split jeopardizes continuation of party rule. Under such circumstances, a referendum is sometimes a useful way to resolve disagreements without alienating either side. It can provide a procedural solution to potential party fratricide and a way of preserving party power amid threatened factionalism.[3]

Another theory, suggested by the research of David Magleby, is that referendums are consequences of efforts by well-financed and well-organized minorities of nonelites who wish to redirect government action.[4] Through petitions, lobbying, and occasional protest, the nonelites cajole governments into holding referendums on policy questions that they are thus far deciding in ways contrary to these mobilized minorities. Referendums from this perspective are a process by which certain organized groups can redress grievances. Magleby expresses skepticism that most people have sufficient financial and organizational resources to initiate referendums. He views referendums as largely tools of the social "haves." Magleby, nonetheless, sees the source of referendums as lying outside elite circles.

A terrifying variant of this general argument made by Magleby is provided by Bachrach, who says his personal political theorizing is strongly democratic. He believes that Americans today are inadequately experienced in making decisions about complicated policies and argues that referendums are most likely to occur when selfish minorities that have money, organization, and rhetorical skills enlist the support of large majorities through "hate" campaigns that play upon the majorities' unreasoned fears. Bachrach contends that recent domestic referendums on busing, pornography, and abortion illustrate just how manipulative referendums can be.[5] One can easily extend Bachrach's argument to the realm of foreign policy, saying that today's international-issue referendums are tools of well-organized and well-financed groups trying to manipulate everyday voters on issues where their emotions run high and their knowledge is low. Such issues might include foreign aid, support for the United Nations, escalation of defense expenditures, and undertaking "winnable" wars.

A third theory concerning the timing of referendums is that international-issue referendums most often occur when government policy is clearly at odds with the wishes of a significant proportion of a country's citizens. This view holds that a referendum does not occur unless there is first a majority of voters who feel troubled by current policy and believe change is necessary. Referendums thus are the result of neither various governing parties' calculations about how to bolster their organizational power nor of small, well-organized interest groups' efforts to manipulate others. Referendums, according to this third theory, occur when there is palpable evidence, such as petitions or demonstrations, that a majority or near majority of the general public is strongly dissatisfied with current policy and believes that its preferences are being blatantly neglected by elites. Referendums are one political tool by which intense, but ignored, blocs of citizens can protect their interests from government.[6]

If any one of these propositions about the origins of referendums is true, its validity logically has implications for the persuasiveness of the strong democrats' and the realists' theses. For example, many advocates of participatory democracy interpret referendums as a consequence of general citizen discontent with government policy and nonresponsiveness. It is said that elites generally will not risk submitting major and controversial policy to an unpredictable citizenry, and that interest groups are reluctant to subject their policy wishes to the glare of media coverage and public debate.[7] Therefore, referendums must be the result of sufficient public clamor to cause elites to want to quell discontent. If, however, international-issue referendums primarily occur either because of political parties' calculations concerning organizational power or because of interest groups' pressures, then many advocates of strong democracy probably would be dismayed. Instead of being natural expressions of the public's concern, this would mean that referendums are ploys by elites or by interest-group minorities seeking goals that are not directly connected to the public good, at least so far as it is understood by large numbers of voters. The alleged natural connection between the referendum process and the public's will would be called into question.

Advocates of realism in making foreign policy also would be troubled if the recent increase in international-issue referendums is a consequence of either party calculations or interest group pressures. Neither, after all, is necessarily connected to studied assessments of foreign affairs and national needs. The realist wants policy to be determined by dispassionate calculations of national needs and not be simply the result of the struggle of special interests for comparative advantage.

It is likely that advocates of realism also would be uneasy, but not necessarily surprised, if the citizenry at large proved to be the normal instigator of referendums. Realists tend to be skeptical of the abilities of everyday citizens to master the intricacies of foreign affairs and to control their private frustrations and moralistic impulses. If referendums are produced by the desires and discontent of an unenlightened public, this would only reinforce the realists' fears. By this standard, referendums would be acceptable to the archetypical realist only if they were generally the result of calculated efforts by experts in foreign policy and not usually generated by partisan concerns, minority pressure, or majority whims. But thus far no major political theorist has made such an argument.[8]

In summary, there are three common propositions about the origins of foreign policy referendums. They focus alternately on the role of (1) intraparty disagreements over major policy questions, (2) interest group activism, and (3) citizens' general discontent. The truth of each proposition has bearing on which theory about referendums—the realist's, the optimistic strong democrat's, or the wary strong democrat's—seems the most reasonable in light of historical experience and therefore deserving of acceptance.

CITIZEN EDUCATION AND REFERENDUMS

Many political theorists who advocate either realism or strong democracy are concerned not only about when and why referendums occur, but also about whether and how voters are educated before they cast their ballots.

Advocates of strong democracy *and* advocates of realpolitik would be concerned if referendums were held without extensive discussions and systematic dissemination of information. Advocates of realism, of course, would not be surprised if serious discussions of the issues do not occur. After all, these theorists presume that everyday voters are not interested in the subtleties and technical issues surrounding referendums and instead act out of moralism or headless passion. Advocates of strong democracy, such as Benjamin Barber, would hope that today's referendums are preceded by serious educational campaigns in which issues are discussed fully and information becomes widely available.[9] Their provisions might include campaign periods to ensure that all sides have sufficient opportunity to voice their arguments, government preparation and mailings of information packets to all qualified voters, and government-appointed commissions responsible for publicizing the different sides.

In addition, many advocates of strong democracy would hope that citizens in referendums would study the available information and then cast ballots in a deliberate manner. Many democratic theorists, moreover, would expect most voters to think independently of government officials' directives and endorsements by the news media.[10] If referendums are approached by vast majorities of voters in a thoughtless manner, despite serious efforts to broaden discussion and provide voters with information, and if voters seem easily duped by either organizational elites or media celebrities, then the participatory-democratic defense of referendums would be seriously weakened. There would be no obvious connection between the institution of referendums and a mature, autonomous spirit of citizenship. Of course, advocates of realism presume that voters will not think seriously about the public good, even if voters' education and dissemination of information do occur.

Thus, two sets of questions for empirical investigation arise. First, do serious educational campaigns precede international-issue referendums? If so, what is the substance of the campaigns? Second, are citizens who vote informed and thoughtful when they enter the booth, or do they approach casting their ballots by uncritically accepting the endorsements of political and social authorities?

WHO PARTICIPATES?

Referendums are, in the opinions of most theorists of strong democracy, an institutional opportunity for citizens at large to participate more directly in policymaking processes. Direct democracy permits, and even reinvigorates an interest in, widespread political participation.[11] But do eligible citizens, in fact, participate in referendums when given the opportunity?

Participation in referendums by *every* citizen is an unreasonable expectation, of course. Personal illness, inclement weather, natural disasters, job obligations, family crises, child care, and other aspects of daily life can dissuade politically concerned people from going to the polls. Another, and arguably more appropriate, standard for judging the extent of citizen participation is conceivable, however. That standard is the average electoral turnout within a nation. Are turnout levels for international-issue referendums comparable to, or even higher than, those for other major, national-level elections? Or are levels for international-issue referendums significantly lower, suggesting that referendums do not in practice significantly enrich citizenship for most politically interested persons?

Some theorists of voting behavior who do not advocate strong democracy might predict that referendums would have significantly lower turn-out rates because of the absence of party cues to simplify voters' choices. In the absence of unambiguous party endorsements, a greater effort is required to become familiar with issues and to choose a position. Because of the effort required, some who vote in national elections stay home during an international-issue referendum rather than undertake the trouble to decide by themselves complex issues. Thus, as an instrument for popular involvement in politics, referendums are bound to fail.[12]

A counterargument by theorists of strong democracy is possible, however. One can argue that unlike modern elections, in which candidates from "catch-all parties" blur positions and issues so as to appeal to as many constituencies as possible, international-issue referendums offer stark alternatives.[13] Perhaps unusual excitement, historical significance, and drama accompany major referendums, and they, at minimum, partly offset the inconvenience of a lack of party cues. Consequently, current turnouts at international-issue referendums might not necessarily be significantly lower than turnouts for national elections. Referendums on a particularly significant issue, in fact, might have a higher turnout than is the norm for national elections.

An advocate of realism in foreign policy would probably not be primarily interested in turnout levels per se, but would stress the social composition of voters. Do well-educated and well-traveled people who realists believe might have cosmopolitan interests and perspectives vote? Or do most of the voters in international-issue referendums consist of "the great unwashed," that is, people with modest-to-small incomes, with modest-to-small experiences in the broader world, and therefore (realists presume) with modest-to-small perspectives on global issues and foreign life? If nonwealthy, largely untraveled, and therefore parochially minded people vote, the fears of the realist are reinforced: uninformed people, lacking minimal experience and knowledge about foreign affairs, are making policy decisions, presumably on the basis of untested prejudices and small-town moralism.

Thus, two sets of questions arise about "who votes?" First, are turn-outs for today's international-issue referendums significantly lower than normal turnouts for national elections? Or are turnout rates comparable, suggesting that a large proportion of everyday nonelites are taking advantage of the opportunities to participate in today's foreign policy referendums? Second, what is the sociopolitical background of people who vote in today's international-issue referendums? Do "the great unwashed vote?" Or are voters on international issues from above-average income and educational strata and therefore likely to have at least some familiarity with events and conditions abroad?

WHO WINS?

Some advocates of strong democracy argue that all citizens "win" from today's international-issue referendums in the sense that citizens' roles are expanded, citizens develop a greater sense of efficacy and responsibility, and the political system's legitimacy is reinforced (see Chapter 2). But other writers, including participatory democracy advocate Peter Bachrach, are more cynical about the alleged general winners of referendums. These skeptics believe instead that referendums primarily help a variety of self-serving special interests at the cost of the general good.

Who are these special interests that allegedly benefit from referendums at the sacrifice of the general good? According to Bachrach and others, it is the inordinately wealthy who primarily benefit. Through their funding of campaigns, which skew the public's understanding of issues, the rich can indirectly control voters' behavior and prevent them from considering the general good.[14]

Some authors focus not on the wealthy but on the national-level electronic media and its celebrities who can manipulate voters' thinking through endorsements and slanted presentations of the news. According to this line of argument, voters are extremely passive in their thinking and are easily manipulated by screens and sound waves and the messages that media leaders prefer.[15]

A third possibility deals with oppositional demagogues, who allegedly play upon the fears and resentments of voters in order to unseat established elites. According to this theory, voters resemble the impulsive, amoral mob described by Gustav LeBon and at times by Sigmund Freud. Voters are said to lack the ability to reason patiently and independently about international issues. They therefore can be easily led by a person skilled in playing on voters' feelings of insecurity, anger, and resentment.[16]

A final possibility involves the incumbent government. Through biased wording of referendum choices and direct and indirect support for particular sides, established elites in effect determine the outcome of the referendums despite the alleged rule of the people. If this occurs, referendums are a method for elites to legitimate their favored policies and thus minimize citizen discontent, rebelliousness, and independence. Through referendums, elites help citizens run to their chains, which are covered by democratic-looking procedures.[17]

To recapitulate, there are at least four distinguishable theories about who wins by using referendums. Each identifies different groups of people who allegedly benefit from international-issue referendums: the wealthy, leaders of the media, oppositional demagogues, and political elites. The different theories lead to the following predictions:

1. The side that receives the most private funding and business support usually wins.
2. The side that is endorsed by the national media usually wins.
3. The side that engages most extensively in emotional appeals and demagoguery usually wins.
4. The side that the government endorses usually wins.

ARE REFERENDUMS SIGNIFICANT IN LONG-TERM FOREIGN POLICY FORMATION?

Some policy-oriented readers might ask: "Don't both theorists of strong democracy and theorists of foreign policy realism exaggerate the historical significance of international-issue referendums? Granted, referendums are more common today than 100 years ago. Still, they play such a minute part in overall foreign policymaking that they do not deserve the attention given to them. Foreign policy is basically unaltered."

Advocates of realism who fear the spreading use of referendums assume, of course, that policy implications are extensive and that referendums disrupt long-term policy continuities rooted in decades of diplomatic experience and tradition. Referendums are for realists a Pandora's box of unpredictable emotion and passion that threaten established diplomatic order.

Theorists of strong democracy are not of one mind concerning the impact of referendums on foreign policy. Some argue that policy impact per se is not as important as the value of the participatory process. The creation of an interested, involved, and reflective citizenry should be the *summum bonum*, the unquestionably "highest good," of politics. Whether the results of referendums disrupt preexisting traditions of policymaking is a secondary issue at best. A policy without active, involved citizens is intrinsically deplorable, this view maintains, regardless of whether or not there is continuity in the content of policy.[18]

A second strong-democracy argument exists that is somewhat compatible with the realists' line of argument. According to this position, which has been forcefully advanced by Bachrach, referendums are usually used by demagogues and wealthy interests to manipulate masses into passing legislation that harms everyday people. Bachrach argues that new "hate" legislation on topics such as abortion and the death penalty is being passed through referendums because voters, lacking practice in making policy decisions in daily life, act on instinct and resentment rather than on reason. Like the realist, this type of strong-democracy theorist insists that a Pandora's box of unreasoned passion is being open. But where the strong democrat's argument differs from the realist's is that even a strong democrat, such as Bachrach, fearful of politically inexperienced masses, would not assume that elites on their own have necessarily made wise and generally beneficial policies in the past.[19]

A third possible argument from a strong-democracy position is that contrary to the realists' presumption most citizens are not reckless when participating in international-issue referendums. Instead, they tend to be cautious when they vote because they appreciate the benefits derived from the policy status quo and are reluctant to change it in radical and unpredictable directions. According to this line of argument, referendums usually function as a desirable check on elites' impulses to innovate. In the words of one British conservative, referendums are "not a spear, but a shield" protecting citizens from unwanted legislative change.[20] Ironically, and contrary to the Madisonian presumptions so deeply entrenched among scholars and citizens in the United States, it is the elites, not the nonelites, who are the primary sources of discontinuous and perhaps thoughtless change in foreign policy.[21]

Once again, several testable propositions arise from these divergent theories about the significance of referendums for ongoing foreign policy traditions. They are:

1. Today's international-issue referendums play a marginal role in the making of foreign policy. Foreign policy remains basically the same as before.
2. Referendums produce radical discontinuity in foreign policy because voters' passions and ignorance result in innovative policies that are at odds with a country's diplomatic tradition.
3. Referendums function as prudent restraints on elites' innovative impulses. Whereas elites often desire new directions in foreign policy and have little commitment to tradition, nonelites are more reluctant to undertake risks that may jeopardize present arrangements and benefits. Therefore, referendums usually are decided in favor of the status quo.

SUMMARY

The increasing use of referendums in deciding international issues can be greeted with enthusiasm or alarm, depending in part on one's theoretical predilections and in part on empirical experience.

In Chapter 1 we compared the strength and weaknesses of each position on the basis of the moral principle of positive freedom. We noted the argument that if one values positive freedom, then one logically should approve of the use of referendums to decide questions of foreign policy on the grounds that this process advances active citizenship.

This chapter has introduced a series of questions and alternate empirical propositions that are also relevant for deciding one's position vis-à-vis referendums. Depending on the answers to these questions, one might be persuaded to adopt either an optimistic strong-democratic view, a wary strong-democratic view, or a realist view of referendums, irrespective of one's commitment to the principle of positive freedom. Stated differently, one can adopt a theoretical position in favor of or against referendums not only a priori, on the basis of logical deduction from a moral principle, but also a posteriori, on the basis of empirical knowledge that makes one theoretical position appear more plausible and convincing than its rivals.

In the following chapters, we will review several recent international-issue referendums in light of the different testable propositions introduced in this chapter. For the sake of convenience, a list of approximately a dozen empirical propositions that guide our inquiry in the remainder of the book will be presented in the appendix that follows this chapter. After surveying examples of referendums in recent history in light of these propositions— and the broader questions about timing, voter education, participation, and policy impact which the propositions imply—we will reconsider the relative validity of the three archetypal ways of thinking about referendums that have been articulated in this chapter. Again, these theoretical perspectives are not value-neutral ways of describing the world. Each perspective encourages different assessments about the relative value and dangers of referendums. Because the different theoretical perspectives entail different judgments about the benefits and costs of international-issue referendums, the data that we will gather will aid us in deciding a posteriori whether the increasing use of referendums should be greeted with approval, ambivalence, or alarm.

APPENDIX: PROPOSITIONS ABOUT
INTERNATIONAL-ISSUE REFERENDUMS

- Propositions About Timing:

  1. International-issue referendums usually occur when factions in a governing party disagree over a major policy question.
  2. International-issue referendums occur primarily as a result of interest group pressure.
  3. International-issue referendums usually occur when a large plurality of the citizenry in a polity is openly and strongly dissatis-

fied with its government's current policies.

- Propositions About Voters' Education:

    1. Extensive information campaigns precede today's international-issue referendums.
    2. Most citizens who vote in an international-issue referendum do not seriously think about the issues involved.
    3. Most voters in international-issue referendums cast their ballots almost entirely on the basis of their government's endorsements.
    4. Most voters in international-issue referendums cast their ballots almost entirely on the basis of news media endorsements.

- Propositions About Participation:

    1. Voter turnouts for international-issue referendums are significantly lower than voter turnouts for national elections.
    2. Voter turnouts for international-issue referendums are significantly higher than voter turnouts for national elections.
    3. Most voters in international-issue referendums are from low-income backgrounds.
    4. Most voters in international-issue referendums are poorly educated.

- Propositions About Victory:

    1. The side that receives the largest amount of business support and private funding usually wins an international-issue referendum.
    2. The side that is endorsed by the national media usually wins an international-issue referendum.
    3. The side that engages most extensively in demagogic "hate" campaigns usually wins an international-issue referendum.
    4. The side that the government endorses usually wins an international-issue referendum.

- Propositions About Significance:

    1. International-issue referendums have little long-term impact on today's foreign policy. Following a referendum, a nation's foreign policy remains basically unchanged.
    2. International-issue referendums lead to significant upheaval in a nation's foreign policy traditions.
    3. International-issue referendums are usually decided in favor of

the policy status quo. They thus function as an institutional check on elites' propensity to innovate.

NOTES

1. Benjamin R. Barber, *Strong Democracy: Participatory Politics in a New Age* (Berkeley: University of California Press, 1984), pp. 281–289. Barber's views are also found in a letter in U.S. Congress, Senate Committee on the Judiciary, *Voter Initiative Constitutional Amendment*, hearings before the Subcommittee on the Constitution on S. J. Res. 67, 95th Cong., 1st sess. (1977), pp. 192–196. For a convenient summary and sympathetic critique of the strong democrat's case for referendums, see Peter K. Eisinger, Dennis L. Dresang, Robert Booth Fowler, Joel B. Grossman, Burdett A. Loomis, and Richard M. Merelman, *American Politics: The People and the Policy* (Boston: Little, Brown, 1978), pp. 479–486.

2. See, for example, Bachrach's testimony in U.S. Congress, *Voter Initiative*, pp. 59–65; Philip Green, *Retrieving Democracy: In Search of Civic Equality* (Totowa, N.J.: Rowman & Allanheld, 1985), p. 177; Christopher Lasch, "Mass Culture Reconsidered," *Democracy* 1 (October 1981), pp. 7–22; Jane J. Mansbridge, *Beyond Adversary Democracy* (Chicago: University of Chicago Press, 1980), pp. 275–276.

3. Vernon Bogdanor, *The People and the Party System: The Referendum and Electoral Reform in British Politics* (Cambridge: Cambridge University Press, 1981), parts 1–2.

4. David B. Magleby, *Direct Legislation: Voting on Ballot Propositions in the United States* (Baltimore: Johns Hopkins University Press, 1984), chapter 4.

5. Bachrach's testimony in U.S. Congress, *Voter Initiative*, pp. 59–65.

6. Statement by People's Lobby in U.S. Congress, *Voter Initiative*, pp. 146–149. A precursor to this argument can be found in Delos F. Wilcox, *Government by All the People, or the Initiative, the Referendum, and the Recall as Instruments of Democracy* (New York: Macmillan, 1912), chapter XVIII. See also Eisinger et al., *American Politics*, pp. 479–486.

7. Barber's letter in U.S. Congress, *Voter Initiative*, pp. 192–195.

8. Bogdanor's argument about political moderation and Tory democracy, however, can be read as anticipating such an innovative line of realist theorizing. Bogdanor, *The People and the Party System*, parts 1–2.

9. Barber's letter in U.S. Congress, *Voter Initiative*, pp. 195–196; Barber, *Strong Democracy*, pp. 285–286; Green, *Retrieving Democracy*, p. 177; Eugene C. Lee, "Can the British Voter Be Trusted?" *Public Administration* 66 (Summer 1988), pp. 165–180.

10. Barber's letter in U.S. Congress, *Voter Initiative*, pp. 193–194; Barber, *Strong Democracy*, pp. 281–289; David D. Schmidt, *Citizen Lawmakers: The Ballot Initiative Revolution* (Philadelphia: Temple University Press, 1989), pp. 26–29.

11. Barber's letter in U.S. Congress, *Voter Initiative*, pp. 193–195; Barber, *Strong Democracy*, pp. 281–289; Bogdanor, *The People and the Party System*, pp. 83–85, 90; Schmidt, *Citizen Lawmakers*, pp. 26–29.

12. Magleby, for example, explores this line of argument in *Direct Legislation*,

chapters 5 and 7.

13. For a famous criticism of the consequences for citizenship of "catch-all parties," see Otto Kirchheimer, "The Transformation of the Western European Party Systems," in *Political Parties and Political Development*, edited by Joseph LaPalombara and Myron Weiner (Princeton: Princeton University Press, 1966), pp. 177–200.

14. Thomas E. Cronin, *Direct Democracy: The Politics of Initiative, Referendum, and Recall* (Cambridge: Harvard University Press, 1989), pp. 90–124, 189–191; Bachrach's testimony in U.S. Congress, *Voter Initiative*, pp. 59–63.

15. On the profound impact of the news media on our understanding of political events, see Todd Gitlin, *The Whole World Is Watching: Mass Media in the Making and Unmaking of the New Left* (Berkeley: University of California Press, 1980). See also, Jane J. Mansbridge, *Why We Lost the ERA* (Chicago: University of Chicago Press, 1986), p. 226; and Lasch, "Mass Culture Reconsidered."

16. Bachrach's testimony in U.S. Congress, *Voter Initiative*, pp. 59–63. For illustrations of the realist position on this issue, see John E. Horton and Wayne E. Thompson, "Powerlessness and Political Negativism: A Study of Defeated Local Referendums," *American Journal of Sociology* 67 (March 1962), pp. 482–493; Henry Fairlie, "The Unfiltered Voice: The Dangerous Revival of the Referendum," *New Republic* 24 (June 24, 1978), pp. 16–17; Cronin, *Direct Democracy*, pp. 187–215.

17. Bachrach's testimony in U.S. Congress, *Voter Initiative*, pp. 60, 63.

18. Barber's letter in U.S. Congress, *Voter Initiative*, pp. 193–195.

19. Bachrach's testimony in U.S. Congress, *Voter Initiative*, pp. 59–65. For illustrations of the realists' fear that referendums would allow swings in popular mood to disrupt long-term policies, see Carl Cohen, *Democracy* (New York: Free Press, 1971), pp. 88–89; Cronin, *Direct Democracy*, pp. 250–251; Fairlie, "The Unfiltered Voice."

20. Bogdanor, *The People and the Party System*, p. 69.

21. Bogdanor, *The People and the Party System*, parts 1–2. See also Magleby, *Direct Legislation*, p. 153; Philip Goodhart, "Reflections on Referendums," in *The Referendum Device*, edited by Austin Ranney (Washington, D.C.: American Enterprise Institute, 1981), pp. 1–2.

5

Referendums, Europe, and International Organizations

This chapter begins analyzing the last chapter's questions, focusing on seven referendums in Western Europe that decided membership in international organizations. The first of these are five 1970s referendums related to membership in the European Economic Community (EEC).[1] These referendums occurred in France, Ireland, Norway, Denmark, and Great Britain. The other two referendums both occurred in 1986. They respectively decided if Spain would remain in the North Atlantic Treaty Organization (NATO) and if Switzerland would join the United Nations.

The 1958 Treaty of Rome, which joined six Western European countries into the EEC, was a landmark in European integration. Further progress occurred along two lines. One was expanding the scope of integration, symbolized by the coalescing of the EEC and other regional organizations into the European Communities (EC) in 1967. The other path to progress was expanding the membership in the EEC and EC.

While EEC membership remained stable for fifteen years, there was an assumption that it would expand. The key was Great Britain because of the size of its economy, its heritage as a European leader, and the probability that a number of other, smaller European countries, including Ireland, Norway, and Denmark, would follow the British lead in seeking membership. In the 1960s, the Conservative government in London sought to join the EEC, but French president Charles de Gaulle vetoed British membership. Prime Minister Harold Wilson's Labour government again sought membership in the late 1960s and was again rejected by de Gaulle.

The passing of de Gaulle from power offered the opportunity to resume European integration, and in June 1970, Great Britain, Ireland, Denmark, and Norway all began negotiating EEC membership. A year later, Great Britain concluded negotiations, and in October 1971 the House of Commons agreed to membership effective January 1, 1973. Negotiations between the other three applicants and the EEC were also successful. In April 1972, French president Georges Pompidou submitted to French voters the question of whether France should support an expansion of the EEC. Sixty-eight percent said yes. The next month, 83 percent of Irish voters favored their county's entry into the EEC, and in

October, 63 percent of Danish voters also opted for membership. On the other hand, 53 percent of Norwegian voters rejected membership in September.

The issue was not fully settled in Great Britain, however. The Conservative government that led the country into the EEC was defeated in 1974, the new Labour government renegotiated membership terms, and the issue of continued British membership in the EEC under the new terms was referred to the voters in June 1975. Sixty-seven percent chose to have their country accept the new terms and remain in the EEC.

Similarly, the issue in Spain was whether to remain in an international organization—in this case NATO. Spain had joined NATO in 1981 under a conservative government. The Socialists had demanded a referendum on the issue as a campaign tactic during the following election. When the Socialists won, they were forced to proceed even though the prime minister had a change of heart and favored remaining in the alliance. Fifty-two percent of Spaniards agreed in a reversal of earlier public opinion, and Spain remained in NATO.

Just four days later, the Swiss voted on joining an international organization, the United Nations. Here again the status quo carried the day. Despite overwhelming support for membership by the government and most of the society's elite elements, three out of four Swiss voters who went to the polls voted no, thereby overwhelmingly rejecting UN membership.

THE TIMING OF THE REFERENDUMS

Why were these European referendums held? For Ireland, the answer is simple: the Irish constitution required a referendum because membership amounted to a constitutional amendment insofar as it bound Ireland to accept EC decisions. This, in effect, limited the legislative power of the Irish parliament. In the other four countries, more complex reasons persuaded leaders to schedule the referendums. Suffice it to say at this point that they were more the result of parliamentary and party politics than any other factor.

The changes in France that ended de Gaulle's decade in power and brought Pompidou to the presidency also ended French opposition to expansion of the EEC. While the French constitution provides for holding referendums, there was no requirement to submit the EEC issue to the voters. Indeed, the more important question of French membership itself had not been referred to the people in 1958.

Analysts agree that Pompidou's desire for a referendum on EEC expansion was largely the result of partisan politics, including the intrafactional struggle among his supporters.[2] Pompidou also sought to refurbish his sagging political image by demonstrating that he could create a strong national consensus on a major policy issue. His political maneuvering was also aimed at political parties across the spectrum. Pompidou wanted to manifest his independence from the hard-line Gaullists who opposed British entry into the EEC and to bedevil the Gaullists by changing policy using a referendum, which had been a favorite tool of de Gaulle. Pompidou saw the referendum as a way to appeal to opposition centrists, who were keen Europeanists, in the hope of winning their support for the government coalition and as a tool to drive a wedge between the parties of the left, which were divided on the issue. All of this, Pompidou hoped, would create favorable conditions for the forthcoming general election. On the international level, Pompidou also expected a referendum victory to strengthen his position at the approaching Paris summit meeting.[3]

The way the referendum was announced was one sign of these motivations. Constitutionally, the president calls for a referendum only after a proposal is forwarded to him by the premier and the legislature. In 1972, however, Pompidou attempted to take political credit by announcing three weeks before parliamentary action that there would be a referendum. It is also notable that the referendum was not occasioned by public pressure to decide the EEC expansion issue by popular vote. In fact, the French electorate was markedly indifferent, as we shall see.

Unlike France, the Norwegian constitution has no provision for holding referendums. Therefore, the popular vote on the EEC was technically advisory. Like France, however, Norway had historical precedent for referendums, with the April 1972 vote on the EEC being the fifth referendum since Norway's independence in 1905. Based on this precedent and on a 1967 government white paper that recommended a referendum to legitimize the decision of the Storting (parliament), there was "a general understanding that...a referendum on the issue would be held."[4]

The decision to hold a referendum was reinforced further by intraparty divisions on the EEC issue, with the MPs of several parties disagreeing among themselves.[5] There were also serious splits between party leaders and rank-and-file members. These divisions convinced the leaders that a referendum would avoid damaging stresses within their parties. At the leadership level, the governing Labour party, for example, strongly supported EEC membership, with about two-thirds of its MPs favoring entry. Still, that left one-third of Labour's MPs opposed or unsure.

Labour and several other parties also experienced splits between their MPs and their local leaders and rank-and-file members. For example, half the Christian People's party MPs favored membership, but a scant 19 percent of the party's formal members agreed, and only 25 percent of its identifiers were promembership. These splits also extended to the general political structure, with political leaders distinctly more promembership than the general populace.[6] Support within the Storting for membership was 60 to 75 percent, given wavering members.[7] That contrasted markedly with public opinion. One poll found that during the referendum debate, opposition ranged from a high of 74 percent to a low of 56 percent; another poll's "no" range was 70 to 52 percent.

Just as Norway's was, the Danish decision to hold an EEC referendum was heavily influenced by both intraparty leadership splits and by intraparty leader-follower splits within the left parties. General public opinion was also a factor.

Two articles of the Danish constitution are relevant to the decision to submit membership in the EEC to referendum. Article 42 specifies that acts of the Folketing (parliament) may be submitted to referendum if requested by one-third of the Folketing's members. The other, Article 20, mandates that legislation involving any surrender of Danish sovereignty to an international body be submitted to referendum unless it commands at least a five-sixths majority in the 179-member Folketing.

Throughout the 1960s, most Danish political leaders and a strong majority of public opinion favored EEC membership. One study estimated that if the issue had been decided in the 1960s, a referendum would not have been held because parliamentary opposition was limited to the relatively small (ten to twenty MPs) Socialist People's party (SPP) and because "the size of the ... opposition in the electorate fluctuated between a mere 5 to 10 percent against a support level stabilized in the 50 to 60 percent range."[8]

Renewed negotiations in the early 1970s and shifts in Danish political attitudes and alignments, however, promoted the referendum option. Danish politics generally veered leftward, and that was accompanied by rising opposition to EEC membership. Public opposition to membership tripled in 1971 to approximately 30 percent, while support sank as low as 35 percent, and the "don't know" group varied around the 30 percent mark.[9]

Opposition in 1971 was strongest among the left parties. This was particularly important for the Social Democrat party (SDP), which was the largest single party but not part of the government. While most SDP MPs favored membership, only 22 percent of SDP rank-and-file members favored EEC membership, 40 percent were opposed, and 30 percent were undecided. With a national election impending, and given the trend of public opinion and its own party identifiers' position on the issue, SDP leaders were afraid that they would be outflanked on the left by the strongly antimembership SPP. To keep the issue out of the 1971 general election and thus avoid the possibility of losing seats to the SPP, one SDP leader, in May 1971, proposed holding an extraconstitutional referendum before a final Folketing vote (expected in 1972) on membership. That proposal quickly was altered by other SDP leaders to a postparliamentary vote, which would be binding (by legislative agreement) even if EEC membership received a five-sixths Folketing ratification.

The governing majority of center-conservative parties acceded to this SDP electoral maneuver for two reasons. First, one of the government coalition parties, the Radical Liberal party (RLP), included several anti-membership MPs, while a majority of RLP voters favored membership. Second, in the estimate of one study, the other governing-coalition parties realized that rejecting a referendum "would . . . cast them in the unenviable role of undemocratic elitists who arrogantly refused to trust major issues to the will of the people."[10] Therefore, the Folketing overwhelmingly voted to submit the EEC question to referendum after the legislative vote, whether or not it received a five-sixths vote. Once the Folketing committed itself to a referendum, there was little chance that the decision would be altered, and any possibility disappeared with the parliamentary elections, which brought the SDP to power in a coalition government dependent on the SPP.

Of the five countries that held EEC-related referendums in the 1970s, Great Britain was historically and constitutionally the least likely to hold a referendum. The British had never held a national referendum, nor was there any provision in British law for holding one. Furthermore, most political leaders opposed the idea. Indeed, in 1970, Prime Minister Harold Wilson specifically rejected the idea of a referendum on EEC membership, arguing, "We have a parliament . . . and I think it is right that it is the Parliament which should take that decision with a sense of full responsibility, with a sense that reflects national views and national interests."[11] Furthermore, under the Conservative government of Edward Heath initial British membership in the EEC was decided by parliamentary action.

When, in the early 1970s, the idea of a referendum was proposed and rejected by the Labour as well as Conservative leadership, one of Labour's leading figures, James Callaghan, predicted that a referendum was "a life-raft into which the whole party [might] one day have to climb."[12] His speculation proved accurate.

The split within the governing Labour party government of Prime Minister Harold Wilson was the most important factor behind the decision to hold a referendum on continued membership in the EEC. The issue clearly threatened the short-term ability of the party to remain in power and arguably also threatened the long-term cohesiveness of the party as an ongoing institution. It is instructive that in his book on the referendum, Anthony King, after having discussed Labour party politics for three full chapters, begins his fourth chapter with this comment:

> Readers of this book must be beginning to wonder whether [this] is a book about the Common Market referendum or about the internal

politics of the Labour party. The answer is that it has to be both. . . . The decision to hold a referendum was a direct outcome of Labour's internal struggle over Europe. The Conservatives played almost no part in the decision. If the Conservatives had won the February 1974 general elections, no referendum would have been held.[13]

The quandary of the Labour party resulted from division and ambivalence within the party, both among leaders and between leaders and party voters. In the 1960s, Labour prime minister Harold Wilson and most of the British political elite had favored entry into the EEC. A May 1967 House of Commons vote supporting application for entry had carried by a strong 488 to 62, with Labour MPs voting 260 to 35 to back the application. Public opinion also favored joining, with a 1966 poll finding 71 percent in favor and only 11 percent opposed.[14]

The attitude of many in Great Britain had changed by the early 1970s, however. A 1970 poll found that after being stung by two French rejections, only 18 percent of British respondents favored entry, 72 percent were opposed, and 10 percent were uncertain. Support for membership then grew slowly, but Labour party identifiers remained particularly opposed. By 1972, for example, overall British opinion had become evenly divided on membership, with about 41 percent on either side of the question and 18 percent uncertain. Labourites, however, were still strongly opposed, with only 25 percent for, 62 percent against, and 13 percent unsure.[15]

Many Labour party activists, including its MPs, also swung into opposition. Partisanship was one factor that motivated this shift, and Wilson announced in 1971 that while he did not oppose membership, he could not support it on the terms being negotiated by the Conservative Heath government. Furthermore, the Labour party's National Executive and its annual conference were dominated by the party's left, which was suspicious that economic integration would stall a shift to a more socialist order in Great Britain. Still others in the Labour party, including Roy Jenkins, the deputy leader in the House of Commons, continued to favor membership even along the terms being negotiated by the Conservatives.

The depth of the split within the Labour party was evident in an October 1971 vote in the House of Commons when 198 Labour MPs voted to reject the Conservatives' negotiating terms, but sixty-nine other Labour MPs, including Jenkins, defied party discipline and voted to support the government. According to King, "Rebellion is too weak a word for what happened. . . . [It] was civil war."[16] All in all, King estimates, the strong pro- and anti-European integration forces accounted for about half of the Labour party, while the other half, including Wilson, "were more concerned with the maintenance of party unity than with achieving any particular outcome on Europe."[17] This pragmatic half of the party saw a referendum as a life raft to save the party.

With Great Britain having joined the EEC in 1973 on the Conservatives' terms, the strategy devised by the Labour party to maintain unity during the 1974 general election was twofold: call for a renegotiation of the terms of entry and submit the final decision on remaining in the EEC, even given new terms, to the British people by referendum.

The 1974 general election was successful for Labour; it achieved a parliamentary majority, and Wilson again became prime minister. The renegotiations with the EEC also progressed rapidly. These twin successes also had negative consequences for the Labour party, however. In the end, Wilson had to proceed with the referendum because, as Vernon Bogdanor put it, "the Labour Government . . . [could not] have been held together without the . . . referendum."[18]

One negative factor was that despite terms that met most previous objections, a strong contingent of Labourites, especially those to the left of the prime minister, remained opposed to membership on virtually any terms. When the House of Commons voted in April 1975 on continuing membership under the terms renegotiated by the Labour government and supported by the prime minister, Wilson had to allow a free vote or risk being defeated within his own party. On that vote, 145 Labour MPs voted against their own leadership, while only 137 supported Wilson, and 33 abstained. Even a third of Wilson's cabinet members and half the junior ministers voted against him or abstained.

A second force behind Labour's continued support for a referendum was the fact that the general population remained divided and confused. Polls in January 1975 showed that when asked, "Do you think that we were right or wrong to join the Common Market?" only 31 percent of respondents thought the move was right, and 50 percent thought it wrong. Asked whether Great Britain should stay in, 33 percent said yes, 41 percent said no, and 26 percent did not know or would not choose. Yet, at the same time, 53 percent (to 22 percent opposed) said that if the government could negotiate terms acceptable to it, then Great Britain should stay in the EEC.[19]

Finally, and perhaps most pivotally, having announced its support for a referendum at a time when it was in the minority and when EEC entry terms had been negotiated by the Conservatives, the Labour government, now in power and having renegotiated terms to its liking, could not renege on its pledge to give the people the final say. As early as February 1971, surveys found that nearly 80 percent of the British people favored a referendum on the EEC issue, and that preponderance of opinion remained steady through the following years' debate.[20]

The referendum in Spain on whether to remain in NATO was prompted, like several of the EEC referendums, by partisan political maneuvering more than by any burst of democratic enthusiasm on the part of either the political leaders or the citizenry. One key aspect of the 1986 NATO referendum is that it involved a complete about-face for the moderately left Socialist government of Prime Minister Felipe González Márquez.

A decade earlier, the rebirth of Spanish democracy after the death of longtime dictator Francisco Franco in November 1975 both accelerated Spain's shift from a quasi-isolationist to a more internationalist stance and made Spanish membership in such international organizations as the EC and NATO acceptable to their member countries. The moderately conservative Unión del Centro Democrático (UCD) party won control of the Cortes (parliament) in 1977; Prime Minister Calvo Sotelo negotiated Spain's entry into NATO; and in October 1981, the Cortes ratified the accession by a vote of 186 to 146.[21]

The main political opposition was provided by the Spanish Socialist Worker's party (Partido Socialista Obrero Español, PSOE), which finished second in the 1977 elections. The PSOE opposed Spain's entry into NATO, and it also wanted to reduce or eliminate the U.S. bases in Spain. In the October 1981 Cortes vote, González and other PSOE deputies voted along with deputies of the further-left parties against membership.

Political fortunes changed in the 1982 general elections. The PSOE campaigned on a platform that included holding a referendum on Spanish membership in NATO. The strategy was that even if the party did not capture control of the Cortes, the referendum could be used to terminate NATO membership.[22] The PSOE won, however, and González was named prime minister. The already fragmented UCD fell into even greater disarray and was replaced as the chief opposition party by the distinctly right-wing Alianza Popular (AP) party led by Manuel Fraga.

Once elevated to power, González changed his view of the political landscape and his position on NATO. The new prime minister wanted to move the PSOE closer to the middle of the political spectrum to bolster its future electoral fortunes. Internationally, he also wanted to end Spain's isolation from Europe. Part of this was based on the urge to rejoin the family of acceptable nations after Spain's quasi-exile during the four decades of fascist Franco rule. Another part of the internationalist movement was based on the wish to improve Spain's economy by joining the EC.

Membership in NATO soon was linked to Spain's application for EC membership. The connection was never formally made by Europeans, but it was made inferentially clear to González during his discussions with other European political leaders.[23] As a result, he was intimating that he favored continued membership in NATO as part of Spain's movement into Europe and away from isolationism. Then, in October 1984, González presented a ten-point foreign policy plan that included staying in NATO.

This new position created several political problems. One was within the PSOE, where many officials and rank-and-file members continued to be against membership in NATO. Complicating this, González did not consult within the PSOE or, some say, even his own government before announcing his ten points.[24] Second, the prime minister's credibility with the electorate was at stake, given his widely commented on, frequently derided about-face.[25] Third, he and the PSOE had earlier called for a referendum to try to overturn the UCD adherence to NATO. Once he turned in favor of remaining in the alliance, he was stuck with the risk of a referendum, which he had proposed, defeating his policy preference.

González escaped potential political traps by pushing the idea of a referendum while also relying on his considerable personal appeal and an all-out campaign to ensure that Spanish voters supported his position. The prime minister's control of his party and of the Cortes were amply confirmed by prereferendum maneuvering. The PSOE approved continued membership during its December 1984 congress. Then, in late December 1985, almost 80 percent of the Cortes voted for continued membership. This was followed in late January by a decision of the Council of Ministers to hold a referendum on March 12.

Thus, the referendum was a product of partisan political maneuvering rather than any commitment to expanding direct democracy in Spain. Nevertheless, most Spaniards supported a popular vote. A February poll found that 67 percent favored holding a referendum, with only 20 percent opposed and 13 percent unsure. The referendum was not greeted with wide enthusiasm by the elites, most of whom supported NATO membership. What worried many elites was that public opinion on the issue had varied greatly since democracy had been reestablished. Early majority support for membership had reversed by mid-1983 to 57 percent of Spaniards opposing membership. By the time the referendum was announced in January 1986, opinion stood at 33 percent favoring membership, 30 percent opposed, and 37 percent undecided.[26] González's maneuver, therefore, was a considerable gamble. The vote was not legally binding, but various members of the government indicated it would be morally binding. As such, it might have resulted in Spain's withdrawal from NATO. Among other implications, this outcome would have considerably distressed the Spanish military, elements of which had nearly overthrown the government in February 1981. To add to the drama, the prime minister put his political life on the line by hinting that a referendum defeat would result in his government's resignation and new elections. In a fledgling democracy, all this created considerable apprehension.

Much of the printed media opposed having a referendum.[27] The conservative morning newspaper *Ya* termed the referendum "an unnecessary risk." Some papers favored holding the referendum, but even these worried that González's maneuver was dangerous. The day after the referendum, *El País* expressed relief that "one of the most controversial and schizoid episodes of the infant Spanish democracy is now over." *La Vanguardia* added that "the nightmare is over," and *Diario 16* concluded, "There was something suicidal about this referendum."

The wording of the referendum, which was determined by the González government, added to the mixed reception in Spain to this exercise in democracy. To make membership palatable to a majority of voters, the referendum specified a limited Spanish commitment to NATO that would not include integration into the alliance's military structure. The prime minister also inserted two tangential clauses that pledged Spain to be a nuclear-free zone and promised to reduce the U.S. military presence in Spain.[28]

The magazine *Cambio 16* called this wording "the candy of sweet and easy digestion," and there can be little doubt it eased passage.[29] One of the magazine's polls, for instance, found that on this language, 47 percent would vote yes, 26 percent no, with 27 percent undecided. When the same poll asked people simply if they favored or opposed alliance membership, only 37 percent said yes, 38 percent said no, and 25 percent were undecided.[30] In addition to appealing to PSOE members, the wording had the salutary effect, in González's view, of confounding the opposition. The AP and other conservative parties favored full membership in NATO without the strings attached by the prime minister's wording. They were left in a difficult position. Voting yes meant both favoring limited membership and also supporting their prime political opponent, González. Voting no meant withdrawal. Rather than do either, the AP decided to urge its members to abstain. As *Ya* commented, the prime minister had performed "the miracle of making it impossible for anyone to vote in accordance with his convictions."[31]

The wording of the Swiss referendum was as straightforward as the Spanish effort was convoluted. Yes or no on joining the United Nations was the simple choice. The results also stood in contrast. Just four days after Spanish voters decided to remain in an international organization, Swiss voters made an opposite choice. On March 16, 1986, the Swiss overwhelmingly voted against a proposal to have their country join the United Nations.

Switzerland is noted for its political stability, and the long evolution of the UN referendum reflected that reputation.[32] The Swiss are somewhat caught between their desire to remain rigidly neutral, on the one hand, and their considerable international involvement and their recognition of the growing importance of international organization, on the other. The viability of the United Nations and the increasing importance of the EC are of particular concern to the Swiss. As a result, the Federal Council (the collective executive) recommended in 1965 that the federal parliament consider UN membership. This idea's genesis lasted more than two decades. A federal-sponsored report in 1981 recommended membership, but further study and intervening general elections persuaded the cautious Swiss to defer deciding the issue. By law, a referendum was required, because joining a theoretically supranational organization, such as the United Nations, is construed as affecting Switzerland's constitutionally proclaimed sovereign neutrality. Finally, after nearly twenty-one years, a date for an exercise of the popular will was set.

VOTER EDUCATION

If elections or referendums are to operate optimally, citizens presumably must cast an informed vote. That can be brought about by providing a high level of balanced information in the form of neutral analysis or the airing of opposing views combined with a high level of voter interest that disposes them to acquire available information.

In the five EEC-related referendums, the information and interest factors ranged significantly. The French referendum was at the low extreme in both areas, with information both scanty and one-sided and with the electorate indifferent and unheeding. From this nadir, information and interest improved, with Great Britain and Ireland in the middle, and Norway and Denmark at the high end. French voters showed little interest in their referendum, but this is a reasonable response inasmuch as President Pompidou devised the referendum for his own political purposes, rather than to ascertain French views on expanding the EEC, and the information in the government-controlled broadcast media was biased.

Vincent Wright's analysis of the April 1972 vote on the EEC and the other referendums held during France's Fifth Republic comments that the official campaigns on radio and television were supervised by the Constitutional Council and were "generally fair." They were preceded and accompanied, however, by "unofficial campaigns which were monstrously biased in favor of the regime and the government." Wright concludes that "no referendum campaign was an educative exercise."[33]

This approach was reflected in 1972 in the knowledge and interest of French voters. Less than two weeks before the referendum, 49 percent of the electorate still was unaware of the question to be decided, and most of those who did know the question thought it unclear.[34] Furthermore, polls indicated that a substantial percentage of the French recognized the referendum as manipulative, rather than politically justified, and therefore viewed it as unnecessary.

The EEC campaign in Ireland saw the distribution of a substantial amount of information, but it was heavily one-sided. The government, the main political parties, the press, and most of the leading economic organizations were promembership. The government spent perhaps £250,000 on the campaign. These public funds were supposed to be for neutral or balance information only, but in fact the government's strong promembership position was reflected. Indeed, the government not only supplied promembership forces with information, but officials from the Industrial Development Authority, the Agricultural Marketing Board, and other public agencies were allowed to campaign for membership. Furthermore, the government directly and indirectly gave the promembership movement approximately £30,000, and it raised another £125,000 from other sources. These sources combined for perhaps £400,000 in promembership campaigning. The antimarket forces, by comparison, were impoverished, raising only about £40,000, or 10 percent of the funds commanded by their opponents. There was also wide television and radio press coverage, but this too, as one study comments, was "on the whole favorable to membership."[35]

The Norwegian referendum, in contrast to its French and Irish counterparts, was marked by a high level of much more evenhanded information. The parliament allocated approximately 10 million kroner (£750,000) for the campaign. Of this sum, almost half was distributed to the political parties in proportion to their parliamentary strength, another 2.5 million kroner was divided evenly between the pro- and antimembership organizations, and the government spent approximately 3 million kroner on its own information campaign. One gauge of this funding's extent is that it equaled more than half of British funding for its 1975 referendum in a Norwegian population that is one-fourteenth the size of Great Britain's.

The government issued a wide variety of free, readily available, and generally balanced booklets and pamphlets on EEC membership issues. There was no unsolicited distribution of literature, however, other than a printed voting appeal just before the referendum. Public television and radio gave extensive and largely even coverage to the campaign. By contrast, the national newspapers, most of which are associated with one or another of the political parties, took stands that corresponded with their particular party affiliation. Therefore, insofar as most of the parties backed membership, so did the press. Local papers were dominated by letter-writing campaigns by the two sides.

With government information largely unbiased, the pro- and anti-campaigning was left to the two umbrella organizations and to the various political parties. The antimarket organization was more organized and effective, distributing, for example, the *EEC News* every other week with a print run of 1.3 million—one for every three Norwegians.

The Danish referendum on the EEC exceeded even the high levels of information and interest exhibited in the Norwegian referendum. Indeed, one study estimates that the "campaign before the referendum . . . was undoubtedly the most extensive political campaign ever undertaken in Denmark. It was also one of the most intensive."[36]

The quality and amount of information in the Danish campaign was impressive. The government appropriated some £1,800,000 for the campaign in a population of just 5 million, an expenditure twice the per capita allocation in Norway and nearly five times the per capita expenditure in Ireland. Also, the loose-knit, pro- and antimembership organizations raised funds, amassing approximately £450,000 each.

The government used its share of the funds to publish a great deal of evenhanded information. Every household received a booklet, for example, that included arguments on both sides of the issue and statements by each of the nine major political parties. The government also encouraged and helped fund the formation of citizens groups to discuss the issues and formulate opinions. In all, one study estimates that 500,000 people, 10 percent of all Danes, were involved in this aspect of the campaign.[37] Like the Norwegian campaign, and in contrast to the Irish and British referendum campaigns, the Danes did not mandate or specifically recognize pro- and antimembership umbrella organizations, although some aggregating of forces on both sides of the issue did informally occur in both Scandinavian countries. There were also several television and radio presentations, and all the major parties and organizations that gained recognition by collecting petition signatures were given equal time to present their positions. However, since most of them favored membership, this resulted in an imbalance for membership during these presentations.

The interest of Danish citizens was high. For example, more than 60 percent claimed to have seen all or most of the television presentations. As a result, knowledge increased. Hansen, Small, and Siune have concluded that political communications flowed well between leaders and the masses, with the views of the two becoming "more congruent as the result of a two way influencing process" and with the electorate benefiting from "the learning process which enabled [it] to use not only more arguments but also more specific and sophisticated ones [on which] to base [its] decision."[38]

The British referendum's level of activity and interest, by comparison, was less than that in the Scandinavian countries, but substantially better than the lackadaisical showing in the French referendum. The British government spent a total of £1,250,000 on the campaign, or about 2.5 pence per citizen. This contrasts poorly with the 25 pence per citizen spent by Norway's government and the 45 pence per citizen spent by the Danish government. Even allowing for economies of scale, it is clear that the British appropriation did not allow for a significant level of official information.

Most of the government's funds were used to print and distribute three pamphlets to each household. One pamphlet set out the pro-membership case, one argued the antimembership case, and the third aired the government's views, and thus, in the words of Anthony King, "was simply another version of the 'yes' case."[39]

The government also gave £125,000 to each of the two established umbrella organizations: (pro) Britain In Europe (BIE) and (anti) National Referendum Campaign (NRC). These two organizations also solicited funds, although the effort greatly favored BIE, which was heavily supported by British commercial interests and was able to raise £1,336,000 in addition to the government grant. The NRC fared poorly, garnering only an additional £8,629 and 81 pence. Thus, the total £133,629 NRC campaign fund was only 9 percent of the BIE's treasury. Insofar as they were able, these organizations conducted referendum campaigns that paralleled the course of parliamentary campaigns, with local meetings and speeches around the country and with canvassers distributing leaflets and knocking on doors.

The broadcast and printed media also played important, but somewhat limited, roles in the campaign. Because there had been two general elections in the previous eighteen months, media leaders assumed that the public appetite for political argument had been sated. There had been particular criticism of the BBC for too much coverage, and, as Philip Goodhart explains, television executives "were anxious to avoid ramming the referendum into the public's ears and eyes."[40] Similarly, David Butler and Uwe Kitzinger observe that while the printed media "was never without referendum stories," it can also be said that "the limit was the digestion of the British public. The newspapers quite early on decided that, while the referendum must be covered, it was something of a bore."[41]

Unlike the broadcast media, the printed press tended to favor one side or the other. The *Times*, for example, in the ten weeks prior to the vote, devoted about 40 percent of its coverage to promembership stories and about 30 percent each to antimembership and neutral stories. And the one-day analysis of column-inch coverage found that in the nine national papers, promembership coverage exceeded antimembership in five, the bias went the other way in three, and only one was balanced.

Public interest in the referendum paralleled the media's: attentive but not excitedly so. Regarding the limited broadcast media coverage, polls found that 14 percent thought that it was too much, 34 percent thought it was about right, 30 percent wanted more, and 22 percent had no opinion. In the campaign's last week, as coverage increased, the "too much" percentage rose to equal "not enough."[42]

There is some indication that the three government-mailed pamphlets had some impact, with 75 percent of poll respondents saying they had at least seen one or another of the leaflets, and 25 percent saying they had read at least one thoroughly.[43] By contrast, traditional local campaigning seemed largely invisible. By campaign's end, only 30 percent could recall having seen "any sign of people campaigning for Britain to stay in or leave the Common Market."[44] The broadcast media had more of an audience.

The eight pro- and antimembership television presentations drew an average of 21 million viewers, and campaign broadcasts on radio averaged 2.2 million listeners.[45]

It is not clear whether these broadcasts, despite substantial audience levels, had an impact on voter preferences. Voting intentions remained relatively stable during the three months preceding the referendum, and only 5 percent thought the broadcasts had affected their views. Furthermore, specific information was not strong among respondents in British polls. After the renegotiated terms were announced, 56 percent of Britons could not think of any new terms, and this included 54 percent of the people who were switching to a promembership position because of the new terms. Another survey asked voters questions about the EEC and found that more than half of the respondents could not correctly answer even one of the six questions.[46]

The official efforts to educate voters before the Spanish referendum and the quality and amount of information available to them were lower than in any of the EEC referendums, except perhaps the French vote. The entire official referendum campaign from its announcement to the day of the vote encompassed only six weeks, although the possibility had been discussed for well over a year. There was no official funding of a mass education effort, nor was there any attempt by the pro-NATO government to encourage, much less fund, groups to urge a no vote in the referendum. As a result, while a large number of grassroots efforts did form to oppose membership, they were ill-organized and had few financial resources to air their views.

That left it to the media to carry on the informational campaign. The dispersal of information to voters and their interest in it were affected in part by the issue of whether to vote at all. The AP and other right-of-center parties had urged citizens to abstain from voting in the referendum, and a minority of the media either joined the conservatives' call for abstention or were ambivalent about whether citizens should vote. The impact of the mixed message about participation was to lessen the interest of the population, part of which reasonably concluded that it did not have to become well versed on a subject on which it would not vote.

The second matter, the particular issues at stake in the decision, received a reasonable amount of attention in the printed media. Many papers were not editorially neutral, however, and they also slanted their reporting to a significant extent. On the membership issue itself, a majority (*Diario 16, Cambio 16, and La Vanguardia*) openly favored a yes vote, while others (*El País*) ambiguously favored membership. No major printed media source openly opposed staying in the alliance. By comparison, the untrammeled bias of the state-controlled television network (TVE) left even the printed media aghast. Information on TVE was one-sided, and it broadcast a long, last-minute appeal by González for a yes vote without affording equal, indeed any, access to the opposition. This TVE performance was roundly condemned by the printed media, with *El País* typically commenting that TVE "has followed the official line in a stifling manner and has not served the society as a whole."[47]

All this constrained citizen interest and knowledge. A late January poll, for example, found that 20 percent of those questioned thought (incorrectly) that Spain was not a member of NATO, and another 16 percent did not want to hazard a guess. When told that Spain was indeed in NATO, only 56 percent had any opinion about whether or not military integration with NATO was desirable.[48] This dearth of opinion reflected a tepid level of interest among Spain's electorate. An early February poll found just 45 percent saying they were "much" or "fairly" (*bastante*) interested in the results of the referendum. Another 26 percent expressed "a little" interest; 24 percent said they had "no" interest, and 4 percent did not respond. The highest (much/fairly) interest was among Spaniards who were left-political identifiers (67%), aged 26 through 40 (54%), and the upper class (58%). The lowest interest (little/none) was among centrists (60%), those older than 60 (61%) and the working class (58%).[49]

Switzerland's democracy and its referendum tradition were as old as Spain's democratic processes were new. In this context, the 1986 Swiss referendum on UN membership was less remarkable than Spain's NATO vote. The Swiss had gone to the polls about every three months during 1985 to decide twelve different issues, ranging from electoral law to vivisection. It was not an unusual year. Eleven referendum questions were decided in 1984; the 1986 UN referendum was only the first of seven that year. Because of this constant round of referendums, the UN referendum was not the subject of the particular focus that often occurs in countries where referendums are less common. It was not, however, business as usual in Switzerland. The UN question carried the potential of a major shift in Swiss policy. In part for that reason, it did not share the ballot with another issue (it is common in Switzerland for several issues to be presented at the same time). That level of interest sparked considerable coverage of the issue, and in a country as highly educated as Switzerland and as extensively served by the media as it is, there was considerable debate and available information on both sides of the issue.

VOTER PARTICIPATION

It is axiomatic that democratic government requires some citizen participation in the process of making choices. We have also contended that democracy is enhanced by a high level of participation by all citizens eligible to vote.

The third set of questions that structure this study concerns this issue of participation. It varied considerably among the five countries along lines that might be expected given the level of interest discussed above. Participation also varied within countries. This occurred for a variety of reasons that related to the individual countries, but in greatest part it related to the classic variations by socioeconomic status (SES) that numerous studies have found in numerous countries.

The lack of interest by the French in the 1972 referendum and their recognition that the campaign was an attempt at political manipulation by President Pompidou was further evidenced by voting turnout. Several opposition parties, most notably the Socialists, urged abstention, and others recommended spoiling the ballots. The right-wing Ordre Nouveau, for example, suggested writing "Yes to Europe, No to Pompidou" on the paper ballot.[50] Lack of interest, the voters' accurate sense of being manipulated, and the organized campaign to abstain or spoil ballots had their effect. Nearly half the electorate (47.6%) did not participate, of which 11.5 million abstained and 2 million cast spoiled ballots. This contrasts with the approximate 75 percent turnout for the 1968 and 1973 general elections, and both the referendum's abstention rate (39.5%) and the spoiled ballot rate (7.1%) were the highest in French electoral history, encompassing both general elections and referendums.

Claude Leleu's analysis of voter turnout indicates that the exceptionally low level of participation was only somewhat related to the left parties' call to abstain from the election. There is evidence that Communist party supporters heeded their party's call, but voters identifying with the Socialist party did not especially do so. Instead, according to Leleu, "correlations all point in the same direction . . . non-participation stem[med] more from the indifference which affected all the political groups than from the role played by the Socialist party."[51] What Leleu's argument misses, however, is that the referendum was widely reported by the press and understood by the public to be a partisan political ploy by Pompidou. Therefore, the lack of interest of many French citizens showed a fair amount of political savvy, not deplorable inertia.

The Irish were as enthusiastic as the French were blasé. This is surprising given the lopsided campaign and the fact that a promarket victory was never in doubt. The 70.9 percent voter turnout was the highest for any Irish referendum, but it was about 4 percent lower than the previous, 1969 general election turnout.

Norwegian voters also exhibited a high level of interest in the EEC issue, with 29 percent describing themselves as "very interested." The 79.2 percent voting turnout was also very high, although a few percentage points below the 1965, 1969, and 1973 general elections.

The social demographics of Norwegian voting participation conformed to the pattern found for many countries by many studies: lower

SES groups were "less interested in the issue, [knew] less about [it], . . . [had] less access to some important channels of information . . . [and had] less confidence in [their] knowledge about the issue."[52] Rating SES from 0 (low) to 8 (high), for example, only 12.3 percent of those in the lowest three SES groups expressed high interest. By contrast, the highest three SES groups had a high interest average of 55.7 percent. Of the low group, 47.7 percent had heard of the government's information pamphlets; 90 percent of the high groups had. Of the low group, 28.7 percent felt competent to take a position on the issue compared to 53 percent of the high group.

It would have been reasonable to predict that this demographic pattern of knowledge and interest would favor a promembership vote in Norway, since higher SES groups supported membership and lower SES groups were opposed. Also, membership was perceived as a particular threat by fishing communities, which tended to be on the lower SES periphery. That, accelerated by the high level of consensus in these communities, heightened interest and participation in them. By contrast, more evenly divided communities, such as urban, industrialized centers, had something of a voting drop-off.[53]

The keen interest of Danes in the referendum was further demonstrated by the extraordinary turnout of 90.1 percent, the highest level in Danish history. Analysis of participation in the Danish referendum indicates that, as could be expected, turnout was affected by social status.[54] This was only marginal, however, and while metropolitan Copenhagen had a lower turnout than rural areas, at 88.9 percent it was only slightly lower than the national average or the vote in any of the other major areas (excluding Greenland). Copenhagen narrowly voted against membership, and that position was strongest in working-class constituencies. But given the high turnout everywhere and the easy victory for membership, even a 100 percent turnout in Copenhagen would have only slightly changed the margin, not the result.

British interest stood between the highs of Scandinavia and Ireland and the low of France. On referendum day in June 1975, 64.5 percent of eligible Britons cast ballots. It was a lower turnout than for any national election after World War II. By comparison, the preceding parliamentary election in October 1974 had occasioned a turnout of 72.8 percent. Still, the voting level was higher than that in many other stable democratic countries, such as the United States.

In Great Britain, as in the other countries holding EEC referendums, participation was affected by SES status. One poll that grouped probable voting according to three SES groupings found that 72 percent of the highest group, 64 percent of the middle group, and only 58 percent of the lowest group were likely to vote.[55] The age factor was also typical, with middle-age voters going to the polls more than the young and the old, and men were more apt to vote than women (68 to 65 percent). Another analysis indicated a relationship between turnout and the percentage of manual laborers in a district or area, with a 2 or 3 percent turnout variation attributable to this factor. This was also related to the drop-off from the 1974 general election, with working-class areas having an even more significant vote decline than areas with higher percentages of professional and white-collar workers. Participation in Spain's NATO referendum was lower than in any of the EEC referendums except France's. The 59.4 percent turnout was also low by Spanish standards. The 40.6 percent abstention rate was the highest in any national election to that time. Another 6.5 percent of the votes were blank. Insofar as these blank votes were political statements, which most were, this would increase abstention to 44.5 percent. Even the 40.6 figure was 20 points higher than abstentions in the 1982 general election and 8 percent higher than in the 1978 referendum on the constitution. One ramification is that while continued NATO membership was supported by 52.6 percent of those who voted (with 39.8 percent against, 6.5 percent blank, and 1.1 percent spoiled), overall less than a third of the eligible electorate voted for NATO.

Mitigating the image of Spanish democratic lethargy is the fact that part of the low turnout resulted from the abstention calls by the conservative parties. Surveys showed that both support for having a referendum and expressed interest in the results were much lower on the right than on the left. Furthermore, the intention to abstain was much more prevalent on the right. When asked whether abstaining was a responsible position, 47 percent of the right identifiers said yes; only 18 percent of the left identifiers agreed.[56] Another study reported that between a third and a half of 1982 CP-UCD voters said they intended to abstain.[57]

The pattern of voting reflected this politically motivated lack of interest and participation. Abstentionism was highest in areas where the conservatives had the greatest electoral strength. There was also a strong correlation (0.62) between the level of blank votes and conservative strength in electoral areas, which indicates that a significant number of blank votes were acts of abstention rather than indications of ambivalence.[58]

Voting participation was reasonably even across the country, although there were a few areas of very low turnout. There was some relationship between turnout and result. Of the fifty-six geographic voting areas, eight had turnouts 5 percent or less than the national average. All of these areas voted yes. Twelve of the voting areas had turnouts 5 percent or more above the national average. Whether high turnout had an impact on outcome depends on interpretation. Six of the thirteen areas that voted no had high turnouts; but of the twelve high-turnout areas, six voted yes and six voted no. The blank vote factor adds another complexity to the analysis. Eleven areas counted blank votes that exceeded 10 percent of the ballots cast. All of these areas voted yes. The three areas with less than 3 percent blank ballots all voted no, and the thirteen areas that voted no averaged 4.7 percent blank votes, 1.8 percent below the national average. If the blank vote was added to the nonvote, this would again tend to indicate that the abstention strategy (low turnout/blank vote) favored the status quo.[59]

There was no thought of politically motivated abstention or casting of blank ballots in Switzerland. The UN membership issue had the portent of a major change in Swiss foreign policy, and it occasioned considerable interest in the country. The turnout of 2.10 million Swiss voters was just below the record turnout of 2.14 million in February 1984 referendums and was more than 600,000 higher (40%) than the average referendum turnouts the previous year. This is particularly impressive in light of the feeling in the press that the public had wearied of the long-contemplated UN referendum and given the fact that polls showed that the referendum would certainly be defeated. Still, in a country that sometimes seems sated on voting, the relatively high turnout amounted to just over half (50.7%) of the eligible voters. But it is also true that this was almost 2 percent higher than the preceding and next general elections in 1983 and 1987. Turnout in the various cantons ranged significantly from a high of 75.5 percent to a low of 36.4 percent. Turnout was higher than the national average in almost all the German-speaking cantons, while French and Italian-speaking cantons averaged less than a 45 percent turnout.

DETERMINANTS OF VICTORY

The crux of any referendum is, of course, the decision of the electorate, and this section examines this crucial factor. It will become evident that a wide range of cues, including nationalism, group/voter self-interest, the positions of parties and political leaders, the stance of the media, and interest group funding all play a role. These roles varied considerably, however, among the five referendums that addressed EEC membership.

In France, partisanship was a key factor in the vote. President Pompidou never quite risked turning the referendum into a personal vote of confidence as President de Gaulle regularly had. Still, Pompidou cast it in terms broader than the immediate issue. Minister of Foreign Affairs Maurice Schuman announced that if the referendum question was "disapproved by the people, it is up to them to designate another president, and we shall have another government."[60] Also, Pompidou asserted that the referendum vote was tantamount to an electoral test of his entire European policy.

Leleu's analysis indicates that the low turnout did not affect the outcome. With the government strongly supporting a yes vote, with the major right and center parties holding that position, and with most of business and the media also urging yes, there was little doubt about the outcome of the campaign.[61]

The Irish campaign was even more one-sided than France's. Indeed, it was so lopsided that it is hard to imagine Irish voters making any decision other than endorsing membership in the EEC. The government strongly endorsed and campaigned for membership, and of the 144 members of the Dail (the Irish parliament), the seventy-five who were members of the Fianna Fail (the government party) and the fifty-two who were members of the main opposition Fine Gael party supported membership.

Only the relatively small (seventeen MPs) Labour party opposed membership. This was based on the antimembership position of the 350,000-worker-strong Irish Trade Union Congress, and, most particularly, its member union, the Irish Transport and General Workers Union, with 150,000 members. The other notable antimembership group consisted of small farmers in West Ireland, who were concerned about markets in the EEC.

The coalition standing behind membership was much more powerful. In addition to the government and major political parties, virtually all of business and industry favored membership, and this helped the promembership forces outraise and outspend their opponents by ten to one. The media also favored joining the EEC. Government-controlled television was neutral, but all six national newspapers endorsed membership.

The issues in Ireland, and in the rest of the countries conducting referendums on the EEC, tended to have a domestic slant. There were several issues that could have spelled trouble for membership. With 7 percent unemployment, there was concern about the fate of such labor-intensive and static or declining industries as textiles and leather. Agricultural and fisheries competition created other worries. The possible sale of land to foreigners and the fear of free immigration, especially from Italy, touched nationalist as well as economic sensibilities. The opposition also argued that joining Europe would inevitably compromise Irish neutrality and lead to NATO involvement and foreign wars. Finally, as in all countries, the opposition maintained that membership would mean loss of Irish sovereignty.

These messages never persuaded the bulk of Irish voters. Part of this failure was because the antimembership forces had scant funds to air their view. Their campaign also was so lacking in good information, strong speakers, and persuasive slogans that the public tended to associate the antis with "the subversive label of militant and violent republicanism. . . . Indeed it was almost impossible to coalesce the opponents who, in the public eye, seemed to be dominated by mavericks and nutcases."[62]

The promembership forces, on the other hand, waged a skilled campaign. Individual groups, such as farmers and fishermen, were targeted with messages that specifically addressed their concerns. The government further eased fears by including specific clauses in the membership agreement that mitigated or extended the impact membership would have beyond a transitional period.

Most analysts view Norway's referendum as a center-periphery struggle with a periphery victory. Hellevik and Gleditsch argue that despite some party influence, "the conflict over the EEC issue was a conflict between center and periphery." They contend that "the EEC [was] a new idea that had not yet penetrated to the periphery," and "membership in the EEC was in the interest of the more powerful, the better educated, [and other elite groups]." Yet, despite the fact that most Storting members, business leaders, the press, and other opinion leaders favored membership, polls during the year leading up to the September 1972 vote showed that a majority of Norwegians consistently opposed membership. The no votes declined from around 70 percent in late 1971 to 53.5 percent in the actual vote, but the elite message was never able to overcome the bases of opposition. This elite-mass split led Hellevik and Gleditsch to conclude that the referendum was "extraordinary" because of "the resistance of public opinion to [the] shift in the direction of the political leaders when these announced their position and pressed for support [of membership]."[63]

The center-periphery dimension can be seen, and membership was rejected in part because antimembership preferences dominated lower SES groups. A study that divided voters into nine SES groups found that voters in the lowest three (26.6 percent of the sample) rejected membership by an absolute majority, and the middle three (57.8 percent of the sample) rejected membership by plurality (with "don't know" holding the balance). Only in the highest three SES groups, comprising only 15.8 percent of the sample, did the promembership position command an absolute majority.[64]

Education had a medium impact; economic status indicators were stronger. The center-periphery split (and the impact of parochial concerns) was also evident in Norwegians' reasons for favoring or opposing membership. Of those who supported membership, the most prevalent reasons cited (48%) were such cosmopolitan explanations as it was good to favor "a united Europe" or that it would promote "peace in Europe." Another 41 percent mentioned economic advantages, such as secure employment, to explain their support of membership. The antimembership reasoning was more diverse. About half explained that membership would be bad for them economically, with a negative impact on farming and fishing seen as the most threatening. Another 40 percent gave generally parochial answers such as fearing the loss of sovereignty, general preference for the status quo, or fear of change or strangers.[65]

The pattern of voter attitudes and decisionmaking in Denmark in many ways resembled Norway's, although the results were markedly different. As in Norway, the struggle occurred along a center-periphery dimension. Most of Denmark's trade and industrial leaders favored membership, and that was reflected in the solid support of the more conservative parties. Trade unions were opposed, although this did not reflect clearly in the moderate Social Democrat party leadership, most of whom favored membership. The farthest-left party in the Folketing, the Socialist People's party, strongly opposed membership. Danish farmers and fishermen, who were more confident than their Norwegian counterparts of their ability to compete in the larger market, favored membership.

The center-periphery pattern was also generally evident in voters' positions. Elklit and Petersen's SES analysis yielded expected results.[66] For example, there was a marked decline in support as one moved from employers to while collar workers to blue collar workers. In Denmark, however, geographical support was nearly the reverse of the pattern in Norway. The areas farthest from Copenhagen were the most favorable, largely because of the support of agriculture and fishing and because of the large, antimembership industrial class in Copenhagen.

The distribution of arguments in the Danish electorate for and against membership also had some parallels to the patterns in Norway and elsewhere. Proponents most often (32%) cited economic reasons for joining, arguing that it would mean greater prosperity. Strong messages from commercial and governmental supporters urged this view. Secondarily, supporters cited specific (self-centered) interests (13%) and ideological concerns (14%), such as the ideal of a united Europe. Opponents, by contrast, most often (35%) cited the loss of sovereignty as the basis of their opposition. Secondarily, they argued that the country would suffer economically (15%), or they held ideological views (11%), such as concern about the bourgeois nature of the EEC.[67]

Several scholars also carefully studied the pattern of opinion formation by studying pro and con arguments in the Folketing and among the electorate.[68] They agree that party position, party identification, and referendum voting decisions were strongly linked. This included, according to one analysis, an intricate pattern of mutual influence that paralleled "the more idealized models of opinion-policy relationships in democratic societies" and indicated the voters were not simply following elite cues.[69]

Voting patterns in the British referendum generally resembled the patterns found in Ireland, Norway, and Denmark. Political position (left-right) and party identification were important; center-periphery/SES status was also a key variable. There were differences, however. Political position was a bit more important and social position a bit less important in Britain than in the other countries. This may well have stemmed in part from two factors. First, the British were voting on the status quo, whether or not to remain in the EEC; Irish, Norwegian, and Danish voters were deciding on change, whether or not to join the EEC. Second, British voters were more apathetic on the EEC issue, and a smaller percentage voted than in any of the other three countries. Since they were more apathetic and lacked strong views, British voters were more open to cues from their parties, political leaders, and other elites. As a result, British opinion on the EEC issue was relatively stable during the three months of the "official" campaign. Once the new, renegotiated terms were announced and the Labour government and the Conservative and Liberal parties endorsed continued membership, public opinion about the EEC improved dramatically to somewhere near the final margin, although some pro-EEC movement (5 to 8 percent, depending on the poll) did occur between March and June.

Several studies have highlighted the importance of elite political cues. Business executives, for example, overwhelmingly (95%) favored continued membership, and 73 percent believed their business would be harmed if Great Britain quit the EEC. These attitudes were widely disseminated to the British public through media reporting and through the promarketeer's extensive public relations campaign, and they had their intended effect.

Political ideology also played a role in voter position. As an overall proposition, left to right self-categorization had a strong relationship to opinion on the EEC, with an increasing right orientation corresponding closely to a propensity to favor continued membership.[70]

The impact of the political parties was even more important. In terms of specific party identification, one analysis concluded that "over the years only small minorities of voters have stayed constant in their support for or opposition to... membership. The great majority changed sides depending on the position of their own and the other parties."[71] As might be expected given this view, promembership opinion (omitting undecided respondents) of the two parties (Conservatives, Liberals) whose leaders solidly favored the EEC was 87 percent and 70 percent, respectively; identifiers with the divided-leadership Labour party favored membership by a narrower 60 percent. Furthermore, only 6 percent of Conservative voters and 7 percent of Liberal voters were undecided a week before the election. Thirteen percent of Labour voters were undecided and thus more likely to sit out the referendum.[72]

The importance of partisanship did not negate, however, the important and related impact of socioeconomic and center-periphery status. Bristow, for example, found partisanship to be the most important index, but he also found strong correlations between a district's industrialization and (lack of) wealth and its percentage of no votes.[73] Other studies confirm age, class, gender, and related demographic patterns found in the other EEC referendums.[74] In addition, there was evidence of geographical center-periphery impact. The percentage of promarket votes was less in Wales than in England and even less in Scotland and Northern Ireland. Even within England, the pro-EEC vote declined as one moved outward from the south, through the Midlands, to northern England.

The specific issues that concerned British voters were akin to those that were on the minds of Irish, Norwegian, and Danish voters. As true elsewhere, economics was the leading concern of promarket voters, but, somewhat differently, few British voters in this category were concerned with ideological issues, such as a united Europe. Because Great Britain was already in the EEC, the tendency of uncertain or apathetic voters to favor the status quo worked in favor of staying in among the British, with about 20 percent citing this reasoning. A bit more than in other countries, economics also dominated antimarket thinking in Great Britain, with rising food prices the particular focus. Nationalism and tradition also were important factors, with 27 percent of anti-EEC voters arguing that continued membership meant a loss of independence, and another 14 percent worried about a decline in Commonwealth ties.[75]

The referendum in Spain demonstrated yet again that voters merge domestic and international policy concerns together when making decisions. It may be, as one purist argued, that "a vital question of international alignment ought to have involved an argument based on principle: the defense of liberty against a Soviet threat."[76] That was not the argument of NATO proponents, however. Instead, Prime Minister González and others urged Spaniards to vote yes based on a range of economic, nationalist, partisan, and emotional arguments.

The desire for economic prosperity and the desire to end the isolation of the Franco era combined to create momentum to join the EC. There was never a formal link between EC and NATO membership, but González contended that Spain's admission to the EC was directly tied to the permanence of Spain in NATO. Spain joined the EC on January 1, 1986, and Foreign Minister Francisco Fernández Ordóñez said that if the NATO vote on March 12 was no, Spain might either have to pull out of the EC or become a "second-rate" partner.[77] Much of Spain's business community endorsed the view that economic prosperity and NATO were connected. The largest banks, for example, joined in a formal statement urging a yes vote, thereby putting some of the country's most conservative capitalists squarely in a political alliance with the socialists. Many Spanish voters were persuaded by this united front. While only 40 percent thought that joining NATO would benefit the country's defense, 54 percent believed that it would improve relations with the EC.[78]

The fact that the NATO and EC memberships were not truly interdependent led some to criticize the government for stampeding the public. *Cambio 16* editorialized that the contention by the foreign minister was "totally unacceptable," as was the implication that "by rejecting NATO we will end up back at the stage of primitive string sandals and horse transport. . . . The PSOE won the referendum with the votes of frail old-age pensioners frightened out of their wits."[79]

González was also able to play on Spanish emotions over the U.S. military bases in the country. The simmering resentment in Spain over the bases boiled up during a May 1985 visit by President Ronald Reagan. Close to a million people joined in antibase demonstrations in most of Spain's major cities. The anti-NATO faction tried to capitalize on these sentiments by linking Reagan's anticommunist hard line, the U.S. bases in Spain, and NATO by arguing that joining NATO increased the danger of nuclear destruction. Leftists also charged that the United States dominated NATO. Therefore, membership was, in the estimation of the leftist leader in Barcelona, the "main proof that we are a province of the empire."[80]

González outmaneuvered the left, however. The language in the referendum barring nuclear weapons from Spanish territory arguably reduced the chance that Spain would be subjected to a Soviet missile barrage. Second, the referendum clause about reducing the U.S. military presence made a yes vote a ballot in favor of fewer Americans and their weapons, while a no vote seemingly supported the *Yanqui* status quo. Few Spaniards favored that. Playing on that sentiment and again coopting one of the left's main issues, the prime minister argued that joining NATO would make Madrid less dependent on Washington, thereby strengthening Spain's position to force a reduction of the U.S. military presence.

Political stability in Spain was a third important issue. There had been an attempted military coup five years earlier. That led many Spanish commentators to argue that "to put a stop . . . to the military's toying with the internal affairs, the government must give them a toy to play with that will turn their minds outward." NATO was the "toy." It would give Spanish officers an external focus and might also have the salutary effect through "contact with the non-political officers of other countries" and through "technical modernization" of fostering "a steady increase in [the] professionalism" of Spain's officers.[81]

Related to this concern, but more general and more important, was the future of the political system in Spain. Many Spaniards feared that the conservatives harbored desires, perhaps in league with the military, to end Spain's democracy. Manuel Fraga and his AP and other right-of-center parties were the main alternative to González and the PSOE government, and the prime minister was able to play on the suspicions of the right by making the referendum a tacit vote of confidence in his government. This ploy raised the specter that a no vote would bring Fraga to power.

González only hinted that he would resign and call elections if continued membership was rejected, but other government officials explicitly made that statement. González himself left little doubt, though, and in his televised speech just prior to the vote he mentioned NATO only twice, stressing instead peace and warning darkly of "political instability."[82] The result of this line of argument, Javier Pérez Royo comments, was that the referendum "lost the character of a referendum and became, for all practical purposes, a general vote of confidence on the conduct of the Socialist government."[83]

The strategy of introducing a vote-of-confidence element into the issues was effective. PSOE loyalists, whose ideology disposed them to vote no, overwhelming decided to support continued membership in NATO and to vote yes in order not to undermine the González government. An early poll showed less than half of all leftist identifiers in favor of staying in NATO along the terms of the referendum's wording.[84] The campaign changed the opinion of much of the left and center-left, however, and in the vote there was a high (0.93) correlation between the voting area strength of the PSOE in the 1982 general election and the yes vote in 1986.[85]

In addition to these three major arguments, the government fielded a host of others, mainly designed to play on Spanish insecurities. The government argued that as a member of NATO it would have more leverage to get Great Britain out of Gibraltar. Some argued that the NATO connection and a modernized military would help Spain retain the colonial cities of Ceuta and Melilla, which are inside Morocco. Other NATO advocates hinted that Barcelona would lose its bid for the 1992 summer Olympic games and that the plans for a World's Fair in Seville would be canceled if the vote was no on NATO. As one opposition leader lamented, the government "warned us of everything except an invasion of AIDS."[86]

The no vote was scattered. Several of the voting areas where there was a majority or plurality were autonomous regions with separatist sentiments, and the no voting was more an expression of antigovernment sentiment than a reflection of opinion on the NATO alliance. There was also a stronger no vote in areas such as Barcelona, where the parties to the left of the PSOE, such as the communists, were strongest. An estimated one-third of both PSOE and AP and other conservative party identifiers also voted no.

The media explained that the vote outcome also resulted because of the public's fear that the proposition would lose and because of González's high personal popularity with voters.[87] Ironically, that fear was caused by almost universally inaccurate polls showing that alliance membership would be defeated. *El País, La Vanguardia, Diario 16*, and other national media sources predicted the no votes would carry the day by up to 11 percent. These polls both spurred the government to its strong final-week efforts, urged yes voters to get to the polls, and convinced abstainers that staying home might have a real impact. One study declared itself "convinced" that the negative polls were "a decisive influence in helping the government win the referendum. Or to say this another way: if it have not been for the polls, the no's would have won."[88]

The Swiss debate on UN membership more clearly focused on the international ramifications of the referendum question than did the debates in the European EEC and NATO referendums. Like the others, though, the issue in Switzerland contained important elements of domestic political considerations. There were three main issues of debate: traditional Swiss neutrality, the benefits of UN membership, and purported power-grabbing by the Swiss central government. Given the lopsided rejection of UN membership, it is tempting to write off the campaign as an exercise in futility, but that was not unalterably the case. In the first place, the vote in Switzerland did not reflect, at least to the Swiss, an isolationist stand. A poll taken after the referendum found that two-thirds of all Swiss favored an active international role. Furthermore, Swiss opinion on UN membership had swung widely. As late as 1979, 60 percent of Swiss favored membership. That declined to 35 percent in mid-1985, with 38 percent opposed and 27 percent undecided. Thus, the fate of membership and, even more, the margin hung in the balance as the campaign began.

Swiss neutrality was first adopted in the early 1500s as a pragmatic measure after a decisive defeat by France. But like many old ideas, it has taken on the patina of ideological doctrine. Membership proponents argued that neutrality and isolationism were different, and that continued refusal by Switzerland to join the United Nations left the country at risk of being outside the mainstream of international interchange. Opponents argued that UN membership would end Swiss neutrality by requiring it to participate in UN-mandated economic sanctions and perhaps even military peacekeeping actions. Opponents further contended that the end of neutrality would detract from Switzerland's important roles as neutral mediator, home of many international organizations, and host to frequent bilateral and multilateral diplomatic negotiations.

Opponents also capitalized on proponents' inability to cite tangible benefits of joining the United Nations. To the contrary, opponents argued that the world body was impotent and inefficient, that Swiss membership dues would be high and wasted, and that Switzerland's one vote among 160 in the UN General Assembly would be insignificant.

The power of the central government was also an issue. Switzerland is a strong federal system, with considerable power residing in the cantons. The Federal Council waged an unusually strong effort to secure a yes vote to membership. That backfired, however. The effort was widely criticized in the press as an effort to propagandize, rather than inform, voters. Moreover, critics charged that this was part of a growing pattern aimed at increasing the power of Bern at the expense of the cantons and the sovereign power of the people exercised through direct democracy. This came at a time when the percentage of Swiss expressing confidence in their government had plummeted from 58 percent in 1977, to 44 percent in 1982, to 38 percent in 1986.

Insofar as the referendum was a question of federalism and the locus of sovereignty, it was a center-periphery struggle like many of the EEC referendums. Along with Norway's, the Swiss referendum demonstrated that the periphery sometimes wins, especially when maintaining the status quo. Most Swiss elites supported membership. In addition to the Federal Council, the three largest political parties (Socialist, Radical Democratic, and Christian Democratic) supported membership, as did the small Communist and Independents' Alliance parties. Groups representing workers, women, and students generally favored membership, but the national business associations remained neutral.

The People's party was the only electorally significant party to urge a no vote, and it was joined in that recommendation by the quite small, but upper-strata Liberal party. But the strongest opposition was on the periphery. Despite the stand of the national parties, about half the canton-level structures of the Radical Democratic and Christian Democratic parties opposed membership.

The more than 75 percent margin against membership was so overwhelming that voting analysis gives only limited insights, but they confirm the center-periphery nature of the campaign. There was also a left-right element in the vote split. All major demographic elements voted no except students; women and those with higher education had yes vote percentages a bit higher than the national average. Workers strongly voted no, and 97 percent of farmers were opposed. The strongest opposition came from the center and right. Two-thirds of all Radical Democrat and Christian Democrat identifiers ignored their national leaders and voted no. The Socialist identifiers provided most of the yes votes, with 54 percent of them voting for membership. Eighty-six percent of unaffiliated voters cast ballots against membership.

Traditionalism played a strong role. The cantons that formed the original federation in 1291 were the most strongly opposed; the small canton of Jura created in 1978 was the only one to have more than 40 percent of its voters favor membership. Exit polls found that a majority of those who had voted no explained their choice in terms of favoring continued traditional neutrality and in terms of supporting traditional decentralized federalism. The antimembership voters also said they could see no benefits from joining the United Nations.

THE SIGNIFICANCE OF THE REFERENDUMS

The final series of questions guiding this study address the long-term significance of referendums. An initial query is whether voters are prone to favor the status quo over change. Then we can ask whether the decisions, positive or negative, had a significant impact on the various countries' foreign policy. Last, we can examine other, domestic impacts of the campaigns. Departing from previous presentation in this chapter, we will address this issue concurrently, rather than on a country-by-country basis.

Whether or not the status quo has the advantage can be easily answered in this case: it does not. In the five EEC-related referendums, "change" carried the day in three: France, Ireland, and Denmark. The status quo was just as clearly victorious in Norway. Great Britain presents a somewhat curious case. Membership in the EEC was clearly a break with British tradition, but the vote itself was about whether or not Great Britain would remain in the EEC, not if it would join. Furthermore, a significant number of voters voted for continued membership because it was the status quo. Therefore, the British referendum was a status quo victory, although, in a greater sense, it was part of a historic change in British orientations.

The referendums also represented important foreign policy decisions. Under de Gaulle, France had stressed nationalism—withdrawing from the NATO military command and blocking the expansion of the EEC. The June 1972 vote was a symbol that under Pompidou, France was again open to expanded European integration. Ireland's yes to membership remains steadfast. There was a second Irish vote on membership in 1987 after passage of the EC's Single European Act (SEA), which mandated members to take full account of common policies in foreign and some domestic policy areas.[89] There was concern among some Irish voters about domestic interference by the EC, but in the end the referendum passed by a wide 70 to 30 percent. Indeed, the outcome was so certain before the vote, that there was only a 44 percent turnout. The one no to the EEC, Norway's, remains in place nearly two decades later, although the historic forces now affecting Europe may someday reverse Norway's decision.

Denmark's accession to the EEC/EC treaties and subsequent events offer an interesting example of the impact of the 1972 referendum, which carried by a 63 to 36 percent margin. During the following fourteen years, membership was not a significant issue in Danish politics, although some parliamentary debate continued because of various concerns by the left-of-center parties. The mid-1980s brought the issue to the fore again because of the SEA. Eleven of the twelve member-country parliaments ratified the act. Ireland also held a constitutional referendum, and Denmark decided to hold a referendum even though it was not required.

The details of the referendum are beyond our scope here, but brief commentary is relevant.[90] The referendum was much akin to the 1972 effort. It was held because the coalition government was shaky, and if the government had pushed the issue it would have failed in the Folketing. Neither a new election nor reopening negotiations with the EC appealed to the government, so a referendum was chosen. It was, therefore, a matter of picking the least unwanted option, rather than a burst of democratic idealism, that prompted the 1986 referendum.

The campaign assumed familiar outlines. The center favored membership; the periphery opposed it. Business and prosperous farmers were overwhelmingly in favor, and the proamendment forces outspent opponents two to one. Voting conformed to SES patterns. Male, middle-aged, and self-employed people were all strong yes voters; young and blue-collar Danes voted no. The farther right one went along the parties' ideological spectrum, the greater probability that the parties' identifiers would vote yes.

Perhaps the most interesting aspect of the vote was the "real" message of the voters. The fundamental issue in the campaign was not outright rejection or acceptance of the EC, but whether Denmark's slide into increasing integration should continue. About 25 percent of Danish voters favored greater integration, 16 percent wanted to get out of the EC, and 57 percent favored the status quo. This last category split narrowly in favor of voting yes, but the final 56 to 44 percent margin of approval was much narrower than in 1972.

The British also remain somewhat unsettled about how European they want to become. Polls indicate that economic ties are not questioned. But British citizens are much more wary about increased political ties than are citizens of the original six EEC countries.[91] From a slightly different perspective, 71 percent of Britons say they have "never thought of themselves as Europeans," again the greatest margin in any EC country.[92] Furthermore, the Conservative party under the leadership of Prime Minister Margaret Thatcher was quite cautious about the political ramifications of Europe 1992. This orientation changed somewhat with the succession of John Major to No. 10 Downing Street. Indeed, Thatcher was brought down by a revolt within the party led by Sir Geoffrey Howe, her foreign secretary. He resigned to protest Thatcher's opposition to monetary integration, explaining to the House of Commons that the vision of benefits of a united Europe was "a good deal more convincing and encouraging for the interests of [Great Britain] than the nightmare image sometimes conjured up by the prime minister who seems to look out on a continent that is positively teeming with ill-intentioned people scheming in her words, 'to extinguish democracy, [and] to dissolve our national identities.'"[93]

Despite these events, Thatcher's political demise was based on many factors beyond her EC position, and the British public remains chary of the slide into Europe. That was reflected again in the maneuvering prior to the December 1991 meeting of EC leaders at Masstricht, the Netherlands. Most European countries, especially Germany, were pressing for a commitment to adopt a single currency (the European Currency Unit, ECU) and for increased power for the European Parliament and other central EC organizations. Germany's Chancellor Helmut Kohl flatly told the Bundestag that "we favor the political unification of Europe."[94]

British reluctance to move toward a federal Europe helped frustrate Kohl's desires. Prime Minister Major was willing to contemplate moving toward greater political integration, but he came under heavy pressure to resist federalization. Former Prime Minister Thatcher, who still held her seat in Commons, called for a new referendum on any treaty that was agreed to in the upcoming meeting at Maastricht and for another prior to adopting full monetary unity in 1996. Major rejected a national vote, arguing that "my view remains that we are a parliamentary democracy, and I see no need for a referendum."[95] That brought an angry retort from Thatcher, who proclaimed that "parliamentary supremacy is the supremacy of the voice of the people. If you deny that to be heard, I think it is arrogant and I think it is wrong."[96]

Prime Minister Major was not forced into a referendum, but he did toughen his stand on EC integration, and at Maastricht he forced the deletion of the word *federal* from the final document and insisted on Great Britain's final right to reject adopting the ECU in 1996. It may well be, then, that the next crucial juncture for Europe will be when the shift from economic to political integration reaches a point where it clashes with residual nationalism. Parliaments, and perhaps the people by referendum, will then face a critical choice of direction.

A last consideration of the impact of the referendums is their impact on the domestic political lineup in the respective countries. There were minimal consequences in Ireland, Denmark, and Great Britain, although many of the elements, especially on the left, that opposed membership were not reconciled to it after the referendums. Analysts diverge over the impact of the vote in France. Leleu argues that in a narrow sense of pushing the center parties to join with the Gaullists and splitting the left parties, the use of the referendum device "confirmed the astuteness of [Pompidou's]...initiative."[97] Yet, Leleu also concedes that the lack of interest, and especially the tepidness of the pro-EEC vote by center party identifiers, indicated that the French were not strongly enthusiastic about European integration, about Pompidou's European policy, or about Pompidou as president. Wright sees the results as an unmitigated failure for

Pompidou, noting that even though the Socialists and Communists split on the issue, they were able to conclude a common electoral strategy only three months later and that Pompidou's inability to galvanize the electorate "clearly tarnished" his political reputation.[98]

The most dramatic domestic ramifications occurred in Norway. In the aftermath of Norwegian voters' rejection of EEC membership, the coalition government dominated by the Labour party, most of whose Storting members favored entry, resigned and was replaced by an alliance of antimembership parties. In the general election in September 1973, the Labour party vote dropped to 35.2 percent compared to the 46.5 percent it had gathered in the preceding, 1969 election. The Labour party was able to form a coalition alliance with the farther-left Socialist Election Alliance, but they held power with a slim, one-vote margin. The alliance was itself a coalition of antimembership groups, including the Communist party, the Socialist Peoples party, and antimembership elements of the Labour party who had formed the Workers' Information Committee. In the political center, the Liberal party split; and on the right, an ultraconservative party formed and gained seats in the Storting.[99] Furthermore, there was strong evidence of voters realigning their party allegiances, especially among EEC opponents who had identified with promembership parties. A significant number of these voters switched their party identification to an antimembership party. As one study noted, "Electoral changes of this magnitude had not occurred in Norway since around 1930."[100]

These shifts in Norway's politics were not the result of the referendum alone. Instead, as one study put it, the referendum "accentuated and accelerated latent tensions and cleavages [up to then] contained by the established political order."[101] This view was seconded by Valen and Martinussen, who concluded that the EEC dispute was "related to practically all areas of national politics" and "stirred up tremendous antagonisms. It broke up old alliances and friendships between and within parties and created political constellations unparalleled in modern Norwegian politics."[102]

Spain's referendum also had subsequent domestic political reverberations, but they were not as profound as Norway's. At least in the short term, the referendum had the impacts hoped for by Prime Minister González. Spain's membership in NATO was reaffirmed and has remained strong. Whether or not they were related to the referendum, the subsidiary clauses have also been implemented. Spain remains nuclear free, and the U.S. military presence there has declined significantly. Domestically, the right was discomfited. The PSOE took the middle ground from its main rival, the AP, which was already having great difficulty formulating alternative policies to those of the socialist government. The right's call for abstention was, in one study's estimate, "self-defeating" and led to "an accentuation of the crisis of the right"[103] The standing of Manuel Fraga, the AP leader, was particularly tarnished. Sixty-two percent of Spaniards thought that Fraga had not been sincere in his comments on NATO, and those who disapproved of him increased to 71 percent, while those who supported him declined to 23 percent.[104] The government quickly sought to capitalize on the referendum aftermath by calling elections for June. In those multiparty elections, the PSOE retained its absolute majority in the Congress of Deputies. The AP was particularly dispirited by its failure to increase its representation in the Cortes, and in December 1986 Fraga resigned as AP president. Since then, the PSOE has continued in power, although the disappearance of the right that some predicted in 1986 has not occurred. Thus, it could be said that the referendum resolved several Spanish foreign policy questions including NATO membership, U.S. bases, and nuclear weapons. The referendum also affected domestic politics, but not in a decisive, long-term way.

The Swiss referendum on UN membership, like the EEC and the NATO referendums, settled its issues at least for the foreseeable future. Switzerland is currently wrestling with the matter of membership in the EC. The Swiss have not applied, but after the 1992 target date of EC economic integration, Austria, Sweden, and other countries may well join. This will increase economic pressure on Switzerland to join also. Membership in the EC would affect Swiss neutrality in much the same way as UN membership because the EC is moving beyond its economic origins to become an increasingly political organization. The organization imposed and relaxed sanctions on South Africa, condemned Iraq's invasion of Iran, and tried to mediate the civil war in Yugoslavia; it has also taken a variety of economic and diplomatic initiatives. In the long term, therefore, EC membership might change Swiss attitudes enough to allow UN membership. This is speculation, though, and especially given the strength of the no vote in 1986, the question of Switzerland's membership in the United Nations is unlikely to be rejoined soon.

NOTES

1. Technically, the referendums being analyzed here involved the issue of whether to join the European Communities, established in 1967, of which the European Economic Community was a constituent part. Because EEC is used in many of the titles in the bibliography, because the economic matters related to the EEC were the main focus of debate in the countries, and because of continuing somewhat greater familiarity with the concept of the EEC rather than the EC, the former designation will be used when discussing the British, French, Norwegian, Irish, and Danish referendums.

2. Vincent Wright, "France," in *Referendums: A Comparative Study of Practice and Theory*, edited by David Butler and Austin Ranney (Washington,

D.C.: American Enterprise Institute, 1978), pp. 123–156; Claude Leleu, "The French Referendum of April 23, 1972," *European Journal of Political Research* 4 (1976), pp. 25–46.

3. Michael Leigh, "Linkage Politics: The French Referendum and the Paris Summit of 1972," *Journal of Common Market Studies* 14 (1975), pp. 157–170.

4. Canadian Unity Information Office, *Understanding Referenda: Six Histories: Australia, Newfoundland, Ireland, Norway, Denmark, United Kingdom* (Ottawa: Minister of Supply and Services, 1978), p. 21.

5. Canadian Unity Information Office, *Understanding Referenda*, p. 21

6. Ottar Hellevik and Nils Petter Gleditsch, "The Common Market Decision in Norway: A Clash Between Direct and Indirect Democracy," *Scandinavian Political Studies* 8 (1973), p. 232.

7. Canadian Unity Information Office, *Understanding Referenda*, p. 21; Hallevik and Gleditsch, "The Common Market Decision in Norway," p. 232.

8. Peter Hansen, Melvin Small, and Karen Siune, "The Structure of Debate in the Danish EEC Campaign: A Study of an Opinion-Policy Relationship," *Journal of Common Market Studies* 15 (1976), p. 122.

9. Jørgen Elklit and Nikolaj Petersen, "Denmark: Denmark Enters the European Communities," *Scandinavian Political Studies* 8 (1973), p. 203.

10. Hansen, Small, and Siune, "Structure of Debate," p. 104.

11. Philip Goodhart, *Full-Hearted Consent: The Story of the Referendum Campaign—and the Campaign for the Referendum* (London: Davis-Poynter, 1976), p. 12.

12. Anthony King, "Referendum and the European Community," in *The Referendum Device*, edited by Austin Ranney (Washington, D.C.: American Enterprise Institute, 1977), p. 69.

13. King, "Referendum," p. 55.

14. Goodhart, *Full-Hearted Consent*, p. 17.

15. Dov S. Zakheim, "Britain and the EEC—Opinion Poll Data, 1970-72," *Journal of Common Market Studies* 11 (1973), pp. 194–196.

16. King, "Referendum," p. 42.

17. King, "Referendum," p. 35.

18. Vernon Bogdanor, *The People and the Party System: The Referendum and Electoral Reform in British Politics* (Cambridge: Cambridge University Press, 1981), p. 41.

19. King, "Referendum," pp. 90–92.

20. Zakheim, "Britain in the EEC," p. 226.

21. The Cortes has two houses: the Chamber of Deputies and the Senate. The Chamber of Deputies is the more powerful, and following common usage, the term *Cortes* will mean the Chamber of Deputies unless otherwise noted. For a discussion of the Cortes and its evolution, see Janet Moriarty and John T. Rourke, "The Spanish Cortes: Democracy Re-established," *Contemporary Review* 232 (May 1978), pp. 234–238.

22. Gary Prevost, "Spain's NATO Choice," *The World Today* (August-September 1986), pp. 129–132.

23. Emilio A. Rodríquez, "Atlanticism and Europeanism: NATO and Trends in Spanish Foreign Policy," in *Spain's Entry into NATO: Conflicting Political and Strategic Perspectives*, edited by Federico G. Gil and Joseph S. Tulchin (Boulder:

Lynne Rienner Publishers, 1988), pp. 55–71.

24. Joseph M. Vallés, Francesco Pallarés, and Ramón María Canals, "The Referendum of 12 March 1986 on Spain's Remaining in NATO," *Electoral Studies* 5 (December 1986), pp. 305–311.

25. For example, see Luis Peiró, "El Gran Vuelco," *Cambio 16*, March 17, 1986, pp. 23–27.

26. *Cambio 16*, March 17, 1986, p. 23.

27. Quotes are from Inocencío Félix Arias, "Spanish Media and the Two NATO Campaigns," in Gil and Tulchin, *Spain's Entry into NATO*, pp. 29–40.

28. The referendum read:

The Government consider it appropriate to the national interest that Spain remain in the Atlantic Alliance...[under] the following terms:

1. The participation of Spain...will not include incorporation in the integrated military structure.
2. The prohibition on the installation, storing, or introducing nuclear arms on Spanish territory will be continued.
3. The progressive reduction of the military presence of the United States in Spain will proceed.

29. Quote provided by Janet Moriarty, professor of Spanish at the University of Connecticut. Professor Moriarty supplied some of the quotes, statistics, and analysis used. She also supplied the Spanish-language sources cited here and translated by the authors. We wish to thank Professor Moriarty for her valuable contribution.

30. *Cambio 16*, February 10, 1986, p. 20.

31. Arias, "Spanish Media and the Two NATO Campaigns," p. 37.

32. A great deal of the subsequent commentary on the Swiss referendum is based on C. L. Robertson, "Switzerland Rejects the United Nations," *The Fletcher Forum* 12/2 (1988), pp. 311–320; Von Luzius Wildhaber, "Das Schweizer Nein zu einer Vollmitgliedschaft in den Vereinten Nationen," *Europa-Archiv* 15 (1986), pp. 461–467.

33. Wright, "France," p. 156.

34. Wright, "France," p. 156.

35. Canadian Unity Information Office, *Understanding Referenda*, p. 18.

36. Elklit and Petersen, "Denmark," p. 206.

37. Canadian Unity Information Office, *Understanding Referenda*.

38. Hansen, Small, and Siune, "Structure of Debate," p. 128.

39. King, "Referendum," p. 122.

40. Goodhart, *Full-Hearted Consent*, p. 156.

41. David Butler and Uwe Kitzinger, *The 1975 Referendum* (New York: St. Martin's Press, 1976), p. 161.

42. Goodhart, *Full-Hearted Consent*, p. 157.

43. King, "Referendum," p. 122.

44. Butler and Kitzinger, *The 1975 Referendum*, p. 158.

45. Butler and Kitzinger, *The 1975 Referendum*, p. 212.

46. King, "Referendum," p. 122; Butler and Kitzinger, *The 1975 Referendum*, p. 213.

47. Arias, "Spanish Media and the Two NATO Campaigns," p. 39.

48. *Cambio 16*, February 2, 1986, p. 22.

49. Poll published in *Cambio 16*, February 19, 1986, p. 23.

50. Leleu, "French Referendum," p. 28.

51. Leleu, "French Referendum," p. 43.

52. Ottar Hellevik, Nils Petter Gleditsch, and Kristen Ringdal, "The Common Market Issue in Norway: A Conflict Between Center and Periphery," *Journal of Peace Research* 12 (1975), p. 42.

53. Henry Valen, "Norway: 'No' to EEC," *Scandinavian Political Studies* 8 (August 1973), pp. 214–226.

54. Elklit and Petersen, "Denmark."

55. Butler and Kitzinger, *The 1975 Referendum*, p. 253.

56. Published in *Cambio 16*, February 10, 1986, p. 23.

57. Vallés, Pallarés, and Canals, "Referendum," pp. 307–308.

58. Vallés, Pallarés, and Canals, "Referendum," p. 308.

59. Calculations are the authors' and are based on the voting reported in *El País*, March 13, 1986, pp. 16–17.

60. Wright, "France," p. 158.

61. Leleu, "French Referendum."

62. Canadian Unity Information Office, *Understanding Referenda*, p. 18.

63. Quotes are from Hellevik and Gleditsch, "Common Market Decision," pp. 234, 233.

64. Hellevik, Gleditsch, and Ringdal, "Common Market Issue," p. 42. The indicators used to establish SES included age, sex, location (generally distance from Oslo), education, occupation sector, occupational position, and income. All had an expected impact, but age and sex were relatively weak indicators.

65. Hellevik, Gleditsch, and Ringdal, "Common Market Issue," p. 51.

66. Elklit and Petersen, "Denmark," p. 206.

67. Hansen, Small, and Siune, "Structure of Debate," p. 120.

68. Hansen, Small, and Siune, "Structure of Debate"; Elklit and Petersen, "Denmark."

69. Hansen, Small, and Siune, "Structure of Debate," p. 128.

70. Roy Pierce, Henry Valen, and Ola Listhaug, "Referendum Voting Behavior: The Norwegian and British Referenda on Membership in the European Community," *American Journal of Political Science* 27 (February 1983), p. 53.

71. Quoted in Goodhart, *Full-Hearted Consent*, p. 53.

72. Subsequent analyses confirm these findings. For example, one study concluded that "party was the most important vote predictor. The analysis considered the possibility that the parties' shifts reflected attitude changes among the electorate, and while it admitted such an interpretation was "technically possible," it concluded that "the...fluctuation in British public opinion...indicates that the voters were taking partisan cues" (Pierce, Valen, and Listhaug, "Referendum Voting Behavior," p. 61). Another aspect of elite cue-giving was the prominent role played by party leaders in the voters' image of the membership question. Antimembership leaders tended to have a poor image among the majority of British voters; the reverse was true for promembership leaders. One poll listed twenty-eight such leaders and asked voter opinion of the leader. Of the seventeen leaders familiar to at least 70 percent of the voters, the ten most popular all favored continued membership, the seven least popular all opposed

it (King, "Referendum," p. 122; Butler and Kitzinger, *The 1975 Referendum*, p. 256).

73. Stephen L. Bristow, "Partisanship, Participation and Legitimacy in Britain's EEC Referendum," *Journal of Common Market Studies* 14 (June 1976), pp. 297–310.

74. Butler and Kitzinger, *The 1975 Referendum*, p. 252; King, "Referendum," p. 133.

75. Goodhart, *Full-Hearted Consent*, p. 251; King, "Referendum," p. 108; Butler and Kitzinger, *The 1975 Referendum*, p. 254.

76. Javier Tusell, "The Transition to Democracy and Spain's Membership in NATO," in Gil and Tulchin, *Spain's Entry into NATO*, p. 17.

77. *Time*, March 24, 1986, p. 44.

78. Poll published in *Cambio 16*, February 10, 1986, p. 23.

79. Quoted in Anthony Gooch, "A Surrealistic Referendum: Spain and NATO," *Government and Opposition* 31/3 (1986), p. 310.

80. Prevost, "Spain's NATO Choice," p. 129.

81. Gooch, "Spain and NATO," p. 302.

82. *Time*, March 24, 1986, p. 44.

83. Javier Pérez Royo, "Repercussion on the Democratic Process of Spain's Entry into NATO," in Gil and Tulchin, *Spain's Entry into NATO*, p. 22.

84. Poll published in *Cambio 16*, February 10, 1986, p. 23.

85. Vallés, Pallarés, and Canals, "Referendum," p. 308.

86. *Time*, March 24, 1986, p. 44.

87. Arias, "Spanish Media and the Two NATO Campaigns," p. 38; Vallés, Pallarés, and Canals, p. 307.

88. Arias, "Spanish Media and the Two NATO Campaigns," pp. 39–40.

89. Michael Gallagher, "The Single European Act Referendum," *Irish Political Studies* 3 (1988), pp. 77–82.

90. All the statistics provided here on the Danish referendum are taken from Ole Borre, "The Danish Referendum on the EC Common Act," *Electoral Studies* 5 (1986), pp. 189–193.

91. *New York Times*, May 28, 1984, p. A6.

92. Elizabeth Hann Hastings and Philip K. Hastings, *Index to International Public Opinion*, 1988–1989 (Westport, Conn.: Greenwood Press), p. 538.

93. *Hartford Courant*, November 14, 1990, p. A9.

94. *New York Times*, December 2, 1991, A11.

95. *New York Times*, November 22, 1991, A6.

96. *Hartford Courant*, November 22, 1991, A16.

97. Leleu, "French Referendum," p. 26.

98. Wright, "France," p. 161.

99. Henry Valen, "National Conflict Structure and Foreign Politics: The Impact of the EEC Issue on Perceived Cleavages in Norwegian Politics," *European Journal of Political Research* 4 (1976), pp. 47–82.

100. Henry Valen and Willy Martinussen, "Electoral Trends and Foreign Policy in Norway: The 1973 Storting Election and the EEC Issue," in *Scandinavia at the Polls: Recent Political Trends in Denmark, Norway, and Sweden*, edited by Karl Cerny (Washington, D.C.: American Enterprise Institute, 1977), p. 39.

101. Johan Jørgen Holst, "Norway's EEC Referendum: Lessons and Impli-

cations," *World Today* 31 (March 1975), p. 115.

102. Valen and Martinussen, "Electoral Trends," p. 60.

103. Pérez Royo, "Repercussions on the Democratic Process," p. 26.

104. Poll published in *Cambio 16*, March 17, 1986, p. 29.

6

Referendums and the Specter of Secession

During the 1970s, groups advocating independence for subregions within Great Britain, Canada, and Spain successfully challenged statewide parties in several local and general elections. Almost overnight, nationalist parties became important electoral forces, sometimes increasing their shares of the regional vote by 50 percent or more. For example, the Scottish National party's share of ballots cast in British general elections rose from 2.4 percent of the 1964 Scottish regional vote to 30.4 percent in October 1974. In Spain's Basque country (País Vasco), the percentage of ballots cast for Basque nationalist parties in general elections rose from 29.8 in 1977 to 44 in 1979. The Parti Québécois's share of the vote in elections for Quebec's National Assembly similarly increased, from 23 percent in 1970 to 41 percent in 1976.[1]

The stated long-term goal of the nationalist parties was to win complete political independence for their regions. In addition, many nationalist leaders, as distinct from the leaders of statewide parties (that is, state leaders) believed that full independence was unattainable in the short run. They therefore advocated federalism as an intermediate goal and struggled either to establish new regional governments with as many constitutionally recognized powers as possible or to expand greatly the powers of preexisting regional governments.

The strategy of expanding the powers of regional governments led to rifts within nationalist organizations. Small but vocal factions maintained that the goal of complete territorial sovereignty was being compromised too much and urged leaders of the nationalist parties to adopt a more militantly pro-independence stance.

Concurrently, the sudden popularity of nationalist parties alarmed many state leaders. Some feared that the nationalists might achieve their long-term goal and secede from the existing political order. A federal structure was one compromise solution, and some government leaders openly considered granting a modicum of self-rule to the apparently restive regions in order to undermine the nationalists' popularity. But even that was problematic, for some factions within state parties foresaw dire consequences. For one, even a modicum of autonomy seemed to increase institutional rivalries within the political system and thus dilute powers the central government needed to combat recessions and other modern problems. Furthermore, partial decentralization might whet the electorates' appetites for more extensive self-rule. Critics of decentralization therefore concluded that, all in all, concessions would reinforce rather than retard the pressure for secession.

Amid these complex factional struggles, a remarkable political coincidence occurred at the close of the 1970s. Regional referendums on partial self-rule were held almost simultaneously in Canada, Spain, and the United Kingdom. Voters in each country were asked to help decide whether the leaders of the state should decentralize its authority. The wordings of the referendums generally did not explicitly refer to the specter of secession. They referred only to greater decentralization of the political system. Still, many leaders and opponents of nationalist movements anticipated significant foreign policy implications, because they hoped, or feared, that the expansion of regional self-rule and diminution of state authority would be first steps toward territorial separation.

This chapter examines the referendums on self-rule during the late 1970s. Attention is given to four themes: (1) why the referendums were held when they were, (2) how voters were being educated about the referendums, (3) who voted, and (4) which side won. Following the discussion of the 1970s referendums, we look at referendums during the early 1990s within the then Soviet republics of Estonia, Latvia, and Lithuania. Unlike the referendums held a decade earlier, the popular votes within the Soviet Union were explicitly about independence. Moreover, groups advocating independence won; and their victories foreshadowed the breakup of the Soviet Union.

TIMING OF THE REFERENDUMS

Given that referendums on regional self-rule seldom occur in advanced industrialized societies, it is important to ask why such referendums were held in Great Britain, Spain, and Canada during the 1970s. The sudden and impressive electoral successes of nationalist parties in all three countries partly explain the timing of the referendums. But other political factors—in particular, stalemates between forces supporting and forces opposing decentralization—were also at work.

In the case of Great Britain, the electoral threat posed by nationalist parties at first simply generated a wish among state leaders to establish elected regional parliaments with strictly limited powers. Referendums were not part of the leaders' original agenda. Following the stunning successes of the Scottish National party (SNP) and the Welsh Plaid Cymru in the two 1974 general elections detailed in Table 6.1, leaders of both the Labour party and the Conservative party felt themselves under pressure

Table 6.1. Nationalist Performance in British General Elections

General Election	SNP's Regional Vote Share (%)	Plaid Cymru's Regional Vote Share (%)
1964	2.4	4.8
1966	5.0	4.3
1970	11.4	11.5
1974 Feb.	21.9	10.7
1974 Oct.	30.4	10.8

Sources: James G. Kellas, *The Scottish Political System*, 3d ed. (Cambridge: Cambridge University Press, 1984), pp. 106-107; Arnold J. James and John E. Thomas, *Wales at Westminister: A History of the Parliamentary Representation of Wales, 1800-1978* (Llandysul, Dyfed: Gomer Press, 1981), pp. 202-204.

to prevent further erosion of their Welsh and Scottish electoral bases. Both parties therefore resolved in their respective party congresses to work for "devolution." This meant the establishment of regionally elected parliaments with limited local powers. It would be a one-sided form of "shared government": the British Parliament would retain sovereignty and have the right to override decisions by the regional parliaments. State leaders hoped, perhaps too optimistically, that this mildly prodecentralization proposal would satisfy voters' desires for more self-rule and thus reduce the growing electoral appeal of the SNP and the Plaid Cymru.

There was a further political motive prompting the Labour government to embrace devolution in the late 1970s. After the October 1974 elections, Labour lacked an absolute majority within the House of Commons. It needed more votes. Members of the Labour government hoped that actively promoting greater regional self-rule might enable them to forge a temporary alliance with parliamentarians from the SNP and the Plaid Cymru. So the government decided to introduce devolution bills in Parliament in exchange for the nationalists' support.

The government's proposals were innovative but hardly revolutionary. In Wales, a popularly elected assembly would be established. Its members would be elected from single-member districts with only a plurality required for victory rather than by a system of proportional representation. The assembly would not have lawmaking powers. Its power was to be limited to executing laws decided in London—particularly laws pertaining to public culture (libraries, museums, etc.), environmental protection, building codes, and transportation. According to political scientist Jim Bulpitt, "In constitutional terms at least, the Welsh assembly was meant to be little more than an enlarged county council."[2]

Furthermore, the assembly would not be able to recruit, train, and oversee its own civil service. Instead, up to 13,000 new civil servants would be provided by London.

According to the Labour government's proposal, the Scottish assembly, unlike its Welsh counterpart, would have a few legislative powers in the areas of education, environmental protection, and social services. But, the British Parliament still could overrule the assembly's decisions at any time. Indeed the entire assembly could be dissolved by Parliament, if it so wished. As in the case of the Welsh proposal, there was to be no separate Scottish civil service and no sources of income or fiscal powers other than those explicitly approved by the British treasury.

In creating regional assemblies, the Labour government did not wish to dismantle all existing political arrangements. Scottish and Welsh affairs would continue being represented in the British cabinet by Scottish and Welsh secretaries of state who were appointed by the British government and were members of the majority party in Parliament. According to the Labour government's devolution proposals, the secretaries of state were to exercise supervisory powers within the assemblies to ensure that decisions by the regional assemblies were in harmony with those of the British government. The assemblies, in other words, were intended to rival the administrative authority of local municipal and county governments, not the legislative authority of the British Parliament. As Bulpitt puts it, "the actual institutional losers were local authorities."[3]

As mild as these proposals for political decentralization were—hardly a dismemberment of the British political system—numerous members of the Labour party opposed them. Many Labour parliamentarians from Scotland and Wales feared that any decentralization of government authority would enhance the prestige of nationalist groups, would give nationalists an institutional foothold in local affairs, and would enable nationalists to expand their constituency base through patronage. The proposals for devolution, in other words, would increase rather than diminish, the nationalist threat.

Some parliamentarians further argued that devolution would contradict the party's own principle of Britishwide proletarian unity. Critics argued that if regionally elected assemblies were established, parochial interests soon would play a larger role in the political thinking and judgment of Labour politicians who would have to pander to narrow, local interests in order to win elections.

Because of these concerns, the Labour government faced an unwanted "backbench revolt" by forty-three of its own parliamentarians when it introduced the devolution bills for Scotland and Wales. The government argued that as a minority government it needed Scottish and Welsh nationalist allies in Parliament to maintain its voting majority and remain in power. Even the Labour rebels were partially responsive to this appeal to party loyalty, but they wanted a compromise and would support the government's devolution plans only if local popular support for devolution was first demonstrated through the use of referendums—an eventuality that many rebels doubted would occur.[4]

In hopes of disrupting the government's strategy for perpetuating its rule, Conservative parliamentarians also called for a referendum. They resurrected the traditional Conservative argument that any extensive change in government structure or activity must first be approved by voters through the use of a referendum. The Tories had argued for a century that referendums were a valuable shield for British citizens against unwanted radicalism by elected elites and party machines.[5]

The combined opposition from the Conservative parliamentarians and Labour backbenchers prevented the passage of the government's original devolution proposal. The Labour government therefore compromised and agreed to hold advisory referendums in Scotland and Wales on the proposed regional assemblies. But this was not all. Parliament further decided that passage of the proposals would need more than just approval from a majority of the citizens who turned out to vote. The numerical size of the yes vote in each region would have to be equal to at least 40 percent of all registered voters in that region. This stipulation was called the 40 percent rule. Under it, an abstention would be the equivalent of a no vote, and a low turnout could invalidate an otherwise positive vote for devolution.

Welsh and Scottish nationalists reacted angrily to the turn of events. Many were already ambivalent about using referendums because they were not necessarily a neutral weapon in the battle for regional self-rule. Much depended on how the referendums were worded. Opinion polls in the 1970s indicated that majorities in both Scotland and Wales liked the idea of greater regional self-rule as an abstract principle. Opinion polls also showed, however, that whenever residents were asked whether they desired a specific form of regional government, overall popular support for self-rule quickly fragmented, with minorities supporting different institutional arrangements, different schemes of representation, and different legislative powers.[6] Scottish and Welsh citizens differed, among other things, over whether assemblies should be able to levy taxes; whether Parliament should be able to override the decisions of an assembly; whether members of the assemblies should be representatives from local governments or directly elected; whether members of the assemblies should be elected through a winner-take-all system of voting or by means of a proportional-representation system; and whether the assemblies should have powers to restructure the local economies.

Second, many nationalists viewed the content of Labour's proposals for regional self-rule as a public relations gimmick rather than a serious transfer of power. Members of the Plaid Cymru were especially disappointed over the lack of lawmaking powers proposed for their region's assembly and wanted a second question added to the government's referendum ballot: "Do you believe that the present Act should have gone considerably further, granting Wales full independent status?" The Labour government, predictably, refused to expand the ballot. [7]

Finally, Scottish and Welsh nationalists were angry about the 40 percent rule, which seemed to have been arbitrarily added to the referendum process. The 40 percent rule obviously increased the likelihood that the proposals would be defeated, and that eventuality could seriously set back the nationalists' struggles. Defeat of the devolutionary proposals, for instance, might convince other members of Parliament that the nationalists' call for regional government was not popularly supported and should not be heeded. Defeat might also damage the nationalists' prestige among voters by making the strategy of patiently working for regional government seem unfeasible and politically irrelevant. Many nationalists therefore saw the referendum procedure as a political minefield that the Labour party had eagerly laid.

Controversy over the use of referendums in deciding questions of regional self-rule was much less heated within Spain than it was within Great Britain. This was partly because of the peculiarities of the Spanish constitution. In hopes of securing support from traditionally restive ethnic groups, the designers of the 1978 constitution included a provision allowing three "historic nations"—Catalonia, Galicia, and the Basque country—to acquire regional governments with legislative powers. But before regional governments could be established, referendums must be used to demonstrate citizens' support for the regional governments. It was expected that elected politicians in each region would first form a temporary government, which would draft an autonomy proposal specifying policy areas in which future regional governments would make laws. The temporary governments then would present their proposal to the Spanish government for its consideration. The Spanish government and leaders of the regional governments would negotiate amendments to the initial proposal and then submit the revised proposal to the Spanish parliament, the Cortes, for consideration and approval. The goal of the lengthy process of reviewing and negotiating the details of an autonomy arrangement was to increase the likelihood of building consensus behind a single plan of regional self-rule among all interested parties. Theoretically, the final bill would first receive the blessing of all major political institutions; then it would be submitted to the population of the relevant region for a final test of broad support. If a simple majority of the voters supported the proposal, it would be implemented.

Controversy arose, however, over whether referendums could be used in other Spanish regions to decide on self-rule. The Spanish constitution permitted "non-national" regions to work toward small amounts of self-rule through a very long procedure of review, negotiation, and implementation. According to one section of the constitution, the Cortes and the Spanish government would make the final decision on each region's autonomy, without the use of a referendum. Regional legislative powers would initially be quite limited. After a five-year trial period, the representatives from a non-national regional government could, if it wished, apply for more extensive powers.

But another and often overlooked section of the constitution allowed disgruntled leaders of a region to call for a referendum if they desired either substantially greater self-rule than the Spanish government wished or a more rapid implementation of decentralization than the government wished. But before the Cortes would consider the results of these special referendums as authoritative, the proposals would need to be approved by a majority of *all eligible voters in each province* that would be under the jurisdiction of one of the proposed regional government. If the proposal failed to pass this rigorous test of popularity—even if in only one province—extensive devolution would not be established. If local representatives then remained dissatisfied with the amount of regional self-rule that the Spanish government granted, they could call for a new referendum on regional self-rule, but only after a five-year hiatus.[8]

Soon after the constitution was in place, the newly elected Spanish government was swamped by autonomy proposals from almost every region. The central government understandably was fearful that it was transferring too many policymaking powers to the new regional governments. Many regional coalitions were disappointed with the few powers that the central government wished to grant. After bitter negotiations, the constitutionally required referendums were called in the three recognized "national" territories of Galicia, Catalonia, and the Basque country.

Most "non-national" regions simply bargained directly with the government for limited amounts of local power, with the possibility of requesting greater amounts of power after five-year trials. Andalusia, however, was different.[9] The Andalusians argued that the Spanish government was being too miserly about sharing powers. They claimed, therefore, that a referendum was needed and permitted by the new constitution.

The designers of Spain's 1978 constitution had not anticipated that representatives of Andalusia would desire a degree of self-government that was far greater than the Spanish government would want to grant. Indeed, the number of non-national regions requesting self-rule astonished most Spanish politicians and seasoned political observers. Besieged with requests for regional self-rule, the Spanish government feared that the process of decentralization would soon get out of hand. The impatient Andalusians epitomized the problem. Moreover, if the Andalusian referendum passed, other regions might also request referendums. The Spanish government therefore only grudgingly recognized the constitutionality of an autonomy referendum for Andalusia and then worked vigorously to defeat the proposal.

Why did representatives of Andalusia press for a referendum instead of taking a more patient and piecemeal approach to self-rule? The movement for self-rule was partly an outgrowth of local politicians' growing fears that once given autonomy, Catalonia and the Basque country (two of the most economically developed and industrialized regions of Spain) would use their regional governments to secure budgetary favors from the Spanish government and to obstruct the Spanish government's efforts to transfer Basque and Catalan wealth to poorer regions of Spain. If impoverished regions, such as Andalusia, were to have their economic interests protected and promoted, they would need as much self-rule as possible, and as soon as possible. This would allow them to bargain directly with the central government and to stand out when requesting financial aid, as it was expected Catalonia and the Basque country would.

There were, in addition, electoral pressures and motivations behind the Andalusians' call for a referendum. Because of its failure to solve the profound and persistent problems of Andalusia's declining agrarian economy, the Franco regime had alienated many residents from the Spanish state. In this environment of constant hunger and joblessness, a newly organized nationalist party, the Andalusian Socialist party (Partido Socialista Andaluz, or PSA), quickly became a major electoral force. The PSA won only 4 percent of the ballots cast in the 1977 elections; but in 1979 it won 11.9 percent of the ballots, which is a large share of votes within Spain's multiparty system.[10] The PSA's sudden success convinced many statewide parties to advocate autonomy in order to expand their electoral base. The regional branches of the Spanish Workers' Socialist party (Partido Socialista Obrero de España, PSOE), the Spanish Communist party (Partido Comunista de España, PCE), and several other major parties began adding Andalusian adjectives to their names in hopes of attracting more voters. With the exception of leadership of the Popular Alliance party (Alianza Popular, AP) and other archconservative parties, party leaders throughout Andalusia were soon declaring their support for autonomy. They were, in effect, bidding for the PSA's apparently growing nationalist constituency; and amid this intense competition for votes, advocacy for a referendum became one litmus test of the sincerity of a party's commitment to Andalusian self-rule.

The political origins of Quebec's referendum differ from both the British and Spanish cases in that Canada's central government never called for the referendum and never viewed the referendum as binding.

The referendum, instead, was unilaterally called for by the government of Quebec province, headed by a precocious nationalist party, the Parti Québécois (PQ).

Formed in 1968, the PQ sought voters largely by advocating national independence. Of course, there had been many nationalist parties in Quebec's history. Still, the PQ was in many ways ideologically unique. Previously, electorally successful nationalist parties had advocated merely modifying Canada's federal system of government, not complete independence for Quebec. In addition, most earlier nationalist parties openly aligned themselves with the Catholic church and advocated the preservation (if not expansion) of the church's role in education and the provision of social services. The PQ was the first electorally successful nationalist party to call outright for independence and the first electorally successful nationalist party in Quebec to distance itself organizationally and ideologically from the Catholic church.[11]

The PQ was hardly a one-issue party, however. It certainly cultivated support among voters who already desired independence, but its leaders also sought out voters who were not interested in Quebec's independence as such in hopes of later converting new supporters to a pro-independence stance. In its campaigns, the PQ promised to end corruption, inefficiency, and favoritism in local government; to legislate union legislation, higher minimum-wage standards, the partial nationalization of mines, and other social-democratic reforms; to reduce unemployment and labor strife; to institutionalize economic planning for the region and gradually to phase in a mixed economy; and to legislate greater use of French within political institutions and in the business world. The PQ further promised that if it became the province's government, it would hold and abide by a referendum that asked the voters if they wanted the government to negotiate a "sovereignty-association" arrangement with Canada's federal government.[12]

What the PQ had in mind by sovereignty-association was an ambiguous intergovernmental arrangement. In theory, Quebec would be able to decide almost all cultural, educational, fiscal, social welfare, and economic policies without interference from the federal government of Canada. Quebec would also be completely responsible for its own defense. At the same time, a free-trade relationship would be maintained with the rest of Canada. There would also be a common Canada-Quebec currency and four joint government projects, such as Air Canada.

The ambiguities in the PQ's notion of sovereignty-association arose over such questions as whether Quebec's government would have sufficient authority to protect the province's infant industries from competition from other parts of Canada and whether Quebec would be bound by economic treaties signed by Canada. On such sensitive policy questions, which government would have final say: Quebec's or Canada's?

Almost all observers agree that the obvious ambiguity or "softness" in the PQ's sovereignty-association proposal was intended to minimize the possible radical implications of the PQ's nationalist aspirations and thus maximize the electoral base of the party. By contrast, a direct proposal for independence might alienate non-nationalist voters.[13] Again, it is worth remembering that almost all PQ leaders wanted a broad electoral base and therefore sought voters outside the region's pro-independence block. This inclusive electoral strategy apparently worked. Opinion surveys in 1976, for example, indicated that while almost one-third of PQ supporters did not favor independence they still supported the PQ because of its stand on economic and good-government issues such as foreign control of the economy and corruption in local government.[14] Indeed, PQ supporters tended to be more concerned about foreign control of the economy, reducing labor strife, and implementing economic plans and less concerned about maintaining law and order and regenerating the influence of the Catholic church than were supporters for other major parties in the region.[15]

After the party captured control of the provincial government in 1976, the PQ's leaders walked a political tightrope. On the one hand, they feared scaring off non-nationalist constituencies by pursuing excessively ambitious proposals for decentralization. On the other hand, the party's leaders wanted to sustain the loyalty and enthusiasm of its many party activists, especially younger grassroots activists in Montreal, who believed a powerful independent regional government was needed if Quebec was to realize its economic, cultural, and political potential.

Under growing pressure from its pro-independence activists and troubled by a Supreme Court of Canada's decision to overrule the government's francophone language policies, the PQ government decided in December 1979 to call for a sovereignty-association referendum. The PQ's chief opponent was the Liberal party. It argued in the Assemblée Nationale, Quebec's parliament, that the PQ's proposal for sovereignty-association was ridiculously impractical because the federal government in Canada neither had agreed nor was required to agree to view the results of a referendum as binding. The PQ spokespersons prudently had earlier prepared a defense of their position. During the dramatic parliamentary debate, which was televised and watched by a remarkably large audience, the Liberals often appeared disorganized and tongue-tied. The PQ spokespersons, in contrast, confidently predicted grand economic benefits resulting from a sovereignty-association arrangement and skillfully evaded the question of whether and how the federal government would respond to the referendum. Following a thirty-five-hour televised debate, the Assemblée Nationale approved the PQ's proposal, and the referendum was scheduled for May 20, 1980.[16]

VOTER EDUCATION

In Great Britain, Spain, and Canada, groups favoring and opposing the proposals launched campaigns to inform and influence voters' decisions. In each country a different constellation of groups participated in the campaigns, and they participated with different amounts of enthusiasm.

A three-week campaign period preceded the Scottish and Welsh referendums. Party involvement was generally incoherent, however, because within the major parties there was significant disagreement about whether and how to participate in the campaigns.

The Labour government, having been dragged into two referendum battles by its own rebellious backbenchers, never adopted a clear position toward either autonomy proposal. As Scottish political scientist James Kellas kindly put it, "The Government's heart was not in the cause of devolution."[17] Even ministers within the Labour cabinet differed greatly in their feelings about whether the proposals should be supported. Almost all of the top civil servants in Whitehall advised the government to oppose devolution. Uncertain where to stand, the government sat out the campaign. One consequence was that official pamphlets discussing the pros and cons of regional autonomy were never published by the British government. This was unlike the extensive papers mailed to all Great Britain's voters before that country's referendum on EEC membership.

It is doubtful that the Labour government, even if it had wanted to, could have generated enthusiasm among the vast majority of its own parliamentarians. Several figures within the Labour party had already begun to campaign vigorously against the proposals. In particular, there was considerable antidevolution campaigning undertaken by the so-called Gang of Six—a half-dozen staunchly anti-autonomy, high-ranking Labour parliamentarians who represented Welsh constituencies.

At the grassroots level, some Labour activists devotedly campaigned for the government's halfhearted yes position. Others, however, chose not to get deeply involved and instead watched the campaign either in bewilderment or with ambivalence. In Scotland, for instance, more than one-third of the local Labour organizations abstained from campaigning either for or against the devolution proposal.[18] Still other Labour activists worked for the maverick Labour no campaign.

Scottish and Welsh nationalists were also divided, at least initially, over whether to campaign for proposals. As noted, many nationalists believed that Labour's devolutionary proposals offered highly limited legislative and administrative powers for the regional assemblies rather than the extensive legislative powers that many militant, especially younger, activists desired. More cautious nationalists tried to dampen dissatisfaction by asking whether a more far-reaching proposal would ever be legislated if the currently mild proposals lost in the upcoming referendums. Probably not, many soon concluded. Therefore, although the proposals for self-rule were disappointingly modest in the eyes of most nationalists, many nonetheless participated in yes campaigns.[19]

The Conservatives were the only major party that officially opposed the Labour government's proposals for devolution. Even within this party, however, there was a maverick Conservative yes campaign. Conservative leaders understandably feared alienating voters in Scotland and Wales. The Conservatives therefore insisted that they were campaigning not against devolution, but against the details of the specific assembly schemes proposed by the Labour government.

The political rhetoric during the referendum campaigns was greatly influenced by the ambivalence and lukewarm attitudes within the Labour and nationalist parties. Disappointed over the details of the proposals, Scottish and Welsh nationalists seldom focused on either the specific institutional arrangements being proposed or the policy benefits that might flow from regional assemblies. The nationalists instead focused on more abstract themes, arguing that the devolution proposals would enhance British democracy both by bringing rulers geographically closer to their constituencies and also by reducing the extensive power of Great Britain's appointed bureaucrats.[20]

By rooting the debate in such abstract grounds, the nationalists inadvertently played into the hands of the antidevolutionists, who skillfully turned the prodevolution arguments about democracy on their heads. For example, opponents of devolution maintained that a new regional government in fact would not decrease the power of bureaucrats in British politics, but ironically would increase bureaucratic power by establishing new, regional tiers of civil servants. This would only further alienate citizens from their government. Moreover, a regional government would gravely weaken the institutional basis of local democracy in Great Britain, because towns and counties would have their resources and responsibilities transferred to regional governments. So government would be further removed from citizens' daily lives.

The antidevolutionists also focused on the possible economic consequences of regional self-rule. Conservatives, for example, often argued that the expense of financing a new layer of government would necessitate either significant tax increases or the siphoning of funds from the central government's already underfinanced social service programs. Conservatives further warned that Labour candidates might easily capture the new Welsh and Scottish parliaments and use those governments either to implement unwise economic policies or to obstruct policies made in London for the well-being of all British citizens.

The Labour party campaigners who opposed devolution in Wales added an ethnic wrinkle to the Conservatives' argument about the dangers of having members of the Labour party govern either Wales or Scotland. Allegedly, if a Welsh assembly were created, it soon would be dominated by members of the region's Welsh-speaking agrarian elite. Because of its upper-class background, this elite would ignore the daily needs of Wales's largely English-speaking urban workers and act only on behalf of the wealthy.

Dozens of organized interest groups also tried to influence voters' thinking. Almost all Scottish and Welsh business associations campaigned against devolution, arguing that the likely tax increases needed to support the assemblies' activities would destroy both regions' already weak business climates. This would increase bankruptcies and joblessness. In Wales, a representative of the National Federation for the Self-Employed and Small Businesses declared that a regional assembly "can spell only gloom to the thousands of small shops and businesses which have been the main-spring of the Welsh economy."[21] According to Kellas, "Some companies even threatened to remove themselves from Scotland if devolution came about."[22]

The creation of regional governments was also opposed by many government employees, especially at the municipal level, because they feared it would reduce local government jobs and duties. Government workers therefore campaigned against the proposals and sometimes even helped finance anti-autonomy campaign organizations with public funds.[23] Almost all unions that represented government workers (and there were almost 100,000 town hall employees in Wales alone) also went on record as opposing the proposals.

The press also generally opposed the proposals.[24] Almost all London newspapers predicted that devolution would be a first step to secession. Many Scottish regional papers initially supported devolution, but a number of traditionally prodevolution newspapers, such as the *Scottish Daily Express*, unexpectedly opposed the referendum proposal, partly on grounds that the powers of the proposed assembly were inadequate. On the front pages of Welsh newspapers, news about local strikes crowded out discussions of the upcoming referendum. A local newspaper strike during the midst of the campaign made information about the referendum even harder to acquire. The few editorials that did appear in Welsh newspapers tended to portray the upcoming referendum as Labour's bill. According to several scholars, this symbolic association damaged the proposal's reputation, because a vote against devolution was increasingly viewed as a vote against the highly unpopular Labour government and its seemingly inept handling of Great Britain's economic troubles.[25]

Some interest groups, of course, supported the devolution proposals. The Welsh Trade Union Council, for one, supported its region's referendum proposal partly out of fear that a decisive no vote would bring down the Labour government. Such an endorsement was a mixed blessing for the prodevolution forces, however, because of growing public hostility toward unions and their recent strikes. Most ministers in the Church of Scotland endorsed the devolution proposal. In general, however, the interest groups supporting devolution lacked the financial resources, myriad of activists, and prestigious endorsements of the no campaigns.

During the three-week devolution campaigns, public support for devolution waned in both regions, particularly in Scotland, where early opinion polls had shown that a large majority of eligible voters initially favored devolution.[26] The reasons for the decline are multiple. Party endorsements played a role, especially among Conservative voters who initially favored devolution and then were encouraged by party leaders to vote against the proposal.[27] Opinion polls also suggest that many adults were increasingly uncertain about the possible economic consequences of the devolution proposals and were fearful about undertaking political experiments during economically troubled times.[28] Finally, some scholars believe that many initial supporters became disillusioned and reconsidered their stand as they became more familiar with the institutional details and political possibilities of the devolution proposals. One typical concern was the possible domination of a Scottish assembly by the more numerous representatives from Scotland's industrial belt and the corresponding loss of power for the representatives from rural districts.[29]

The near unity of the political parties in Spain stands in contrast to the extensive inter- and intraparty squabbling before the British referendums. Almost all major statewide parties in Spain endorsed the referendum proposals for self-rule for the traditional nations. For example, the then governing party, the Union of the Democratic Center (Unión Centro Democrático, UCD), the PSOE (the major opposition party), and the PCE all endorsed the autonomy proposals for the Basque region, Catalonia, and Galicia. In addition, all major nationalist parties in Catalonia and two of the three largest Basque nationalist groups endorsed the proposals. The Basque region's People's Unity coalition (Herri Batasuna, HB) was the only electorally powerful nationalist organization that actively campaigned against the autonomy proposals.

The HB was a recently formed electoral coalition indirectly connected to a paramilitary wing of the Basque Homeland and Freedom (Euzkadi ta Askatasuna, ETA) movement, an evolving and fissuring nationalist effort loosely held together by visions of a future Basque socialist order.[30] The HB had enjoyed considerable electoral successes in the 1979 general and municipal elections and had become the third largest electoral force in the region behind the long-established Basque Nationalist party and Spanish Socialist party. The HB leaders insisted that all Spanish police and armed forces be removed from the territory and believed that the specific wording of the Basque autonomy proposal was too vague to be satisfactory. The coalition's leadership further contended that the proposal, even to the extent that it was clearly stated, failed to give the region adequate self-rule. In the opinion of HB spokespersons, a good autonomy statute would at minimum give the region independence in reconstructing its economy, direct representation in international bodies, and recourse during jurisdictional disputes with the Spanish government to a constitutional court whose bench would include several members from the Basque country's highest court. Without these and other promises, HB leaders said, the substantive impact of the autonomy proposal would be anti-Basque and antiworker. The HB electoral coalition, therefore, urged voters to boycott the referendum, as many had done earlier during the ratification of the Spanish constitution, so that the referendum's results could not legitimately be read as a sign of popular approval.

Meanwhile, a paramilitary faction within ETA launched a campaign of armed attacks against Spain's armed forces and prominent politicians. This faction hoped to provoke the Spanish police into indiscriminate brutality against Basque civilians that, in turn, would anger the Basque population, further alienate Basque voters from the Spanish political system, and persuade them that the modicum of freedom promised in the autonomy statute would not effectively protect their interests.

In the case of Galicia, almost all nationalist parties in the region disliked the watered-down substance of the government's proposal for regional self-rule. They lacked significant electoral clout, however, jointly attracting less than 12 percent of the vote in the 1979 general elections.[31] In terms of voting behavior, Galicia traditionally has been one of the most conservative regions within Spain. The wording of its autonomy statute therefore had been largely decided by elected politicians of either the highly conservative AP or the moderately conservative UCD and not by nationalists.[32] The leaders of both the AP and UCD wanted only few, limited constitutional powers transferred from Madrid to Galicia. As a result, the wording of the proposed autonomy statute on the one hand explicitly referred to Madrid's supreme legislative authority and on the other enumerated very few economic or other policy areas in which the regional government would have legislative power.

Andalusia was the only region in which a major statewide party opposed a referendum for autonomy.[33] As noted, leaders of the governing UCD feared that extensive autonomy for Andalusia might obstruct swift and decisive actions by the central government. Moreover, UCD leaders feared the growing popularity of their chief electoral rivals, the PSOE. Since Franco's death, the PSOE electoral base in Andalusia had been steadily growing, and many members of the UCD believed that the Socialists might soon be able to capture a newly established regional government in Andalusia, transform it into a left-wing stronghold, and use it to obstruct the controversial program of economic austerity that the UCD was pursuing. Finally, many UCD leaders feared that if Andalusia

succeeded in attaining extensive amounts of policymaking authority, political leaders in other non-national territories might imitate the Andalusians and press for equal amounts of autonomy. Such an eventuality
might lead to a far more confederal system of government in Spain than
most UCD leaders thought was desirable.

The decision by the UCD leadership to oppose autonomy for Andalusia split the party at the grassroots level. Many UCD activists in Andalusia
openly supported autonomy. In part this was because many had been
members of regionally based Andalusian parties prior to joining the UCD,
and they retained a sense of regional loyalty. In addition, many local UCD
activists feared that they would lose a significant amount of electoral
support if they publicly opposed regional self-rule. After all, the pro-
autonomy Andalusian Socialist party had come out of nowhere to win 11
percent of the region's votes, and almost all statewide parties in the region
were appealing to residents' sectional sentiments. With such political
considerations in mind, numerous UCD notables and activists resigned
from their party and began to campaign for the proposal.

Three-week campaigns preceded the referendums in the Basque
country, Catalonia, and Galicia. In contrast to the Welsh and Scottish
experiences, Spanish trade unions, business associations, church organizations, and most other major interest groups endorsed the proposals for
regional self-rule. Most newspapers also supported this position. In the
dramatic words of one high-ranking executive of a major Basque bank,
"God liberate us from the Spanish administration! We presently are
traveling on a road of concubinage and nepotism. . . . This country needs
to be decentralized."[34]

Opinion polls indicated sizable majorities in almost every socioeconomic group in the Basque country, and Catalonia supported autonomy.
Even immigrants to the regions tended to support the autonomy proposals.[35] In Galicia there was also considerable support in the towns and cities.
A large number of rural residents, however, seemed indifferent to the
vote. This disinterest, some scholars speculate, was partly attributable to
the superficiality and vacuousness of the region's autonomy proposal.[36]

There was consensus among major parties in Galicia, the Basque
country, and Catalonia that the autonomy proposals should be ratified at
the referendum. Only in Andalusia did the referendum campaign become
bitter. A major source of the contention was the UCD's methods of
campaigning against the autonomy movement. The UCD used its authority over state-run media, especially televised news, to reduce popular
knowledge about, interest in, and support for the referendum. Newscasts
repeatedly failed to report on day-to-day developments in the referendum
campaigns, and public service debates over the referendum were scheduled for inconvenient hours. The Spanish government also arranged for
the referendum campaign in Andalusia to last only two weeks.

The pro-autonomy forces were hardly passive, however. The president of Andalusia's provisional government launched a hunger strike to draw attention to the importance of the upcoming vote. More than 2,000 street parties, informational meetings, and marches were held by pro-autonomy groups; and more than 3 million pieces of pro-autonomy literature were distributed.[37] The PSOE alone held 1,500 informational meetings in 750 towns, while the relatively small Communist party printed more than 100,000 pieces of pro-autonomy literature.[38] The Catholic church's leadership also campaigned for autonomy, declaring that "Andalusia cannot tolerate a degree of autonomy inferior to that given to other regions and nationalities."[39]

Results from Andalusian opinion polls indicated widespread and growing support for the autonomy proposal throughout the two-week campaign. Majorities favoring autonomy were found in virtually every income group, although urban, middle-income residents were especially apt to support autonomy. Even about half the UCD identifiers favored autonomy.[40]

The referendum campaign in Quebec informally began with the PQ government's early decisions on how to phrase the proposal. After analyzing opinion polls, strategists for the PQ government concluded that a sizable majority of Quebec's residents wanted the province to have more policymaking power, while only a little more than a third desired complete political independence from Canada. The party's leadership therefore chose ambiguous wording for the referendum proposal.[41] They presented sovereignty-association as a way of conserving existing ties with Canada yet achieving a measure of independence. The referendum's wording also intentionally sidestepped the sensitive questions of how much and what sorts of self-rule were being sought, since the proposal merely asked voters if they wanted the government of Quebec to *begin* negotiations with Canada's federal government. Sovereignty-association, in other words, was presented as an initial bargaining position. The actual number and content of Quebec's new powers would be known only after negotiations were completed.

Finally, the PQ's referendum proposal included an explicit promise that a second referendum would later be held to give residents an opportunity to review the results of the intergovernment negotiations. Thus, the proposal's wording implied that since any negotiated change would require popular ratification, voters need not fear that the province's representatives would seek an excessive range of powers for a Quebec government.

To give the appearance of nonpartisanship, the advocates and opponents of sovereignty-association organized themselves under two umbrella groups. Each received $1.1 million from public funds to finance its campaign.[42] But it was well known that the PQ dominated the pro side and the Liberals the opposition.

Once the referendum campaign formally began in April 1980, both sides hired advertising consultants, organized concerts and other media events, printed brochures, posted stickers, and canvased house-to-house. The opposing sides also held rallies throughout the territory, including even the small towns and villages in the remote eastern and northern areas. Sports personalities and entertainers endorsed the rival sides; federal civil servants, Inuits (Eskimos), small business, and other organized interest groups also campaigned.[43]

Other than the business community's general suspicion of the PQ's periodic socialist rhetoric, there was no clear pattern to the pro and con endorsements by interest groups. The French-speaking community, for example, was divided over the wisdom of sovereignty-association. Many churchgoing rural francophones, in particular, were nervous about the growing power of the urban-based and social-democratic PQ. At the same time, some urban francophones feared that if there were negotiations over a sovereignty-association arrangement, the PQ might seek a greater economic independence from the rest of Canada than was desirable.[44]

In this situation of rough parity between interest groups favoring and opposing sovereignty-association, perhaps the single most important campaigner was the popular and eloquent Liberal prime minister of Canada, Pierre Trudeau.[45] Trudeau made four well-publicized campaign appearances in Quebec, during which he promised (in a misleading way, according to his nationalist critics) that if the sovereignty-association proposal were defeated, his government would acquire more powers for Quebec through reform of Canada's federal constitution. Trudeau also contended that the PQ's proposed method of securing greater self-rule through an ambiguously phrased referendum about sovereignty-association was utopian because the leaders of Canada's other regions had already rejected the idea of negotiating economic association with a sovereign Quebec. He argued that the advocates of sovereignty-association were woolly-minded idealists with "a sense of honour more highly developed than their sense of reality."[46] Finally, he accused PQ's leaders of intolerance toward English speakers and warned that under PQ rule an independent Quebec would resemble Cuba or Haiti because of endless economic problems and limited political freedoms for large numbers of citizens who do not speak French.

Trudeau's arguments about an economic malaise were not unique. Opponents of sovereignty-association often raised questions about the economic implications of the referendum's proposal. They alleged that if Quebec had to survive on its own, severe economic dislocations would result because normal trade and currency relations with the rest of Canada would not immediately resume. For example, there soon would be shortages of petroleum, which Quebec imported from Canada's western provinces. Without access to traditional markets in other parts of Canada and without agricultural and petroleum imports, opponents predicted that Quebec's economy would soon collapse.

Advocates of autonomy made the predictable counterarguments. They insisted that economic growth would result from a sovereignty-association arrangement because of the region's largely untapped export potential, underutilized hydroelectric potential, and already advanced industrial base. Any dislocation and joblessness would be minimal and temporary and would soon be offset by the appropriateness of economic policies designed by regional policymakers highly sensitive to local needs and aspirations.

During the campaign period, the PQ's leadership was fairly confident that the proposal would receive support from the party's past supporters, who were primarily urban, white-collar, public-sector, and francophone families. Therefore, the PQ's yes campaign courted more conservative middle-class voting blocks, with a particular emphasis on rural families and small capitalists whose livelihoods depended on the rough-and-tumble private sector. This required modifications of the PQ's traditionally social-democratic program, which had emphasized increased planning by the government. PQ leaders now argued that the province had a native entrepreneurial dynamism, but it was currently fettered by rules and regulations imposed by Canada's federal government. A powerful Quebec government would reduce interference in the market and leave enterprises freer to generate regional prosperity.

During the two-month campaign, spokespersons for the yes campaign made a few tactical blunders that, some observers believe, affected the referendum's outcome. First of all, a highly visible PQ feminist, who was also a member of the provincial cabinet, used a negative stereotype of traditional housewives in a campaign speech. She derogatorily referred to such housewives as "Yvettes" and insinuated that women who planned to vote no in the upcoming referendum were culturally backward Yvettes. The activist had intended to shame women listeners into supporting the PQ's sovereignty-association proposal, but the stinging rhetoric backfired. Influential newspapers in the region depicted the negative stereotype as evidence of the activist's intolerance toward housewives. Outrage spread, and a pro housewife mobilization, the "Yvette movement," emerged and denounced the PQ and its sovereignty-association proposal. With its numerous marches and demonstrations, the Yvette movement soon monopolized headlines in local newspapers and captured the imaginations and hearts of many Quebec residents.[47]

Ironically, the PQ's campaign was further hurt by its leaders' normally low-key, highly polite campaign style designed not to offend any social group.[48] Since its inception, the PQ had taken great pains to maintain an image of respectability. Unlike other militant nationalist groups of the

1960s, the PQ had carefully avoided participation in extraparliamentary demonstrations and combative rhetoric. Fearing that broadsides and invectives might backfire, PQ activists eschewed mean-spirited statements. Local Liberal activists slung a considerable amount of mud during the campaign, sometimes even equating the PQ's "hidden" political agenda with fascism. PQ activists, however, appealed to voters' economic hopes and interests and provincial pride. Through positive and patiently argued higher appeals, the yes side could win, or so the PQ leaders believed.

Opinion polls indicated that popular support for sovereignty-association oscillated considerably during the referendum campaign. Before the referendum proposal was introduced in December 1979, about 37 percent of the province's eligible voters supported sovereignty-association, 47 percent opposed it, and 16 percent expressed no opinion. During the first weeks of campaigning that immediately followed the televised parliamentary debate, almost 50 percent of the eligible voters had favorable attitudes toward the proposal, with slightly more than 40 percent opposing the proposal, and with less than 10 percent of eligible voters reporting no opinion. After a month of formal campaigning, eligible voter support for sovereignty-association had declined and stood on a par with opposition. By the end of April, eligible voters expressing approval for the proposal were in the minority. They trailed those expressing disapproval by 10 percent, with another 10 percent of the voters reporting no opinion.[49] Popular opinion toward sovereignty-association had come full circle.

Many voters' understanding of the substance of the proposal was fuzzy, however. Less than 40 percent of the Québécois interviewed by poll takers could correctly articulate what the PQ meant by *sovereignty-association*, and about 25 percent openly admitted that they did not know what the phrase meant.[50] Although the vast majority of residents were willing to make judgments about *sovereignty-association* when queried by pollsters, few were confident of the exact meaning of the phrase.

There were many causes for the shifting tides of public opinion concerning the PQ's proposal. It is likely, as some scholars have argued, that short-term factors such as Trudeau's skillful oratory, the Yvette affair, and the PQ's nonassertive rhetorical style influenced voters' opinions. It is also conceivable that, over time, the ambiguity of the referendum's proposal made some citizens edgy; for as we have seen, voters frequently lacked a clear picture of what economic and political consequences might result from a yes vote.

VOTER PARTICIPATION

Popular participation in the referendums on regional self-rule varied considerably. Voter turnout in Scotland and Wales was quite low, far below the typical regional turnouts for British general elections. The Spanish referendum turnouts were generally higher than those in Scotland and Wales. Furthermore, the difference between turnouts in preceding general elections and turnouts in the referendums was far less dramatic in the Spanish cases than in the British ones. Quebec had the highest voter turnout among the referendums considered here. The turnout in Quebec's referendum also exceeded those of recent general elections.

In Scotland, the average voter turnout for general elections during the 1970s had been around 76 percent of the electorate. Election turnouts in Wales had been slightly above 78 percent.[51] Slightly less than 63 percent of the electorate voted in the Scottish referendum; slightly less than 59 percent of the Welsh electorate participated in the Welsh referendum.[52] So in the two regions, referendum turnouts were roughly 15 percent lower than turnouts at general elections.

One could argue that these comparatively low turnout figures partly support a common proposition in the literature on referendums: that most citizens are politically apathetic by nature, tend to be preoccupied with private concerns even during referendums, and without directions from parties are seldom informed, interested voters. This proposal, as we mentioned earlier, is often advanced by critics of referendums who emphasize the political incompetence of voters. Competing interpretations of the low turnouts are possible, however.

First of all, it is possible that some voters stayed home not because of apathy or indifference but because they remained dissatisfied with the alternatives that the government had offered. The substance of the Labour government's watered-down devolution proposals, after all, satisfied few political activists—including many members of the Labour party and the nationalist parties. Perhaps many Scottish and Welsh voters also were ambivalent and chose neither to vote against the government's offer for regional self-rule nor to embrace it in the form the government had designed. Instead, many citizens chose to stay home.

It is also possible that the low turnout was more the result of the major parties' contradictory mobilization efforts than it was due to voters' innate apathy. Almost all parties were internally divided over the devolutionary proposals. Consequently, their voter-mobilization efforts were often half-hearted. Indeed, different wings of the party were at times working at cross purposes: some urged voters to support devolution, some urged voters to defeat the proposal. It is not unreasonable to speculate, therefore, that a larger than normal proportion of voters stayed home because they were exposed to contradictory instructions and conflicting information.

Finally, the low turnouts may have been a by-product of economically uncertain times. Great Britain was in the midst of a recession during the late 1970s. The economic downturn was especially severe in Scotland and Wales. Moreover, there had been recent and bitter industrial struggles that had lowered many residents' standard of living and had divided the nation. Founding a new system of government is always a leap into the dark. To try to create a new political order when so many economic arrangements are being shaken requires remarkable courage, because the long-term implications of a major change in political arrangements are unclear and disaster may result. Thus, because they were already living amid highly uncertain economic times, Scottish and Welsh voters arguably and understandably were hesitant about making a potentially momentous constitutional decision.

Referendum turnouts in Spain were remarkably consistent across the country's geographically and sociologically diverse regions. Seldom did more than 60 percent of eligible voters in a region participate in the referendum; seldom did less than 55 percent do so, as Table 6.2 details.

The referendum turnout in each Spanish region was only moderately lower than was the turnout for the most recent general election. In the Basque country, for example, the turnout for the autonomy referendum was 57 percent, while the turnout for the 1979 general election was 65.9 percent.[53] The referendum turnout in Catalonia was 60 percent, while the 1979 general election turnout was 67.6 percent.[54] In both cases, the difference between the referendum turnouts and general election turnouts was less than 9 percentage points, noticeably smaller than the differences found in either Scotland or Wales.

An anomalously low turnout did occur in Galicia, however, where less than 30 percent of the eligible voters cast their ballots. In light of local

Table 6.2. Voter Turnout in Spanish Autonomy Referendums

Referendum Date	Region	Percentage of Eligible Voters Casting Ballots
October 1979	Basque Country	57
October 1979	Catalonia	60
February 1980	Andalusia	64
December 1980	Galicia	29
October 1981	Andalusia	54

Sources: Antonio Porras Nadales, "El Referéndum de Iniciativa Autonómica del 28 de Febrero en Andalucía," *Revista de Estudios Políticos* 15 (May-June 1980), p. 189; Mike Newton, "The Peoples and Regions of Spain," in *Democratic Politics in Spain: Spanish Politics After Franco*, edited by David S. Bell (New York: St. Martin's Press, 1983), pp. 110, 118; Robert P. Clark, "The Question of Regional Autonomy in Spain's Democratic Transition," in *Spain in the 1980s: The Democratic Transition and a New International Role* (Cambridge, Mass.: Ballinger, 1987), p. 145.

history, the low turnout is not entirely surprising. Galicia traditionally has had comparatively low turnouts in almost all elections. For example, less than 50 percent of the Gallego electorate voted in the 1979 general elections. This was the lowest turnout in all of Spain. Still, the referendum's turnout of less than 30 percent was unusually low, even by Gallego standards.

As scholar Mike Newton points out, the low turnout for the autonomy referendum in 1980 was partly due to "general public disillusion" with the small amount of autonomy being considered.[55] The issue was too tangential to people's lives to ignite interest.

Local social conditions, however, probably also contributed to the citizens' inertia. Galicia has the lowest literacy rate among Spain's regions and is the least industrialized and most impoverished region in Spain. Research on voting behavior and political culture suggests that illiteracy and chronic poverty often inhibit voting, partly because they nurture feelings of personal helplessness and futility that, in turn, can debilitate one's faith in the efficacy of political action.[56]

Intraregional differences in referendum turnouts within Catalonia and Andalusia indirectly corroborate this socioeconomic interpretation of Galicia's unusually low turnout. If Galicia's social conditions contributed to voters' passivity, it follows that low turnouts should have also occurred in other regions whose rural areas have social conditions similar to those of Galicia. Scholars have in fact found some supporting evidence in both Catalonia and Andalusia. In these regions, unlike in Galicia, a considerable amount of regional self-rule was being decided. Overall turnout in the two provinces was higher than in Galicia, but within the two, voting was noticeably higher in urban areas than it was in predominantly rural districts, where both literacy rates and standard of living are quite low.[57]

In comparison to turnout rates in Great Britain and Spain, participation in Quebec's sovereignty-association referendum was remarkably high, with 84 percent of the electorate voting. Even in terms of local political history, this is a remarkably high level of popular participation, easily surpassing the 76 percent turnout in the 1979 general elections.[58] Part of the explanation for the comparatively high turnout in Quebec may involve the region's relative prosperity and economic stability, especially in comparison to the deep recessions and industrial dislocations occurring in Scotland, Wales, and Spain during the late 1970s. The PQ and Liberal party also took consistent and strong stands during the referendum and vigorously pursued votes, unlike the often confused and fragmented campaigns in Great Britain. Finally, the PQ referendum, unlike most referendums in Spain, could not be predicted. The anticipated closeness of the vote arguably prodded additional citizens to go to their polls.

DETERMINANTS OF VICTORY

The results of the regional self-rule referendums were, like the turnout rates, quite diverse. In both Quebec and Wales, the proposals were defeated by surprisingly large margins. The proposals almost always easily passed in Spain. Most of the voters in Scotland supported the Labour government's devolution proposal, but it was defeated because of the controversial 40 percent rule.

As noted, voter turnouts in Scotland and Wales were relatively low in comparison to turnouts in general elections. The low turnout proved significant because of the 40 percent rule, which stipulated that in order for the devolution proposal to pass, the number of yes votes had to be equal to or greater than 40 percent of all registered voters. In Scotland, the turnout was only 64 percent. Therefore, to pass, the proposal needed to receive approximately twice as many yes votes as no votes. This did not happen. Fifty-two percent of the voters cast yes ballots, but they represented only 33 percent of the region's total electorate.

Within Scotland, support for devolution was especially strong in the industrial belt that runs along the Clyde River. The industrial belt is also a Labour party stronghold, although some SNP candidates with socialist beliefs had recently made inroads there. In many rural and most outlying areas of Scotland, the proposal was not as strongly supported and was sometimes defeated. According to Vernon Bogdanor, many rural residents believed that the regional assembly proposed by the Labour government would be monopolized by urban, Labour party interests to the detriment of more traditional, rural communities. Out of sectional interests, therefore, many rural residents voted no.[59]

In Wales, the proposal was soundly defeated: only one voter in five supported the bill. Even in the two nationalist counties, where Welsh was commonly spoken and where Welsh nationalists had been recently elected to Parliament, the proposal lost by similar lopsided ratios of two to one.[60] In the four counties that had been Labour party strongholds and also had been home districts for the outspoken Gang of Six opposition leaders to devolution, only 17 percent of the voters supported the Labour government's proposal.[61]

The results in Spain stand in sharp contrast to the Scottish and Welsh experiences. Almost every autonomy proposal in Spain easily passed. Ninety-five percent of the voters in the Basque country opted for autonomy; 88 percent did so in Catalonia; 75 percent in Galicia; and 87 percent in Andalusia. These consistent and impressive victories are partly explained by the breadth of the interparty coalitions that supported the proposals. As mentioned, a considerable amount of negotiation and consensus building among elites preceded the presentation of the proposals to the voters. By the time the referendums were held, only a few parties openly opposed the proposals, with the most obvious cases being the UCD in Andalusia and the HB in the Basque country.

Results of referendum-day polls indicate that most citizens who voted yes had also voted in earlier elections for one of the parties that endorsed the autonomy proposals. Conversely, most of the citizens polled who voted no reported supporting either the highly conservative AP, the Basque HB, or the Andalusian UCD. So, partisan loyalties seem to be a partial explanation for the voters' behavior. Still, party allegiance was only one of several factors influencing voters' behavior; according to some polls, supporters of the HB and Andalusian UCD frequently broke ranks during the referendums and voted yes.[62]

Andalusia was a curious exception to the overall pattern in Spain. It was the only region where the referendum proposal technically failed to pass. This resulted from the procedural requirement that majorities of all *eligible* voters in *every* province approve the proposal. Large majorities of those who cast their ballots approved of the proposal in all eight Andalusian provinces. In one province, however, the proposal was not approved by a majority of all *eligible* voters. There were constitutional ambiguities about whether these results meant passage or failure, and the UCD government interpreted the constitution to support the government's position and declared that the referendum had been defeated.

Non-UCD politicians in Andalusia immediately protested the government's strict interpretation of the law governing the referendum and argued that autonomy had been strongly supported throughout the region and that, therefore, the referendum's results should be treated as morally binding on the Spanish parliament and government. There was, furthermore, troubling evidence of ballot tampering by the UCD government. For example, there were reports of poll watchers allowing voters to cast multiple no votes and of no ballots mysteriously being cast by deceased citizens. Bombarded by protests in parliament and embarrassed by a growing scandal, the government agreed to a second referendum, which the pro-autonomy forces won even more handily than they had in the 1979 referendum.

While the story of the Spanish referendums is one of repeated victories for groups favoring regional self-rule, the referendum story from Quebec is one of disappointing defeat for the PQ. During the campaign, opinion polls periodically showed a majority of citizens supporting regional self-rule, and many PQ activists had faith that their position would win. On the day of the referendum, however, 40.5 percent of the citizens who cast ballots voted yes and 59.5 percent voted no.

There was a fairly clear partisan pattern to the referendum voting. Most citizens who voted yes also had voted for the PQ in recent elections, while no voters tended to have voted for parties other than the PQ.[63] There is, furthermore, some opinion poll data suggesting that partisan loyalty frequently overrode policy preferences in determining how a citizen voted. One study found that 16 percent of those who cast ballots for sovereignty-association opposed any increase in regional self-rule. They had voted yes to support their party, the PQ. Meanwhile, 28 percent of those who voted against sovereignty-association actually desired significantly greater regional self-rule but voted no to demonstrate support of parties other than the PQ.[64]

Interestingly, unlike the votes in Spain where many non-Basque speakers and non-Catalan speakers either voted for regional autonomy or abstained, large numbers of nonfrancophones in Quebec voted in the referendum and voted overwhelmingly against sovereignty-association. Given the nonfrancophones' more than 90 percent opposition to sovereignty-association, the proposal needed support from a very large majority of French speakers to pass. Only about 50 percent of the French-speaking voters who went to the polls cast yes ballots, however. French-speaking voters in the countryside were especially reluctant to support the PQ's proposal, perhaps because of ongoing hostility to the PQ's highly urban, pro growth, and semisocialist platform and rhetoric.[65] It appears, then, that the sovereignty-association proposal that was sponsored by the economically reform-oriented PQ simply had too narrow a partisan backing and too qualified a linguistic appeal to win.

THE SIGNIFICANCE OF THE REFERENDUMS

Once the referendum ballots had been counted, did much change? Were the referendums empty spectacles that dazzled observers but did not significantly alter public policy, or were there noticeable consequences following from the proposals' defeats or ratification?

Although the Scottish and Welsh referendums did not immediately produce any long-term change in the constitutional rights and political status of the two regions, the referendums had immediate consequences for Great Britain's preexisting system of parties and party rule. Frustrated and angered by the entire referendum process, the SNP withdrew its parliamentary support from the Labour party. This action facilitated the success of a Conservative-sponsored vote of no confidence, which in turn provided an opportunity for Prime Minister Margaret Thatcher and her Conservative government to enter office and retain power for over a decade.

The two nationalist parties, in the meantime, were reeling internally from the decisive defeats of the devolution proposals. Accusations of incompetence were made within both parties; factional purges commenced within the SNP; and many young nationalists left politics altogether. Voting for Scottish and Welsh nationalist candidates, meanwhile, declined sharply, with the Plaid Cymru losing two of its three parliamentarians in the 1979 general elections and the SNP losing nine of its eleven.

Aspirations for regional self-rule did not die, however. Opinion polls taken immediately following the defeat of the devolution proposals showed that many residents in the two regions expected that the British Labour government would propose a new decentralization plan. Few anticipated that the issue would be dropped altogether by the Thatcher government.[66] From this nadir, opinion polls during the 1980s showed that public approval for devolution grew steadily in both regions. This encouraged many Labour activists in Scotland and Wales, including the former members of the antidevolution Gang of Six, to embrace extensive regional self-rule in hopes of weakening the Conservatives' hold in Parliament.[67]

In Spain, the four autonomy referendums clearly helped redefine the government's political agenda. After the referendums, the clarification and development of relationships between Madrid and the multiplicity of regional governments became a dominant issue in Spanish politics. Questions about the exact extent of the regions' educational, labor, economic, and social service policymaking powers had to be clarified; and bitter battles between Madrid and the regional governments ensued.[68] Political leaders in Spain, however, ceased to use referendums to help decide autonomy policy. Instead, intergovernmental relations were refined through ongoing and seemingly endless negotiations between the central government and coalitions of politicians from each region, with Spain's constitutional court system playing an increasingly important role in adjudicating differences.

The failure of Quebec's sovereignty-association referendum combined with the sudden death of René Lévesque, the PQ's highly skilled leader, resulted in the party's rapid organizational disintegration and electoral decline. Just as the failures of the devolution proposals in Wales and Scotland led to widespread disappointment within the Plaid Cymru and SNP, many younger activists in the PQ who had hoped that Quebec's self-rule would lead to widespread social and political change dropped out of nationalist politics; and some dropped out of politics altogether.[69] The impact of the world recession further reduced the saliency of autonomy in this especially hard-hit industrialized and exporting region.

Since the referendum's defeat, Canadian leaders repeatedly have tried through initiatives at the federal level of government to preserve Canadian unity while advancing the linguistic rights and economic interests of French Canadians. Various constitutional revisions have been proposed to give provincial governments new powers. These ideas, however, have faced strong opposition from leaders of English-speaking provinces. Objections have been especially virulent in western Canada, where leaders maintain that too many scarce resources and political rights have already been granted to Quebec while the western provinces' economic needs have been repeatedly neglected. The belief of regional elites that their provinces are being unfairly exploited by other provinces within the federation is apparently also commonplace among Canadian citizens. In each province, the citizenry generally "sees itself as altruistic but exploited by others and disliking them for it."[70]

Meanwhile, opinion polls in Quebec have shown a steady increase in favorable attitudes toward independence. In 1978, only 12 percent of the residents in Quebec approved of separation from Canada. By 1991, however, 42 percent of the residents in Quebec supported separation.[71] Thus, despite the defeat of the PQ's referendum, the question of redesigning Canada's constitutional order clearly remains a lively one. As one Canadian political scientist has pointed out, the words of Yogi Berra seem apropos in the context of Quebec's ongoing struggles for greater self-rule: "It ain't over 'til it's over."[72]

RECENT REFERENDUMS IN THE SOVIET UNION

Many citizens of the then Soviet republics of Estonia, Lithuania, and Latvia voted during 1991 in what local government officials cautiously called opinion polls. The officials avoided calling the votes referendums largely because their constitutional standing within the Soviet Union was unclear and because an apparent violation of the Soviet constitution could provide the Kremlin with a pretext for a full-scale invasion of the republics.[73] Nonetheless, these "opinion polls" were in effect advisory referendums through which citizens of the republics could express whether they desired independence from the Soviet Union.

These instances of direct democracy both resembled and differed from the referendums held in Great Britain, Spain, and Canada a decade earlier. One striking similarity was the sudden rise of nationalist parties immediately prior to the referendums. In 1990, elections were held for the parliaments of the three Soviet republics. Pro-independence candidates won a surprisingly large number of seats—so many that nationalist parties became the premier electoral forces within the republics.

In contrast, the republics' Communist parties, which had been staunchly anti-independence, suffered numerous election-day losses. Some individual Communists responded to these widespread setbacks by adopting a pro-independence posture in order to retain a modicum of popularity and to be more competitive in later elections.[74] Lithuania's Communist party openly advocated Lithuanian self-rule and renamed itself the Lithuanian Democratic party despite heavy pressure from the Soviet Union's Communist party. The courage of the Lithuanian Democratic Party in resisting pressure from Moscow quickly resuscitated its sagging popularity.

Almost immediately following the 1990 elections, the parliament of each Baltic republic declared its wish to secede from the Soviet Union and form a sovereign state. Soon thereafter, Soviet tanks rolled into the republics' capitals and forcibly repressed pro-independence demonstrators. These actions apparently were taken with the prior approval of Soviet president Mikhail Gorbachev, who feared that the republics' declarations of independence might spawn secessionist movements throughout the Soviet Union, encourage a right-wing backlash within the Communist party, jeopardize already controversial liberal economic reforms, and greatly harm the Soviet Union's international stature.

Prior to the central government's military action, the republics' parliaments had opposed holding referendums on independence on grounds that the election process had invested the parliaments with sufficient authority to decide the issue of independence.[75] This common stand changed, however, after Soviet troops had entered the capitals, surrounded government institutions, and attacked and even killed Baltic citizens. Fearing an imminent full-scale military invasion and martial law, the local parliaments quickly called for referendums to substantiate their citizens' desire for national independence before world opinion.

As was true in the Quebec referendum, the advisory referendums in Estonia, Latvia, and Lithuania were never recognized by the central government. Gorbachev maintained that the Baltic parliaments were ignoring constitutionally established procedures for securing independence. He advised the republics' parliaments to work patiently through the Soviet system, utilizing legal procedures of petition and review. From the nationalists' perspectives, a problem with Gorbachev's recommendation was that the established appeals procedure could take five years to complete and could result in significant reductions in the republics' territories. Moreover, Gorbachev's deep distrust of decentralization was well known, so a favorable outcome to the appeals procedure was hardly guaranteed.

The wording of the three republics' referendums did not ask voters if they approved the creation of a specific type of political order that had particular powers, procedures, and institutional arrangements. Voters instead were asked a more abstract question: "Are you in favor of a democratic, independent Latvia (or Estonia, or Lithuania)?" Potentially divisive questions about institutional arrangements—such as what fiscal, educational, and economic powers an independent republic should have, or how minorities' rights should be protected—were thus sidestepped.

Organized interest groups, including Soviet trade unions, the Catholic church, and diverse ethnic associations, participated in informational campaigns prior to the republics' referendums. Opponents of the proposals prophesied that independence would lead to economic collapse and terrible hardships for all. Allegedly, the economies of the Baltic republics were too intertwined with those of the other Soviet republics to ignore their trade, fiscal, transportation, monetary, and tariff policies. Only coordination by a centralized interrepublic government could ensure economic health in the Baltics, opponents claimed.

Critics further argued that if the Baltic republics became independent, ethnic minorities, particularly ethnic Russians and Poles, would become second-class citizens suffering, among other things, linguistic discrimination at school and at work. Gorbachev himself charged that the independence movements were thinly veiled expressions of "nationalist totalitarianism."[76] Parenthetically, it should be noted that ethnic discrimination was not an entirely imagined problem invented by pro-Soviet demagogues. The Estonian Citizens' Committee and some other important Baltic nationalist organizations wanted citizenship rights restricted to direct descendants of those who were citizens of the Baltic republics prior to their 1940 incorporation into the Soviet Union.[77]

Advocates of independence naturally offered a different picture of what would happen if independence was attained. They alleged that the republics no longer would have to follow Moscow's poorly informed directives and economic policies and would, therefore, be free to enact policies appropriate for each republic. This would also avoid inefficiencies caused by corruption within the Communist party. After independence, separatists claimed, government officials would be far more sensitive to regional economic needs because they would be accountable to a regionally elected government. The result of all these changes would be prosperity.

Many advocates of independence also tried to reassure ethnic minorities that citizenship in their new country would be extended to them once independence was achieved. Most church leaders in ethnic-minority enclaves, for instance, tried to discredit xenophobic arguments and urged a yes vote on independence.

Compared to the turnout for the British and Spanish referendums, the more than 80 percent turnouts for each of the three advisory referendums was quite high.[78] The exceptional turnout levels are especially remarkable given Gorbachev's repeated condemnations of the votes and the presence in the streets of Soviet tanks and soldiers.

Perhaps as important as the turnout levels was the almost religious spirit of the participants. Many voters were so impressed by the potential historical significance of their acts that they brought children to the polls to watch the event. Declared one elderly voter after casting her ballot, "We are moved to tears this day."[79]

Large majorities voted yes in each republic. Seventy-seven percent of Estonian voters supported independence; 78 percent of Latvia's voters did so; and 91 percent voted yes in Lithuania.[80] In each of the three republics, the indigenous ethnic populations voted in favor of independence by an overwhelming ratio of nearly 9:1. Surprisingly, many Russians and other non-Baltic residents also voted for independence. In some Russian enclaves, large majorities of voters understandably either cast no ballots or silently protested by staying away from the polls. In other enclaves, however, turnout was as high as its republic's average. Even more remarkably, in some ethnic districts the yes vote was as high as 98 percent.[81]

Weeks later, the Soviet government tried to offset the international impact of the republics' referendums by holding a referendum on reforming the federal structure while retaining the unity of the Soviet Union. Soviet leaders campaigned hard, hoping that a large yes vote would delegitimize the results of the earlier Baltic referendums. The exact substance of the Soviet referendum was difficult to identify, however. The proposal read: "Do you consider it necessary to preserve the union of Soviet Socialist Republics as a renewed federation of equal, sovereign republics in which human rights and freedoms of any nationality will be fully guaranteed?" Gorbachev maintained that the referendum promised both a stronger central government in certain policy areas and greater self-determination for the republics in other areas. Boris Yeltsin, a charismatic Russian leader and Gorbachev's chief rival, argued that the proposal's phrasing was so obscure and ambiguous that it was almost meaningless. Even to the extent that meaning was clear, however, it reinforced the principle of an overriding central government. Therefore, in Yeltsin's opinion, the referendum was "aimed at the preservation of the imperial, unitary nature of the union and its current political system and allows for only superficial renovation."[82]

During the referendum campaign, Gorbachev used state-run television and Communist party newspapers to rally support. Government and party publications and campaign literature associated a vote for the unity proposal with security and prosperity, while they associated a no vote with chaos and bloodshed. For example, one drawing on the front page of *Pravda* on the eve of the referendum showed two hands. One hand, next to the word yes, held grain; the other hand, next to the word *no*, held bullets.[83]

The yes campaign was government funded and relied heavily on television to convey its message. The no campaign was dispersed, grassroots based, and uncoordinated. It also lacked access to statewide electronic media. Yeltsin, for example, was barred from campaigning on state television.

To the government's surprise, the yes vote was quite weak, especially in urban areas. In Moscow, Leningrad, and Kiev—the three largest cities in the Soviet Union—and other metropolitan centers, the referendum barely passed and occasionally failed. Furthermore, turnout in many urban and industrial areas was between 50 and 65 percent, which was low by Soviet standards.[84]

In the Ukraine and some other republics, the local parliaments added subsidiary questions to the government's ballots. These local additions asked questions such as whether the voters desired their republic's independence from the Soviet Union. In the western Ukraine, a small majority of voters supported Gorbachev's unity proposal. But a much larger percentage (80%) of the voters supported an independence proposal, which explicitly referred to the creation of a Ukrainian army and currency. As a result, even though Gorbachev's proposal was supported by a majority of those who voted and won a technical victory, it was considerably overshadowed by the larger victories of the supplementary pro-independence votes.[85]

Further diluting Gorbachev's victory, the three Baltic republics—Armenia, Georgia, and Moldavia—refused to participate in the referendum. Unable to use public buildings in the Baltic republics, the Soviet government resorted to placing ballot boxes within military bases. Moreover, local governments in several other republics reworded the original referendum question that appeared on the ballots so that it sounded far less appealing to voters. In the end, only four republics carried out the referendum exactly as the Soviet government wished.

Gorbachev was not totally unsuccessful, however. The referendum easily passed with over 90 percent of the vote and the turnout often exceeded 75 percent in Kazakhistan, Uzbekistan, and the other extremely poor, rural republics of central Asia. The strength of the yes vote in this region is partially a result of the considerable strength, resources, and authority of the Communist parties in the Asian republics.[86] The economies of the Asian republics are also heavily dependent on imports from and trade with other Soviet republics. Therefore, voters may have had an economic incentive to support the unity of the Soviet Union.[87]

The personal rivalry between Gorbachev and Yeltsin was another factor that possibly influenced the geographic variance in the vote on Soviet unity. Although the referendum was purportedly about preserving the unity of the Soviet Union, many voters saw the referendum as a vote on the relative merits of the two leaders. Not surprisingly, Yeltsin solidly outpolled Gorbachev in Svendlovsk, Yeltsin's home region, where almost 70 percent of the voters rejected the unity proposal and instead indirectly voted for their favorite son.[88]

By the time the ballots had been counted, it was clear that the amount of support for the Soviet referendum on unity was so uneven and qualified that it could hardly bolster either the slumping popularity of Gorbachev or the deteriorating authority of the central government of the Soviet Union. Furthermore, the results of the referendum failed to delegitimize the results of the earlier referendums on independence for Estonia, Latvia, and Lithuania. The referendum results suggested that both the Soviet regime and Gorbachev were out of step with popular opinion. Within a year, Gorbachev's crumbling leadership would be challenged by a coup.

The last independence referendum held in what was soon to become the former Soviet Union, occurred in the Ukraine on December 2, 1991. The preamble to the referendum question referred explicitly to the August 1991 attempted coup against Gorbachev. The ballot presented the coup as a justification for Ukrainians to reconsider their political standing. The referendum campaign was hard fought, partly because of the immense economic resources of the territory and also because of the location of nuclear weapons on Ukrainian soil. The advocates of independence envisioned a radically self-reliant Ukraine that would have full control over its economic resources, currency, and use of weapons and that would coordinate economic and foreign policy through bilateral treaties with the other former Soviet republics. Outside political leaders, such as Yeltsin and Gorbachev, warned the Ukrainians not to support the independence proposal as written because it would make coordination of economic policy among the former Soviet republics extremely difficult.

Both sides tried to mobilize voter support by appealing to the voters' economic worries through countervailing predictions of economic collapse if independence was or, alternately, was not supported by the voters. The two sides also appealed to ethnic loyalties. The pro-independence forces used indigenous non-Russian languages in many campaign rallies, while the anti-independence forces warned ethnic Russians that an independent Ukraine would discriminate against non-Ukrainian speakers.

As in the other independence referendums, turnout was quite high. Over 80 percent of all Ukrainian voters cast ballots, and in several districts turnout exceeded 90 percent. Throughout the republic, overwhelming majorities of voters supported independence. Even in ethnic-Russian enclaves, majorities voted for independence. Support for independence also cut across class boundaries, with relatively well-off urban districts, working-class districts, seaport communities, and farming towns all giving majority support for independence.[89]

After the results were in, there was considerable debate about what the voters had approved. Gorbachev maintained that the referendum for an independent Ukraine was compatible with a revamped Soviet Union, while Yeltsin foresaw a new confederacy in which the Ukraine and Russia would be the primary leaders. But Leonid Kravchuk, the newly elected president of the Ukraine, viewed the vote as approving a more radical form of self-rule. In his words, "A new Ukraine has been born. A great historical event has occurred which will not only change the history of the

Ukraine, but the history of the world."[90]

REFERENDUMS ON SELF-RULE: PARTY
COALITIONS AND REFERENDUM OUTCOMES

Referendums have been used repeatedly since the mid-1970s in struggles over national self-rule within a wide range of advanced industrialized societies. This phenomenon has also been evident in other parts of the world, as discussed in Chapter 3. Both supporters and opponents of regional self-rule have advocated the use of referendums, but in almost all cases they were proposed by political actors who momentarily saw themselves at a disadvantage. Labour activists in Wales and Scotland who feared the government's proposal for devolution, Andalusian politicians who believed Madrid was neglecting their calls for regional self-rule, and Lithuanians who faced threatening tanks all looked to referendums as an alternative to a decisionmaking process that they felt was stacked against them. One might generalize that in struggles over regional self-rule, referendums are typically used defensively—not as political weapons of first choice.

The referendums on regional self-rule also illustrate the many possible abuses of the referendum process. Sometimes to ensure that they win the struggles, political leaders carefully word proposals to maximize the proposals' chances of being passed or defeated. The case of Quebec's sovereignty-association referendum and the more recent and vaguely stated Baltic referendums serve as examples. Leaders also frequently have tampered with procedural rules in order to affect the outcome. Recall, for instance, the 40 percent rule in Great Britain, the abbreviated campaign period and ballot-box fixing in Andalusia, and the local republics' modifications of the original ballot during the Soviet Union's referendum on unity. These manipulations deviate from some commonplace pictures of referendums as fair, impartial applications of democratic ideals but should not be surprising, much less shocking. Nor do they condemn direct democracy. Referendums, after all, are political phenomena: they affect public policy and therefore people's conditions and interests. Because people are affected, they have a stake in the outcome of referendums and will try to affect the result by sometimes manipulating the process as well as debating the issue and casting their votes.

Besides illustrating some of the seamier sides of past referendum politics, this review of British, Spanish, Canadian, and Soviet referendums has shown how electoral upheavals—often in the form of unprecedented surges of support for nationalist parties—have usually preceded the use of direct democracy in deciding questions of regional self-rule. Referendums were initiated and used by the rapidly growing pronationalist forces in some cases to increase their moral leverage vis-à-vis the state. Several cases also show that incumbent governments tried to weaken the growing appeal of nationalists by using referendums to legitimize a *limited* transfer of power to regional governments. We can say, therefore, that dramatically changing electoral fortunes and calculations of political self-preservation seem to have been the key conditions affecting the timing of the referendums.

In all the cases under consideration, political parties and a myriad of groups tried to inform and mobilize voters during the referendum campaigns. Religious orders, economic associations, political personalities, and sports and entertainment celebrities typically participated in the referendum campaigns. Activists tried to influence voters' behavior by discussing a broad range of issues, not simply by discussing the potential international implications of decentralization and possible independence. Through discussions of economic prosperity (or disaster) and overt appeals to ethnic and partisan loyalties and xenophobic sentiments, campaigners tried to change voters' opinions. Furthermore, opinion polls have shown that many voters' evaluations of the proposals did in fact change. Voters often were using highly parochial concerns, especially economic ones, to decide policies pregnant with international significance.

The intensity of the mobilization efforts by established parties and interest groups, or the lack thereof, had obvious impact on the outcome of the vote. The case of the British Labour government's failure to campaign for the devolution proposals is one obvious example. A contrasting illustration is provided by the intense, antidevolution effort of the Gang of Six, without which the extent of the failure of Welsh devolution would be difficult to imagine. Moreover, aspects of the campaigns that might at first glance appear tangential to relative merits of the written referendum proposal, such as the popularity of advocates such as Trudeau or Yeltsin, seem to have had impact on how some people voted.

It would be misleading, though, to focus narrowly on the efforts of single individuals and groups when trying to explain the outcomes. Too many counterexamples come to mind. The governments' embarrassing failures in the Andalusian and Soviet-unity referendums illustrate that vigorous campaigning by party-run governments cannot ensure the referendum results they desire. Nor can biased coverage by state-run electronic media ensure that a proposal will be passed or defeated according to the government's wishes.

Rather than focusing on individuals or specific groups as determinants of the outcome of referendums, the observer who wishes to predict outcomes on the basis of a few variables might be wiser to compare the relative size and the breadth of the coalitions campaigning for and against a referendum proposal. Generally speaking, the side supported by the broadest coalition of political parties and interest groups emerged victorious at the polls. Consider the example of Spain, where the autonomy proposals had been designed and supported from the beginning by broad coalitions of electorally strong parties. The self-determination proposals for Estonia, Latvia, and Lithuania were also designed by parliaments composed of diverse parties.

In contrast, the referendum proposals in Quebec, Scotland, and Wales were defeated—sometimes very easily. In none of these cases did extensive interparty consultation, compromise, and negotiation precede the announced proposal for regional self-rule.

The popular vote, in other words, often—but not always—echoes the earlier jarring or harmonious sounds of interelite politics. Elites can increase the likelihood that a proposal for regional self-rule will be passed, but only through a syncretic, noncombative style of politics. Broad coalition building *before* the announcement of the referendum's proposal seems a precondition for victory.

NOTES

1. Cyrus Ernesto Zirakzadeh, "Economic Changes and Surges in Micro-Nationalist Voting in Scotland and the Basque Region of Spain," *Comparative Studies in Society and History* 31/2, p. 319; François-Pierre Gingras and Neil Nevitte, "Nationalism in Quebec: The Transition of Ideology and Political Support," in *Political Support in Canada: The Crisis Years*, edited by Allan Kornberg and Harold D. Clarke (Durham: Duke University Press, 1983), pp. 302–303.

2. Jim Bulpitt, *Territory and Power in the United Kingdom: An Interpretation* (Manchester: Manchester University Press, 1983), p. 189.

3. Bulpitt, *Territory*, p. 190.

4. On the rival schools of reasoning within the Labour party on referendums and devolution, see Vernon Bogdanor, *The People and the Party System: The Referendum and Electoral Reform in British Politics* (Cambridge: Cambridge University Press, 1981), pp. 47–56; Barry Jones and Rick Wilford, "Further Considerations on the Referendum: The Evidence of the Welsh Vote on Devolution," *Political Studies* 30/1, pp. 17–19; Denis Balsom and Ian McAllister, "The Scottish and Welsh Devolution Referenda of 1979: Constitutional Change and Popular Choice," *Parliamentary Affairs* 32/3, pp. 395–397; Jack Brand, "Political Parties and the Referendum on National Sovereignty: The 1979 Scottish Referendum on Devolution," *Canadian Review of Studies in Nationalism* 13/1, p. 33; and James G. Kellas, *The Scottish Political System*, 4th ed. (Cambridge: Cambridge University Press, 1989), pp. 151–153.

5. On the Conservatives' thesis that referendums can and should be used to prevent radical change, see Bogdanor, *People and the Party System*, pp. 11–33.

6. Kellas, *Scottish Political System*, pp. 148–151; Balsom and McAllister, "Scottish and Welsh Devolution," p. 407; Bogdanor, *People and the Party System*, p. 57; Paul Luke and David Johnson, "Devolution by Referendum? A Look at the Welsh Situation," *Parliamentary Affairs* 29/3, p. 337.

7. Arnold J. James and John E. Thomas, *Wales at Westminister: A History of the Parliamentary Representation of Wales, 1800–1979* (Llandysul, U.K.: Gomer Press, 1981), p. 269.

8. For further discussions of the constitutional processes for designing and passing autonomy statutes, see Mike Newton, "The Peoples and Regions of Spain," in *Democratic Politics in Spain: Spanish Politics After Franco*, edited by David S. Bell (New York: St. Martin's Press, 1983), pp. 100–108; Robert P. Clark, "The Question of Regional Autonomy in Spain's Democratic Transition," in *Spain in the 1980s: The Democratic Transition and a New International Role*, edited by Robert P. Clark and Michael H. Haltzel (Cambridge, Mass.: Ballinger, 1987), pp. 143–151.

9. For further discussion of the origins and evolution of the Andalusian movement for autonomy, see Newton, "Peoples and Regions of Spain," pp. 119–123; Jack Brand, "Andalusia: Nationalism as the Strategy for Autonomy," *Canadian Review of Studies in Nationalism* 15/1-2, pp. 1–10; Antonio Porras Nadales, "El Referéndum de Iniciativa Autonómica del 28 de Febrero en Andalucía," *Revista de Estudios Politícos* 15 (May-June 1980), pp. 175–194.

10. Brand, "Andalusia," p. 10.

11. For a comparison of the PQ and earlier nationalist parties, see Gingras and Nevitte, "Nationalism in Quebec."

12. For discussions of the PQ's syncretic platform, see Gingras and Nevitte, "Nationalism in Quebec"; and Kenneth M. Glazier, "Separatism and Quebec," *Current History* 72/426, p. 154.

13. See, for example, Peter T. Sherrill, "Separatism and Quebec," *Current History* 79/460, p. 137; Glazier, "Separatism and Quebec," p. 154; and Gingras and Nevitte, "Nationalism in Quebec," p. 304.

14. Gingras and Nevitte, "Nationalism in Quebec," p. 317.

15. Gingras and Nevitte, "Nationalism in Quebec," pp. 318–319.

16. For a colorful and insightful description of the debate over the referendum, see Graham Fraser, *PQ: René Lévesque and the Parti Québécois in Power* (Toronto: Macmillan of Canada, 1984), pp. 217–218.

17. Kellas, *Scottish Political System*, p. 153.

18. Balsom and McAllister, "Scottish and Welsh Devolution," p. 398.

19. Jones and Wilford, "Further Considerations," p. 21; Kenneth O. Morgan, *Rebirth of a Nation: Wales 1880-1980* (Oxford: Oxford University Press, 1981), p. 403.

20. For detailed discussions of the arguments used in the Scottish and Welsh referendum campaigns, see J. Barry and R. A. Wilford, "The Welsh Veto: The Politics of the Devolution Campaign in Wales," Working Paper Number 39 of the Centre for the Study of Public Policy, University of Strathclyde, 1979; Jones and Wilford, "Further Considerations," pp. 397–409.

21. Barry Jones and R. A. Wilford, "The Welsh Veto," p. 20.

22. Kellas, *Scottish Political System*, p. 157.

23. Jones and Wilford, "The Welsh Veto," pp. 29–32.

24. For brief descriptions of the media's coverage of the referendum, see Jones and Wilford, "Further Considerations," pp. 23, 26; Kellas, *Scottish Political System*, p. 157; Balsom and McAllister, "Scottish and Welsh Devolution," p. 399.

25. See, for example, Jones and Wilford, "Further Considerations," p. 24;

Morgan, *Rebirth of a Nation*, p. 404.

26. Balsom and McAllister, "Scottish and Welsh Devolution, pp. 401–403, 408; Jones and Wilford, "The Welsh Veto," pp. 33, 35–36; Hugh Berrington, "Centre-Periphery Conflict and British Politics," in *Centre-Periphery Relations in Western Europe*, edited by Yves Meny and Vincent Wright (London: George Allen & Unwin, 1985), pp. 194–195.

27. For interpretations of the changes in Scottish and Welsh public opinion on the topic of devolution that emphasize the role of party endorsements, see Balsom and McAllister, "Scottish and Welsh Devolution"; Brand, "Political Parties."

28. Brand, "Political Parties," pp. 39, 42; Berrington, "Centre-Periphery Conflict," p. 194.

29. Bogdanor, *People and the Party System*, p. 58.

30. For brief histories and ideological analyses of ETA and the Herri Batasuna, see Robert P. Clark, *The Basque Insurgents: ETA, 1952-1980* (Madison: University of Wisconsin Press, 1984), pp. 3–119; Cyrus Ernesto Zirakzadeh, *A Rebellious People: Basques, Protests, and Politics* (Reno: University of Nevada Press, 1991), pp. 145–200. For useful overviews of the Basque referendum campaign, see Javier Cuercora Atienza and Alberto Pérez Calvo, "En Torno al Referéndum del Estatuto de Autonomía del País Vasco," *Revista de Estudios Políticos* 12 (November-December 1979), pp. 179–196; Newton, "Peoples and Regions of Spain," pp. 112–116.

31. Richard Gunther, Giacomo Sani, and Goldie Shabad, *Spain After Franco: The Making of a Competitive Party System* (Berkeley: University of California Press, 1988), p. 349.

32. For useful discussions of the Galician referendum campaign, see Newton, "Peoples and Regions of Spain," pp. 116–118; Gunther et al., *Spain After Franco*, pp. 249–251.

33. For useful discussions of the Andalusian referendum campaign, see Newton, "Peoples and Regions of Spain," pp. 120–122; Brand, "Andalusia," pp. 6–8; Porras Nadales, "El Referéndum," pp. 177–185.

34. Zirakzadeh, *A Rebellious People*, p. 106.

35. Gunther et al., *Spain After Franco*, p. 322.

36. For example, Newton, "Peoples and Regions of Spain," p. 118.

37. Porras Nadales, "El Referéndum," p. 181.

38. Porras Nadales, "El Referéndum," pp. 182–184.

39. Porras Nadales, "El Referéndum," p. 184.

40. Porras Nadales, "El Referéndum," p. 185.

41. This argument is suggested, for example, by Sherrill, "Separatism and Quebec," pp. 136–137.

42. Sherrill, "Separatism and Quebec," p. 137.

43. For detailed descriptions of the Quebec campaign, see Sherrill, "Separatism and Quebec"; Fraser, *PQ*, pp. 190–240; John Fitzmaurice, *Québec and Canada: Past, Present and Future* (New York: St. Martin's Press, 1985), pp. 295–307.

44. On the city-country split in PQ support, see Gingras and Nevitte, "Nationalism in Quebec." On the urban voters hesitating to support sovereignty-association, see Fitzmaurice, *Québec and Canada*, pp. 305–306; Sherrill, "Separatism and Quebec," pp. 137, 144.

45. For an interpretation of the campaign that stresses the importance of

Trudeau, see Fitzmaurice, *Québec and Canada*, p. 301; Fraser, *PQ*, pp. 224–228.

46. Fraser, *PQ*, p. 225.

47. For discussions of the Yvette movement, see Fraser, *PQ*, pp. 222–224; Sherrill, "Separatism and Quebec," p. 137.

48. The problems of the PQ's grave, sincere, and almost dull campaign style have been discussed by Fraser, *PQ*, pp. 224, 229–233.

49. For various measurements of the constant changes in public opinion during the campaign, see Fitzmaurice, *Québec and Canada*, pp. 300–301; Fraser, *PQ*, pp. 219–220, 234; Sherrill, "Separatism and Quebec," pp. 36–37.

50. Jon H. Pammett, Harold D. Clarke, Jane Jenson, and Lawrence LeDuc, "Political Support and Voting Behavior in the Quebec Referendum," in Kornberg and Clarke, *Political Support in Canada*, pp. 331–332, 350.

51. William Miller, *The End of British Politics? Scot and English Political Behaviour in the Seventies* (Oxford: Clarendon Press, 1981), p. 130; James and Thomas, *Wales at Westminster*, p. 123.

52. Bogdanor, *People and the Party System*, pp. 51, 57.

53. Francisco José Llera Ramo, "Caracterización Sociopolítica del Sistema de Partidos de la Comunidad Autónoma Vasca y Navarra," *Revista de Estudios Políticos* 20 (March-April 1981), p. 63.

54. Mario Caciagli, *Elecciones y Partidos en la Transición Española* (Madrid: Centro de Investigaciones Sociologicas, 1986), p. 124.

55. Newton, "Peoples and Regions of Spain," p. 118.

56. See, for example, Gabriel A. Almond and Sidney Verba, *The Civic Culture: Political Attitudes and Democracy in Five Nations* (Boston: Little, Brown, 1965); John Gaventa, *Power and Powerlessness: Quiescence and Rebellion in an Appalachian Valley* (Urbana: University of Illinois Press, 1980).

57. Equipo de Sociología Electoral, "El Referéndum del Estatuto de Autonomía en Cataluña," *Revista de Estudios Políticos* 12 (November-December 1979), p. 200; Porras Nadales, "El Referéndum," p. 185.

58. Vincent Lemieux and Jean Crête, "Quebec," in *Canada at the Polls, 1979 and 1980: A Study of the General Elections*, edited by Howard R. Penniman (Washington, D.C.: American Enterprise Institute, 1981), p. 220.

59. Bogdanor, *People and the Party System*, p. 58.

60. Balsom and McAllister, "Scottish and Welsh Devolution," p. 401.

61. Jones and Wilford, "Further Considerations," p. 25.

62. On the imperfect correlations between party voting and referendum voting, see Porras Nadales, "El Referéndum," pp. 185–191; Cuercora Atienza and Perez Calvo, "El Torno," pp. 194–196.

63. Fitzmaurice, *Québec and Canada*, p. 304; Pammett et al., "Political Support," pp. 339–340.

64. Pammett et al., "Political Support," pp. 339–340.

65. Fitzmaurice, *Québec and Canada*, pp. 305–306.

66. Miller, *The End of British Politics?* pp. 252–253.

67. For a discussion of the rise of devolutionary sentiment and politics in Scotland during the 1980s, see James G. Kellas, *Scottish Political System* and "Prospects for a New Scottish Political System," *Parliamentary Affairs* 42/4, pp. 519–532.

68. For an overview of the political struggles over autonomy after the refer-

endums, see Clark, "The Question of Regional Autonomy."

69. On youth's declining involvement in nationalist politics, see Gérard Pelletier, "Quebec: Different But in Step with North America," *Daedalus* 117/4, pp. 270–274; Léon Dion, "The Mystery of Québec," *Daedalus* 117/4, pp. 301–302.

70. Joel Smith and Allan Kornberg, "The Quebec Referendum: National or Provincial Event?" in Clark and Kornberg, *Political Support in Canada*, pp. 374, 379.

71. *World Opinion Update* 15/3, p. 26.

72. Rory Leishman, "Quebec and the Constitution: Completing the Patriation Process," in *Perspectives on Canadian Federalism*, edited by R. D. Olling (Scarborough, Ont.: Prentice-Hall Canada, 1988), p. 410.

73. On the efforts to depict the referendums as "opinion polls," see *New York Times*, February 6, 7, 9, 1991.

74. On the Communists' responses to nationalists' victories, see Martha Brill Olcott, "The Lithuanian Crisis," *Foreign Affairs* 69/3, pp. 30-46; Steven L. Burg, "European Republics of the Soviet Union," *Current History* 89/549, pp. 321–324, 340; *Economist*, February 17, 1990.

75. As Olcott points out, it was the Soviet Union's leadership that initially wanted a referendum held, not the Baltic nationalists. Apparently, centrists like Gorbachev believed that either an independence proposal would be voted down or the size of the no vote would be so large as to render the project of independence impractical.

76. *New York Times*, February 9, 1991.

77. Burg, "European Republics," p. 322.

78. *Washington Post*, February 10, 1991; March 4, 1991.

79. *New York Times*, February 10, 1991; March 4, 1991.

80. *Washington Post*, February 10, 1991, March 4, 1991.

81. On the ambivalence of ethnic minorities in the Baltic republics toward the idea of independence, see Olcott, "The Lithuanian Crisis," p. 41; *Los Angeles Times*, February 10, 1991, March 4, 1991; *New York Times*, February 10, 1991; *Washington Post*, March 4, 1991.

82. On Yeltsin's and Gorbachev's disagreements over the unity referendum, see *Chicago Tribune*, March 16, 18, 1991; *Los Angeles Times*, March 16, 1991.

83. *Chicago Tribune*, March 19, 1991.

84. *Chicago Tribune*, March 19, 22, 1991.

85. *Chicago Tribune*, March 20, 1991; *New York Times*, March 19, 20, 1991.

86. *Chicago Tribune*, March 20, 1991.

87. *Chicago Tribune*, March 22, 1991.

88. *Chicago Tribune*, March 19, 1991.

89. *New York Times*, December 2, 1991; *Hartford Courant*, December 2, 1991.

90. *Hartford Courant*, December 2, 1991.

7

Referendums and
International Politics:
The United States

The call in the United States to utilize referendums as a tool for resolving international issues and making foreign policy has grown louder with each passing crisis since the late 1960s. Twice in that time, large numbers of U.S. citizens have been given the opportunity to express their views in international-issue referendums. One group of referendums focused on Vietnam, the other on nuclear weapons.[1] During the Vietnam War, several end-the-war initiatives were proposed and voted upon locally. In the 1982 election, a nuclear freeze initiative appeared on the ballot in ten states and forty-nine cities. This latter group of referendums was particularly significant because fully 30 percent of the American people had an opportunity to vote on the freeze as a new foreign policy direction.

Because the United States has no national referendum mechanism, these votes were not binding on national decision makers. Yet, they anticipated, and arguably helped promote, major shifts of direction in U.S. foreign policy, if not actual changes in the way that policy is formulated. Compared to the other countries we have discussed in previous chapters, the United States offers its citizens few if any opportunities to influence foreign policy directly between elections. However, the Vietnam and nuclear freeze initiatives, although locally administered, captured national attention and ultimately influenced U.S. foreign policymakers. Thus, they warrant our attention as possible bellwethers of political change in the United States' foreign policy process. While it is still premature to predict when national referendums might become a formal part of U.S. politics, the Vietnam and nuclear freeze initiatives were clear steps in that direction.

Additional steps toward the introduction of national referendums were taken by the U.S. Supreme Court in the 1970s and 1980s. During these two decades, the Court gradually articulated a much more significant place for referendums in the "normal" politics of the United States. By allowing the use of referendums to decide a number of local and statewide issues, the Court effectively "deradicalized" referendums and opened wider the door for national initiatives.

Because much of the recent history of referendums in the United States is legal history, we will begin this chapter by exploring the series of

151

court decisions that have fundamentally changed U.S. referendum politics. Though the courts have yet to consider the issue of a national referendum, the Supreme Court's decisions in other cases make it clear that no constitutional change is required to adopt a national referendum process. After we have traced the judicial journey of a possible national referendum in the United States, we will again take up our propositions in the context of the Vietnam and nuclear freeze ballots of the last decades.

THE COURTS, THE CONSTITUTION, AND DIRECT LEGISLATION

Given the populist heritage of referendums in the United States, it is not surprising that the referendum device has often been viewed as an excessively democratic, even radical method for making political decisions. As early as 1847, a federal judge noted in *Rice v. Foster* that as a nation, Americans chose representative rather than direct democracy institutions to guard against "rashness, precipitancy, and misguided zeal; and to protect the minority against the injustice of the majority."[2] More recently, President Reagan suggested in a 1982 speech that supporters of the freeze initiative were "inspired not by the sincere, honest people who want peace, but by some who want the weakening of America and so are manipulating honest people and sincere people."[3] This fear of direct democracy stems partly from the elitist attitude of conservatives reminiscent of the eighteenth-century British thinker, Edmund Burke. A member of Parliament, Burke contended that "the representative betrays his constituents if he sacrifices his judgement to their opinions."[4]

However, as we noted in Chapter 2, referendums are increasingly accepted as nonthreatening to representative government. Many reasons explain this shift in the United States. Some have to do with the sheer numbers of referendums now on local and state election ballots in every election, making them seem less mysterious and threatening. But increased use of referendums cannot by itself account for the altered environment of opinion about their use. To understand why referendums now enjoy legitimacy as part of normal politics in the United States, we need also to explore their legal and constitutional pedigree as progressively adumbrated by the Supreme Court.

Throughout its history, and especially during the past twenty years, the Court has been the major player in the gradual acceptance of referendums as a normal part of politics in the United States. Surveying this normalization process is a necessary first step before we apply our propositions about referendums to politics in one of the few remaining Western democratic countries without a national referendum.

The Supreme Court has made decisions in three areas affecting the political and constitutional status of referendums. First, the Court has made it clear that state laws adopted by referendum are subject to the same judicial review and determination of constitutionality as any law passed in the traditional way. Second, the Court has stipulated that legislating via referendum is not an unconstitutional delegation of legislative power. Third, the Court has concluded that individuals and, significantly, corporations, have few restrictions on the amount of financial resources they may expend to promote or defeat a referendum issue.

Referendums and Judicial Review

Since its articulation in *Marbury v. Madison* (1803), the power of judicial review has been exercised by the Supreme Court over legislation at both federal and state levels. This power has functioned as a check on presidential and congressional authority and has worked to increase federal supremacy over the states. Today, this unwritten power of the Court is accepted as part of our constitutional system, although individual exercises of judicial review often still stir controversy. What has been less clear, however, is whether the Court may use the nullifying power over legislation passed by the people themselves in referendums.

The Court has considered cases arising from referendums as far back as *Phillips v. Payne* in 1875,[5] but it did not consider power of judicial review over referendums until *Pacific States Telephone and Telegraph v. Oregon* in 1912.[6] In *Pacific*, the Court declined to determine whether a state law concerning licensing fees that had been enacted by state popular vote initiative was indeed constitutional. The Court maintained that the question of the legality of such initiatives was a political, rather than a justiciable, matter relating to the structure and political character of state government and thus was not open to review. Later that year, it again upheld the political question designation and also extended the nonjusticiability criterion to local referendums in *Kiernan v. City of Portland.*[7]

Beginning in the late 1960s, the Court issued a series of opinions that reassessed its role regarding judicial review of referendum-generated state law. Beginning with the 1967 case of *Reitman v. Mulkey*, the Court has used the equal protection clause of the Fourteenth Amendment to pass judgment on the constitutionality of a variety of state and local practices in the areas of taxation, housing and zoning, busing, and amending state constitutions.[8] In *Reitman*, the Court invalidated California's Proposition 14, a constitutional amendment approved by referendum that banned state interference with the right of residential property owners to rent, sell, or lease to whomever they pleased. The Court held that complying with referendum results would involve official state action that was discriminatory on the basis of race and, therefore, unconstitutional.

The Court further extended its right of review two years later in *Hunter v. Erickson, Mayor of Akron.*[9] Again on the grounds of unconstitutional racial discrimination, the Court invalidated an Akron charter amendment, approved by referendum, that required further city referendums before any transfer or use of property on the "basis of race, color, religion, national origin, or ancestry." The Court majority stated that the charter amendment unfairly burdened racial minorities and, therefore, violated the equal protection clause. Two years later, the Court allowed similar zoning ordinances to stand if they turned on economic rather than racial distinctions. In the case of *James v. Valtierra*, the Court upheld restrictive zoning ordinances that required referendums to approve de facto economic segregation through low-income housing projects.[10] Here the Court decided that the question was not one of equal protection, but of the right of local home rule and of the people to hold referendums. On the latter score, Justice Hugo Black delivered the majority opinion that "provisions for referendums demonstrate devotion to democracy, not to bias, discrimination, or prejudice."

Finally, the Court decided two cases in 1982 involving state referendums regarding busing that cemented the Court's right to review laws and state constitutional amendments promulgated through referendum votes.[11] Although these decisions took different views of the right of states and localities to regulate busing via referendum vote, their combined authority completed the Court's expanded authority over referendums. It was now clear that laws enacted by referendums shared an essential feature of constitutionality with laws passed by legislatures: they were both subject to judicial review. To those who feared an unrestrained and uncontrollable public able to pass at will legislation that could not be overruled except by the action of elected political leaders, the Court's expansion of its power meant that referendums were less threatening to the political order.

Referendums and the Power to Delegate

Article I, Section 1 of the U.S. Constitution states that "all legislative Powers herein granted shall be vested in a Congress of the United States, which shall consist of a Senate and House of Representatives." Does this mean that legislation by referendum constitutes a delegation of legislative authority away from Congress, a move that would on its face seem unconstitutional? The answer from the Supreme Court is an unequivocal no. It is true that the Court has never decided this question at the national level, even though it has heard and decided many cases involving the act of delegation. It is also the case that when a possible national referendum process was last debated in Congress in the late 1970s, both proponents and opponents assumed a constitutional amendment would be required to institute the referendum without violating Article I, Section 1. They were wrong, however, and the Supreme Court has already denied the validity of their assumption. It has enunciated the basic principle that referendums do *not* represent delegations of legislative authority. This means that, in the Court's view, instituting a national referendum would not require the extraordinary measure of constitutional amendment. Indeed, the referendum should already be a part of normal politics.

The Court's language in the 1976 case *City of Eastlake v. Forest City Enterprises, Inc.* clearly indicates it would support the constitutionality of a national referendum.[12] *Eastlake* was a zoning case similar to *Hunter v. Erickson* and *James v. Valtierra* and concerned a town charter provision stating that rezoning could be undertaken only with prior approval of 55 percent of the voters in a citywide referendum. The Court upheld the charter provision on grounds explicitly relating the nature of referendums to the constitutional requirement of nondelegation of legislative authority. Speaking for the majority, Chief Justice Warren Burger defended the power of the people to legislate via referendum as a basic democratic right. Furthermore, he argued that there were two reasons why this right could not be construed as a delegation of power from the legislature. First, it is a power the people have never lost even though they have established legislative bodies. Specifically, the chief justice held that

> a referendum cannot, however, be characterized as a delegation of power. Under our constitutional assumptions, all power derives from the people, who can delegate it to representative instruments which they create. See, e.g., *The Federalist No. 39* (J. Madison). In establishing legislative bodies, the people can reserve to themselves power to deal directly with matters which might otherwise be assigned to the legislature.[13]

As seventeenth-century English political philosopher John Locke had argued, the establishment of a representative government does not presume the transference of the rights of the people to the government. Instead, what is transferred is only the execution of those rights. Thus, the right of the people to give itself laws is never actually lost or given up. So in the case of referendums, as Burger points out, no additional delegation of the right back to the people is required. It is a right already reserved to the people through the Tenth Amendment and has never been transferred anywhere else.[14]

The chief justice also articulated a second reason why referendums do not constitute a delegation of legislative power. Before *Eastlake*, whenever the Court had found unconstitutional delegations of legislative authority, there had always been a basic difference drawn between those cases and those involving referendums. As Burger pointed out in *Eastlake*, unconstitutional delegations, where they have existed, have always designated "a *narrow segment* of the community, not the people at large" as the recipient of the power to legislate.[15] Only the people *as a whole* possess the untransferable right of legislation. Any delegation to but a part of the whole people is suspect; but any supposed delegation to the whole is not, because it is not delegation at all.

The *Eastlake* decision therefore effectively alters the entire constitutional discussion of referendums. Though the case, and therefore Burger's opinion, does not explicitly involve Congress or a national referendum, the implications of Burger's logic is inescapable for every level of government. The people in their political organization have never lost the right to legislate themselves. They have merely loaned that right and power, so to speak, to Congress and other legislative bodies. Thus, the people have the power reserved to them to reclaim the exercise of that right at any time. This is the meaning of the Tenth Amendment, and indeed of democracy itself—the right of the people to govern themselves. In the eyes of the Supreme Court, the chief interpreter of the Constitution, referendums at any level of government should be understood as an unexceptional part of U.S. politics.

Referendums, Money, and Politics

It often seems cynical to emphasize the role of money in U.S. politics. Still, its place cannot be denied, though Congress has tried various ways to downplay its effect in electoral politics. Since its inception during the Progressive Era, the referendum has been viewed as a way to give political voice to Americans regardless of their social or economic status. Especially today, in the era of federal matching funds for presidential races, fund-raising political action committees (PACs), and millionaire senators, referendums appear to their supporters as the common voters' access to decisionmaking. Referendums seem ironically out of sync with the apparent historical movement of U.S. politics toward capture by the moneyed set. At least, that is how referendums appeared before a landmark Supreme Court decision in 1978 in *First National Bank of Boston v. Bellotti, Attorney General of Massachusetts.*[16]

Bellotti gave judicial license to the flood of big-time money into referendum politics. As appellant in the case, the Bank of Boston argued that its constitutional right of freedom of speech had been denied by enforcement of a state law preventing it from making expenditures or contributions "for the purpose of . . . influencing or affecting the vote on any question submitted to the voters, other than one materially affecting any of the property, business or assets of the corporation."[17] The Bank of Boston had wanted to spend money to defeat a referendum question seeking to establish a state income tax. The state statute forbade such expenditure, and the Massachusetts attorney general had persuaded a state court to issue an injunction against the bank. The Massachusetts Supreme Court upheld the statute; the U.S. Supreme Court reversed the decision.

In what became a very controversial decision, the Court accepted three important claims that have affected referendums ever since. First, the Court declared that corporations are individuals with individual rights, including rights of free speech. Moreover, the corporation's speech was especially protected in this instance because it "is the type of speech indispensable to decision making in a democracy, and this is no less true because the speech comes from a corporation rather than an individual. The inherent worth of the speech in terms of its capacity for informing the public does not depend upon the identity of its source, whether corporation, association, union, or individual."[18]

Second, the Court argued that since the "people in our democracy are entrusted with the responsibility for judging and evaluating the relative merits of conflicting arguments," corporations had a proper, even essential, role to play in referendum politics.[19] The corporations provided, the Court argued, a needed second opinion or alternative point of view. This further justified the expenditure of corporate funds to defeat the proposition.

Third, the Court declared that even huge expenditures of corporate funds in referendum battles did not violate congressional provisions for campaign spending.[20] There is an intrinsic difference between elections and referendums, the opinion asserted, since "referenda are held on issues, not candidates for public office."[21] Thus, the threat of corruption that such financial largesse so clearly poses for free elections "simply is not present in a popular vote on a public issue."[22] Therefore, the Court refused either to apply campaign finance law to corporate activity in referendum politics or to limit in any way the amount of money a corporation (or anyone else) could spend in a referendum campaign.

By legitimating the impact of big money in referendums, the Court did two seemingly contradictory things. It both bestowed unique political status on referendums and paved the way for their acceptance as noncontroversial political devices. Unlike the major players in elections, referendum participants were now exempted from cumbersome campaign financing and disclosure statutes. At the same time, this made referendums more palatable to the part of the electorate more likely to be opposed to them: established political actors with more money than votes. The referendum no longer looked like the progeny of the Progressive Era.

It is somewhat ironic, then, that the increasing use and acceptance of referendums have distanced them from their original progressive goal. As we have seen, the Supreme Court has played a major role in this evolution. Whether the normalization of the referendum as an noncontroversial political practice is ultimately good for either referendums or democracy itself remains for our discussion, though scholars are not in agreement on this score.[23] But one general result of the Court's decisions is that the players in referendum politics now largely resemble those in electoral politics. Indeed, as we will see in the next section, there are some new specialists, such as professional signature gatherers and proposition framers, that come with referendum politics.[24] But, as we will also conclude, they simply join the ranks of political elites that already populate U.S. politics.

In short, referendum politics in the United States is no longer radical. Its juridical evolution has resulted in laws reviewable by the courts, as are laws that result from legislative action. The use of referendums does not constitute a loss of power through delegation from the legislature. And referendums are open to manipulation by elites and by money—just like normal politics in the United States. Does this mean that referendum politics has gained acceptance at the price of its soul as a participatory democratic practice? That is one of the questions our propositions about referendums seek to answer. It is to those propositions that we now return.

REFERENDUMS ON VIETNAM AND THE NUCLEAR FREEZE

The Court decisions in the *Hunter*, *Eastlake*, and *Bank of Boston* cases fundamentally altered the nature of referendums in the United States. As those cases are all relatively recent, the number of international-issue referendums that manifest that new nature is quite small. Two recent referendums that do fit into the new clothes with which the Court dressed referendum politics are the various, late 1960s local initiatives on the Vietnam War and the state and local votes on the freezing of nuclear weapons in 1982.

The Vietnam Referendums of 1966–1968

As we saw in Chapter 2, the U.S. House of Representatives defeated the Ludlow amendment by a narrow margin in 1937, even though polls showed that nearly three-fourths of the American people favored its stipulation that war could be declared only by national referendum.[25] Since that time, no statewide (or national) plebiscites have been held on the topic of war. Between 1966 and 1968, however, several cities and towns held local referendums on the issue of the continuation of the Vietnam War. These votes obviously were not binding in any national policy sense, and how well they measured public sentiments about the war is open to question. Nevertheless, they offer some interesting and unexpected findings in light of our propositions about international-issue referendums.

Referendums about the war were held in seven cities: Dearborn, Michigan; San Francisco, California; Cambridge, Massachusetts; Madison, Wisconsin; Mill Valley, California; Lincoln, Massachusetts; and Beverly Hills, California. Voters in all of them displayed slightly more support for withdrawal of U.S. troops than most public opinion surveys suggested. Support for an end to U.S. participation in the war ranged from 39 percent of the voters in Cambridge to 57 percent in Dearborn.[26] The Dearborn voters actually voted twice on the issue, the first time in the midterm elections in 1966, when only 41 percent supported withdrawal. Thus the two-year period between referendums in Dearborn actually increased support for a policy change, though the second vote was subsequent to the decision by President Johnson to limit bombing to North Vietnam.[27]

The locations of these referendums for the most part support the proposition that interest group activity was responsible both for the timing of the referendums and for their results. Except for Dearborn and Beverly Hills, these cities are college towns and/or bastions of liberal politics. Students and local celebrities from the entertainment industries played significant organizational roles in circulating petitions to place referendum issues on the ballots. Though there was growing dissension within President Lyndon Johnson's Democratic party by 1968, it is significant that candidates for public office did not disagree widely on the Vietnam issue. This was true even for the Democratic and Republican presidential candidates and meant, as Benjamin Page and Richard Brody point out, that the 1968 election was itself not a referendum on Vietnam issues, since "in reality there was little difference between the candidates" concerning war policy.[28] We should not, of course, discount the role that antiwar Democrats Eugene McCarthy and Robert Kennedy played in changing war policy, but actual candidates after the nomination process at most levels of government downplayed their position on the war until the 1970 and 1972 elections. Thus, dissatisfaction with war policy, though it clearly existed, was not notably related to the positions of political candidates in the election year.

But overall national disillusionment with the war does not really explain the timing of the referendums, since they were not held in a sociologically random set of U.S. cities. What is ironic is that the motivating force behind holding the referendums was interest group success among voters assumed to be in favor of continuing the war effort. It was widely assumed at the time that only students and assorted radicals actually opposed the war, whereas middle-class voters—and especially working-class citizens (the so-called "silent majority")—were solidly behind the war effort. What the referendums in Dearborn especially made evident, however, and what was also true in all the other referendums except in Cambridge, was that socioeconomic status was *inversely* related to support for the war. Disapproval of the war, Harlan Hahn's correlation coefficients indicate, "appeared to be related to working-class rather than to high-status characteristics. In most communities, as the proportion of voters possessing relatively low-status attributes grew, the vote against the Vietnam War also tended to mount.[29]

The role of working-class voters in the Vietnam referendums also supplies somewhat unexpected responses to other of our propositions concerning educational level among participants and about who votes in referendums. Knowledge about the war was not great for most voters on war issues; though, again, working-class voters expressed greater confidence in the accuracy of their opinions. Hahn and Sugarman point out that "upper middle class voters expressed little confidence in their own evaluations of the issue and tended to borrow ideological rationalizations from either proponents or critics of the war."[30] Blue-collar voters, on the other hand, had considerably more first-hand experience with the war either as soldiers or relatives of soldiers, as is well documented, and thus claimed to know more about the issues involved.[31] Whether such personal intimacy with the war itself constituted a higher educational level about the issues is debatable. What is certain is that support for holding the referendums was nearly unanimous among such groups, and that participation in the referendums was much higher among blue-collar voters than it was among higher socioeconomic status groups.[32]

It is difficult to generalize about who won in the Vietnam referendums or about the overall significance of these mostly small-city plebiscites on the eventual ending of the war. Except for San Francisco, none of the referendum localities was a major media outlet, and none of the referendums generated heavy media coverage. Though they all were referendums on current government policy, for the most part government officials and (especially) local candidates avoided comment on the referendum issues themselves. U.S. participation in the war eventually ended, however, and that occurred in part because public opinion swung solidly against it. But the impact of the referendums is unclear, other than speculation that they laid the groundwork for future participation by citizens in the foreign policy process. Harlan Hahn agrees with this assessment, contending:

> Since many [opinion poll] respondents may have become aware that their opinions will have less impact on international than on domestic issues, perhaps their replies have been shaped by special influences or constraints that have not affected policy preferences on other issues. Increased opportunities for direct popular participation in the development of foreign policy, therefore, could have a major effect on public attitudes toward war.[33]

By the early 1980s, the referendum experiences during the Vietnam War provided a model for a new referendum campaign aimed at changing the public attitudes toward a different kind of conflict—thermonuclear war.

The Nuclear Freeze Referendums

The nuclear freeze movement in the early 1980s was unlike any other in U.S. history. Yet, it has been compared to many: abolitionism in the nineteenth century, women's suffrage and prohibition in the early twentieth century, and civil rights and the antiwar movement in the 1960s.[34] It resembles each of these in some ways but remains unique among them for its use of the referendum and the speed of its organizational effort. This was a mass movement that launched and streaked across the political sky like one of the weapons it aimed at freezing. In a mere five years, it galvanized political opinion, won votes, overcame a popular president's jingoistic scorn, and was approved by the U.S. House of Representatives. But it landed with a thud as its electoral and congressional success resulted in a mainly symbolic victory for disarmament.[35] By 1986, it had largely disappeared as both a movement and an idea, while nuclear stockpiles continued to grow.

Many aspects of the freeze campaign placed it solidly within the tradition of other U.S. political movements.[36] In its origins it relied heavily on both a handful of charismatic leaders and an already established network of politically active groups, in this case made up of a variety of peace and social justice activists. The freeze campaign lived and died with the media, both perhaps more quickly than past movements. The freeze effort began as a grassroots campaign unaffiliated with any particular party or elected leader, but it eventually won the endorsement of a wide and bipartisan array of elected officials. Finally, coming from outside normal political channels, the freeze idea swept the nation and successfully forced its way onto the political agenda. Once there, it followed a deeply furrowed path toward political obscurity and irrelevance.

There is, however, one aspect of the freeze movement that sets it apart and prevents us from dismissing it as just another short-lived, one-issue political movement. It was tied to the referendum and initiative device, which it used more successfully than any other movement in U.S. history. In doing so, the freeze campaign offered more Americans the opportunity to vote on an issue of foreign policy and international politics than they had ever had before. In the process, the freeze raised the prospect of an enduring change in the substance of democracy in the United States.

By the end of the referendum campaigns concerning the freeze, roughly 30 percent of the U.S. electorate had been afforded the opportunity to express their views on nuclear policy via the ballot box. The referendums took place in the 1982 elections in ten states, the District of Columbia, and forty-nine cities and counties.[37] Sixty percent of those voting approved the freeze propositions; the only defeat was in Arizona. After the referendums, President Reagan effectively dropped his opposition to the idea and denied he had ever associated the freeze with subversive Soviet influences. In May 1984, the U.S. House of Representatives passed a much diluted version of a freeze proposition, and later in the year, Democratic presidential candidate Walter Mondale promised a freeze on new weapons if elected. He lost, and support for the freeze melted away at virtually all levels, both public and governmental. But, as we will see, a new process for decisionmaking remained, the substance of which could potentially include both domestic and foreign policy questions.

Origins, Conduct, and Significance of the Freeze Referendums

In examining our propositions about referendums with reference to the freeze campaign, it is important to remember that this national referendum movement proceeded without constitutional or statutory mandate. It happened because the people made it happen. This is the defining characteristic of initiatives, of course, but in this instance the relative unimportance of elected leadership—or even nonelected but traditional leadership—out in front at the start of the freeze campaign is striking. Certainly there was disagreement within Congress and between Congress and the White House about defense policy, specifically nuclear deterrence strategies. But other than Senator Mark Hatfield's 1979 amendment to the (ultimately unratified) SALT II treaty calling for a freeze on production of existing weapons, widespread congressional support—not to mention leadership—on the freeze issue did not really exist.[38]

The momentum for a nuclear freeze and for the referendums supporting it came from two sources: the public at large and a small group of leaders who represented a new breed of political elites. The latter are particularly interesting for the development of referendum politics, since they occupy a role in politics ill-defined by traditional offices or interest group affiliations. Yet, in the freeze campaign they showed great success in mobilizing public support for their issue, and in the process they carried traditional polite elites in their wake.

Before looking at this new kind of political opinion leader, we need to note the role of the public itself before and during the freeze campaign. Public opinion supported a freeze on building nuclear weapons, but it was not the precipitating cause of the freeze referendums. Yet, the movement would have soon withered without an early and enthusiastic public following (and resulting media coverage). But, as political scientist Everett Ladd points out, the freeze campaign had not been prompted by a recent change in attitude within the public mind about nuclear weapons. According to Ladd, the public attitude in the United States toward such weapons has always been both complex and distinctly ambivalent. Americans never learned to "love the bomb," and in fact their attitudes toward it have changed very little in four decades of living in its shadow.[39] Since the very beginning of nuclear time in 1945, approximately 20 percent of the electorate "categorically opposed making, much less using, the bomb. In November 1946, Gallup found that 21 percent of the populace thought their country 'should stop making atom bombs and destroy all those we have now.' Only 42 percent of Americans believed in October 1948 'that in the long run atomic energy will do more good than harm.'"[40]

Thus, the origins of the freeze movement lie in forty years of anxiety within U.S. public opinion concerning the use and effects of nuclear warfare. These amorphous fears and deep-seated loathing did not by themselves spawn the freeze campaign; but they did supply a receptive environment for a new approach toward nuclear strategy and toward how that strategy should be made. This new approach was largely developed by two people, who worked independently at first, then collaborated to make the freeze referendums happen. The idea of the freeze itself is often credited to Randall Forsberg, a once little-known, thirty-eight-year-old defense analyst. Her 1980 pamphlet, "Call to Halt the Nuclear Arms Race," began discussion of a new, comprehensive freeze proposal to halt all production of existing weapons and to bar the development of new ones. The idea of using referendums to achieve the freeze began with another Randall, Randall Kehler, who organized the first freeze referendum in three western Massachusetts senate districts in 1980.

The story of Forsberg's "Call" has been told in several places.[41] A graduate student in arms control at MIT in the late 1970s, Forsberg was frustrated both with the academic and peace-activist communities for their approaches to arms control. She asserted that within these settings there was no "attempt to undertake a systematic investigation of the conflicting assumptions held by scholars, educators, and activists about the causes of war and the possible route to a stable, disarmed peace."[42] What was needed, she urged, was a proposal ambitious enough to unite the panoply of peace groups already in place around the country, sophisticated enough to be respectable within the arms control community, and yet simple enough to appeal to the typical U.S. citizen. Her offering, a mere four pages long, became that proposal and that rallying point. The preamble to the "Call" makes its objectives clear:

> To improve national and international security, the United States and the Soviet Union should stop the nuclear arms race. Specifically, they should adopt a mutual freeze on the testing, production and deployment of nuclear weapons and of missiles and new aircraft designed primarily to deliver nuclear weapons. This is an essential, verifiable first step toward lessening the risk of nuclear war and reducing the nuclear arsenals.[43]

At the time of Forsberg's "Call," Randall Kehler was already involved in some 1980 freeze referendums in state senate districts in western

Massachusetts. His proposal followed that of Senator Hatfield, but it was not as comprehensive or as sophisticated in nature as the one outlined by the "Call." Still, the referendums won with a 59 percent vote, even though Ronald Reagan carried thirty of thirty-three towns in the districts.[44] Within a month of the November election, peace and disarmament groups around the country had heard of both the "Call" and the Massachusetts referendum results and had started to organize similar campaigns. In March of 1981, as McCrea and Markle report, the First National Strategy Conference of the Nuclear Weapons Freeze Campaign met in Washington, D.C. It was attended by 300 representatives of various activist groups from thirty-three states.[45] From there the issue took off with dizzying speed, headed for the major referendum votes in the general election of 1982.

That the freeze movement could accelerate so quickly from so modest a beginning makes it obvious that this was a national political issue waiting to be born. By 1981 and 1982, so many national interest groups, religious organizations and denominations, political action committees, citizen groups, and just plain citizens had signed on to the effort that it was a blockbuster political happening. The freeze was only very briefly the property of liberal peace groups. By 1982 it had a mass base of support, had attracted the attention of politicians at every level, and was widely followed by the media.

The freeze movement was clearly not the result of disagreement among government factions, but of a deep antipathy toward nuclear weapons in the public at large, joined with a novel idea supplied by a new set of political elite. It was grafted onto an organizational infrastructure— already in place in 1980—that was somewhat subterranean in that it did not revolve around either political parties or interest groups. And the freeze movement relied heavily on the media to educate voters, to get them to participate at least by voting, and to make the issue persist after the referendums were over. The media cooperated to a degree sufficient to meet the first two of these goals; the third was never accomplished.

The media played a dramatic role in both the rapid ascent of the freeze as an issue and in its precipitous plummet from the public agenda. The freeze as a referendum movement differed from the Vietnam War ballots in several ways, not the least of which was the nature of its media coverage and its intended target group. The role of television in the Vietnam War has been well documented, but the media focused on the event itself, not on the ballots surrounding it. That is, the *substance* of the issue—the war and its effects—provided the story; the *procedures* of decisionmaking concerning the war, including the referendum votes, were largely ignored by the press.

The opposite was true for the freeze issue. As noted, U.S. ambivalence concerning nuclear weapons was nothing new. What was novel was this new mechanism for expressing nuclear fears. The process—the freeze movement and referendums—was the story. What this meant for media coverage was that it would last only as long as the process itself persisted, that is, until the referendums were over in 1982. Arguably, the real impact of the freeze was not felt until 1984, when national and state freeze political action committees numbered thirty-four in all, raised and spent $3.4 million in 244 House and twenty Senate races, and directed the work of 25,000 volunteers. However, as Christopher Paine notes, by that time the media had moved on. According to Paine,

> In the news media the set of serious interlocking arms control proposals known as "the freeze" was treated like the political equivalent of the hula hoop: the sudden feast of coverage was matched only by the instant famine when the media-pack moved on, leaving behind the partially digested remains of an issue and a movement struggling to recover from a drastically "oversold" condition. . . . The freeze movement, for example reached its peak of organization, expenditure, and political influence during the 1984 election, long after the media had lost interest in it.[46]

That the press is a fickle lover is not a revelation in U.S. politics. What is significant about the freeze affair, however, is that media attention made the referendums a great success as events, if not as policy. In a sense, the eventual freeze legislation approved by the U.S. House of Representatives was not the significant legacy of the movement, although the success of the freeze referendums helped persuade representatives to vote for the congressional measure.[47] More important was the freeze effort's achievement, with the media's help, of establishing the use of international-issue referendums.

This ascendancy of process over substance as one legacy of the freeze should not be taken cynically as evidence of the meaninglessness of voting in referendums. That so many middle-class Americans were swept along in the freeze movement, and that they asserted their presence in the referendums, was the reason that the media—and ultimately Congress and the president—paid attention to the issue. Unlike the Vietnam anti-war referendums, the freeze was a white-collar phenomenon, "made up of family people, business and professional people, the clergy, educators, and scientists," occupying "community centers, town halls, church basements, and living rooms all over the country."[48] This demographic profile is the one the media and the politicians hope to see when looking for consumers and voters.

It is possible, of course, that the involvement of such a wide portion of the U.S. middle class in support of the freeze had to do with the fact that the initiative petitions only supported *pursuing* a policy of mutual freeze. The wording of the petitions did not stipulate that a freeze be immediately effected. In other words, the consequence of the success of the referendums would only be continued "talking" about the freezing of nuclear weapons—first in Congress, then in conjunction with the Soviet Union—not the actual implementation of a freeze. Some rational choice theorists make much of this distinction between "expressive" and "consequentialist" voting, arguing that when, and in this case because, "votes are words and not deeds," the appeal of the freeze was wide because its approval would cost the middle- and upper-class voters little in terms of security or wealth.[49] Thus, the rational choice argument concludes, the freeze success does not indicate a willingness on the part of voters actually to make policy in this participatory democratic way, but only to encourage talking about policy.

We will take up this criticism again in the last chapter, since it applies broadly to many international-issue referendums in Europe as well as potentially in the United States. But it is important here to understand how much the rational choice position misconstrues the meaning and substance of democracy. Talking is an (and perhaps the) essential feature of democratic politics. Thus continued talking is not an insignificant consequence of any decision, regardless of whether it is made by referendum or legislative action. Furthermore, referendums institutionalize political talking—they make political discussions more than mere grumbling or cocktail party small talk. They make political discourse part of the substance of political decisionmaking. That the freeze referendums succeeded for a time in stimulating discussion of nuclear weaponry among a large portion of the U.S. public was, then, no small accomplishment.

The success of the freeze should therefore not be measured only by its impact on the nuclear arms race. That race has slowed because of a complex set of circumstances, only one of which is the effect of public opinion as expressed through the freeze campaign. The singular effect of the freeze campaign was to introduce U.S. voters to direct involvement in foreign policymaking. In so doing, the movement's enduring impact should be assessed according to the likelihood of this decision process being used again.

FOREIGN POLICY REFERENDUMS IN THE UNITED STATES

The Vietnam and freeze referendums succeeded in a variety of ways. Both were supported by a large number of voters, in most cases a clear majority of those casting ballots. Both overcame initial derogation by elected leaders as "radical" or "unrealistic" idealizations of political possibility. Both anticipated and contributed to eventual policy outcomes in the "real" world of politics. It should not be forgotten that these referendums were instances of mass political *leadership*—what they put to the decision of the voters became the policy of the leaders thereafter. As political moments in the United States, they were democratic inversions: followers leading leaders, the many guiding the elite.

Yet, both movements also partially failed in that they achieved only short-term, largely symbolic victories that fell short of their proclaimed goals. Furthermore, and more significantly, they did not extensively change the manner in which foreign policy is made in the United States. A referendum is a process that when employed should alter the substance of democracy. As we argued in Chapter 1, participation is not just a method, but the point, of democracy. Thus, symbolic victories alone are not enough. To succeed in making politics more democratic, referendums must spawn more referendums—participation must make further participation both more appealing and more effective. The Vietnam and freeze referendums remain the only two widespread U.S. experiments in popular policymaking (even advising) for international politics.

This failure of foreign policy referendums to reproduce themselves in the United States must lie at least partly with their "normalization" as political devices. By means of several controversial decisions, the Supreme Court has rendered referendums both more possible and less meaningful as methods of decisionmaking. The decisions in the *Bellotti* and *Meyer* cases changed the source of money and the nature of elitism in referendum politics but did not affect their amounts. Already in state and local referendums, the effects of these decisions are being felt, as corporations and referendum specialists take the field. Recent elections in California offered ballots that carried up to fifty initiative and referendum propositions on them and required the distribution of information booklets of hundreds of pages to explain the issues to voters. Though there is evidence that voters were not overwhelmed and, in fact, showed considerable sophistication in their decisions, the future of referendums as methods of participatory decisionmaking for international affairs seems perhaps even more controversial and cloudier now than immediately following the freeze successes.[50]

That conclusion is ironic given the present nature of international affairs, where democracy's praises are being sung in more places than ever around the globe and where, as we have seen in the preceding chapters, referendums are increasingly being used in countries with less (or at least more recent) claim to the title of "democracy" than the United States. It is with a discussion of these final ironies that we close our exploration of the place of referendums in the relations between "democratic" states.

NOTES

1. There have been other, smaller-scale instances where citizens have voted on international-issue referendums. In 1989, for example, Maine voters were given

the opportunity to protest the U.S. Navy training launches of cruise missiles in their state. Also in the late 1980s, several communities, including Cambridge, Massachusetts, Chicago, and San Francisco, voted in referendums to declare themselves "nuclear-free zones."

2. 4 Del. (4 Harr.) 479 (1847).

3. See Pam Solo, *From Protest to Policy* (Cambridge, Mass.: Ballinger, 1988), p. 94; Frances B. McCrea and Gerald E. Markle, *Minutes to Midnight* (Newbury Park, Calif.: Sage, 1989), chapter 5; David S. Meyer, *A Winter of Discontent: The Nuclear Freeze and American Politics* (Westport, Conn.: Praeger, 1990).

4. Edmund Burke, *Collected Works* 89 (7th ed., 1881), p. 96.

5. 92 U.S. 130 (1875).

6. 223 U.S. 118 (1912).

7. 223 U.S. 151, 164 (1912); these cases are also discussed in Harlan Hahn and Sheldon Kamieniecki, *Referendum Voting* (New York: Greenwood Press, 1987), chapter 1.

8. 387 U.S. 369 (1967).

9. 393 U.S. 385 (1969).

10. 402 U.S. 136, 141 (1971).

11. *Crawford v. Board of Education*, 102 U.S. 3211 (1982); *Washington v. Seattle*, 102 U.S. 3187 (1982).

12. 426 U.S. 668 (1976).

13. *City of Eastlake v. Forest City Enterprises, Inc.*, 426 U.S. 668 (1976), p. 672.

14. *City of Eastlake*, p. 675.

15. *Eastlake*, p. 677, emphasis added.

16. 435 U.S. 765 (1978).

17. *Bellotti*, p. 768.

18. *Bellotti*, p. 768. This general line of thinking was not new. The Court has sometimes found corporations to be constitutionally protected, as in *Grosjean v. American Press Co.*, 297 U.S. 233, 244 (1936).

19. *Bellotti*, p. 791.

20. The Court had upheld these provisions for electoral campaigns in *Buckley v. Valeo*, 424 U.S. 1, 17 (1976).

21. *Bellotti*, p. 790.

22. *Bellotti*, p. 790.

23. See David B. Magleby, *Direct Legislation* (Baltimore: Johns Hopkins University Press, 1984).

24. The impact of these new elites and their practices on referendum politics has yet to be fully measured. In *Meyer v. Grant*, 108 U.S. 1886 (1988), the Supreme Court held that a Colorado law prohibiting the use of professional signature gatherers was unconstitutional, on the grounds that it was an unacceptable limitation on political speech. Some have argued that the Court's decision effectively altered the nature of referendums, rendering them ineffective as alternatives to elitist, money-dominated politics as usual. See Daniel Hays Lowenstein and Robert M. Stern, "The First Amendment and Paid Initiative Petition Circulators: A Dissenting View and a Proposal," paper presented at the American Political Science Association convention, August 1989. See also, Larry L. Berg and C. B. Holman, "The Initiative Process and Its Declining Agenda-setting Value," *Law and Policy* 11 (October 1989), pp. 451–469.

25. Richard Dean Burns and W. Addams Dixon, "Foreign Policy and the 'Democratic Myth': The Debate on the Ludlow Amendment," *Mid-America* 47 (October 1965), pp. 288-306.

26. Harlan Hahn, "Correlates of Public Sentiments About War: Local Referenda on the Vietnam Issue," *American Political Science Review* 64/4 (December 1970), pp. 1189–1190.

27. Hahn, "Correlates," p. 1190.

28. Benjamin I. Page and Richard A. Brody, "Policy Voting and the Electoral Process: The Vietnam War Issue," *American Political Science Review* 66/3 (September 1972), p. 985.

29. Hahn, "Correlates," p. 1190. Hahn, in Table 1, p. 1191, shows correlation coefficients ranging from .83 in Dearborn to .57 in Madison between low socioeconomic characteristics and the vote against U.S. participation in the war between 1966 and 1968. Only in Cambridge is the correlation reversed, showing decreasing support for the war as SES increased.

30. Harlan Hahn and Albert Sugarman, "A Referendum on Vietnam," *War/Peace Report* (May 1967), p. 15.

31. James Davis, Jr., and Kenneth M. Dolbeare, "Selective Service and Military Manpower: Induction and Deferment Policies in the 1960s," in *Political Science and Public Policy,* edited by Austin Ranney (Chicago: Markham, 1968), pp. 83–121. Also see, "Negroes and Military Service—Latest Facts," *U.S. News and World Report,* August 15, 1966, pp. 60–63.

32. Hahn and Sugarman, "A Referendum on Vietnam"; Hahn, "Correlates," p. 1190 and passim.

33. Hahn, "Correlates," p. 1187.

34. James Clotfelter, "Disarmament Movements in the United States," *Journal of Peace Research* 23/2 (1986), pp. 97–102.

35. Most analyses hold that constituency opinion, and therefore presumably the referendums, did not significantly influence later action in the executive and Congress. Member ideology, for example, was the key variable in congressional voting on freeze, according to James McCormick, "Congressional Voting on the Nuclear Freeze Resolutions," *American Politics Quarterly* 13 (1985), pp. 122–134. A recent, contrary view that argues that "constituency preferences exercised considerable influence on the [congressional] disposition on the freeze issue" is L. Marvin Overby, "Assessing Constituency Influence: Congressional Voting on the Nuclear Freeze, 1982–1983," *Legislative Studies Quarterly* 16/2 (May 1991), p. 297.

36. There is a growing literature placing the freeze movement in the context of social and political movements in U.S. history. See, for example, Clotfelter, "Disarmament"; McCrea and Markle, *Minutes to Midnight*; Seymour Feshbach and Michael J. White, "Individual Differences in Attitudes Towards Nuclear Arms Policies: Some Psychological and Social Policy Considerations," *Journal of Peace Research* 23/2 (June 1986), pp. 129–141; Kim Salomon, "The Peace Movement— An Anti-Establishment Movement," *Journal of Peace Research* 23/2 (June 1986), pp. 115–128; Ulrike C. Wasmuht, "A Sociological Survey of American Peace Movements," *Alternatives* 9/4 (Spring 1984), pp. 581–591.

37. The states (and the percentage of voters favoring the freeze) were Arizona (41%), California (52%), Massachusetts (74%), Michigan (57%), Montana (57%), New Jersey (66%), North Dakota (58%), Oregon (62%), Rhode Island

(59%), and Wisconsin (75%).

38. McCrea and Markle, *Minutes to Midnight*, pp. 101, 113 (note 8).

39. Everett Carll Ladd, "The Freeze Framework," *Public Opinion* 5/4 (August-September 1982), 20–41.

40. Ladd, "Freeze Framework," p. 41.

41. In addition to McCrea and Markle, *Minutes to Midnight*, see J. Bentley, *The Nuclear Freeze Movement* (New York: Franklin Watts, 1984); Keith B. Payne and Colin S. Gray, *The Nuclear Freeze Controversy* (Boston: University Press of America, 1984); Solo, *From Protest to Policy*.

42. Quoted in McCrea and Markle, *Minutes to Midnight*, p. 98.

43. Quoted in McCrea and Markle, *Minutes to Midnight*, p. 100.

44. McCrea and Markle, *Minutes to Midnight*, p. 102.

45. McCrea and Markle, *Minutes to Midnight*, p. 103.

46. Christopher E. Paine, "Lobbying for Arms Control," *Bulletin of the Atomic Scientists* 41/7 (August 1985), p. 126.

47. Overby, "Assessing Constituency Influence," pp. 108–109.

48. Douglas C. Waller, "The Impact of the Nuclear Freeze Movement on Congress," in *The Nuclear Weapons Freeze and Arms Control*, edited by Steven E. Miller (Cambridge, Mass.: Ballinger, 1984), p. 48.

49. Susan Feigenbaum, Lynn Karoly, and David Levy, "When Votes Are Words Not Deeds: Some Evidence from the Nuclear Freeze Referendum," *Public Choice* 58 (September 1988), pp 201–216.

50. Lowenstein and Stern, "The First Amendment."

8

Democratic World Politics: Performance and Prospects

There can be no doubt that the role of referendums in democratic politics is slowly but steadily increasing. What is less sure is whether this is a trend we should welcome. As we mentioned in Chapter 4, those who judge the expanding role of referendums in policymaking tend to adopt one of three theoretical positions. First, there is the pessimistic view advanced by foreign policy realists. They warn that direct democracy facilitates uninformed policymaking and therefore can be used by demagogues for self-interested ends. Everyday citizens, realists argue, are not adequately trained to handle intricate questions involving treaties, defense, international trade, and so forth. Such complex policy questions require careful deliberation, patience, wisdom, and experience. If, therefore, referendums continue to be widely used, foreign policy will soon become reflections of (at best) people's moral enthusiasm and (at worst) people's headless passions. Meanwhile, demagogues, skillfully manipulating popular passions, will become highly influential. The result will be wild swings in a country's foreign policy, corresponding to voters' superficial thinking and demagogues' mypoic and unscrupulous search for power.

The realist perspective is not the sole theoretical position from which to decry the use of referendums in deciding international issues. Some advocates of participatory democracy also have advanced a pessimistic view that rests on a dismal picture of contemporary industrial societies. These theorists argue that until more radically participatory traditions evolve in advanced industrial societies, referendums will produce more harm than good. Allegedly, such nondemocratic characteristics of advanced industrial societies as the anonymity and loneliness of urban life, the staggering inequalities of wealth and income within all modern economies, the impact of electronic mass media on people's thinking, and the repetitiveness and overspecialization within bureaucratized organizations render everyday citizens unready to cast ballots in a thoughtful and responsible way. Citizens are too impoverished, frustrated, fearful, and inexperienced to act in politics in a deliberate, reflective manner. Instead, the managers of corporations, directors of the electronic media, and a few other officials in the "command posts" of modern society regularly manipulate the referendum process to their own advantage by playing on voters' insecurities and resentments. Despite their purportedly democratic meaning, referendums are another weapon in the arsenal of the socially and politically powerful.

Not all observers, however, view referendums as either facades or dangers. Some analysts advocate referendums on grounds that they facilitate the participation of everyday people in politics, indirectly enrich policymaking by introducing concerns that government officials often overlook, and allow the people to assert their will against the preferences of the elites. According to these democratic defenders of referendums, they seldom have been tools of demagogues, the wealthy, or political elites. Citizens are not passive clay that can be easily shaped by elites. Citizens think for themselves and typically use referendums to draw elites' attention to overlooked grievances.

We thus have three very different assessments about the meaning of modern referendums. Each viewpoint describes referendums in a very different light. Each encourages us either to decry and oppose the current wave of direct democracy in international affairs or to applaud and support it. How well do these alternative pictures of referendums represent recent historical experience, as explored in the preceding chapters?

TIMING OF REFERENDUMS

If we look first at the timing of recent referendums, it appears that the pessimists are partly correct. In many countries, organized political parties and incumbent government leaders are the primary impetus behind international-issue referendums. Self-regarding calculations of how to maintain institutional power largely explain why referendums on EEC membership were called in Norway, Denmark, and France, and why referendums on Scottish and Welsh devolution and EEC membership were called in Great Britain. Referendums often are called by leading politicians who face sudden and immediate threats to their careers. For instance, elites' beleaguered positions partially help explain why referendums on Soviet unity and on the Baltic republics' independence occurred when they did.

Timing is not always controlled by government leaders, however. Sometimes referendums are constitutionally required, as the Irish EEC vote was. The U.S. nuclear freeze initiatives remind us both that elites' struggles may also be quite peripheral to the holding of a referendum, and that sometimes referendums are products of grassroots agitation over which government leaders have a miniscule role. The Andalusian autonomy referendum and the Danish EEC referendum further illustrate how electoral tides can entice elites to advocate referendums on momentarily popular issues, and in Quebec, a young, opposition party came to power in part because it had promised pro-independence voters that it would utilize a referendum on sovereignty-assocation. In the cases just cited, the idea of a policy referendum enjoyed a groundswell of popular support *before* state officials openly called for a popular vote.

In sum, although the argument that referendums are by-products of elite politicking contains much truth, it is only partly true. Referendums are not always proposed by politically beleaguered elites and then presented as a fait accompli to the citizenry. On several occasions, nonelites have been the primary impetus for an international-issue referendum.

VOTER EDUCATION

A key issue in deciding on the advisability of referendums is whether voters in international-issue referendums are as politically ignorant and as easily manipulated as some critics maintain. It is true that political leaders have often phrased proposals in slanted and ambiguous ways. Consider the cases of the NATO referendum in Spain, the sovereignty-association referendum in Quebec, or the Soviet-unity referendum. And sometimes, pluralities of voters do not fully understand the meaning and policy implications of a referendum proposal, as occurred during Quebec's sovereignty-association referendum. So, apparently voters in referendums are sometimes confused and poorly educated about issues, and in part this is because leaders often try to manipulate the question to their advantage.

Still, whenever voters are asked in surveys to explain why they cast their ballots as they did, many can cite highly pragmatic considerations—such as the possible economic implications of a government policy. This suggests that voting is not always a simple, mechanical response to political leaders' cues but in part a reflection of voters' deliberation. Furthermore, the periphery's triumph over the wishes of the international business community and the ruling class during Norway's EEC referendum, and the inability of the González government and Gorbachev's state apparatus to secure victories in controversial referendums over regional self-rule show that voters are hardly passive clay in the hands of determined elites. Finally, the documented swings in public opinion during the Swiss referendum over UN membership and the Quebec sovereignty-association referendum suggest that voters do not follow lockstep behind established business and political leaders.

Of course, there are several countries in which partisan cues have correlated strongly with voting behavior. Referendums in Canada, Spain, and Great Britain come to mind. But even in these cases, many voters did not follow their parties' recommendations. So again, the picture of an overwhelmingly passive electorate during referendums needs significant modification.

What about the impact of modern electronic media? It would be foolish to argue that the media plays no role in how people vote in foreign policy referendums. As Todd Gitlin has cogently pointed out, the more a given policy option is foreign to the day-to-day experience of a citizen, the more he or she depends on mass media to clarify and define issues.[1] Still, while voters have been influenced by media reports and endorsements, there have been dramatic cases of voters disregarding media messages. Recall both the inability of the González government, despite its control over television, to determine the outcome of the Andalusian vote and Gorbachev's failure to produce an overwhelming victory during the Soviet-unity vote. These cases demonstrate that the voters' political opinions are not simply created by the media. There is always some unpredictability and independence in voters' thinking, and even if only a minority of voters do not blindly follow media, party, and elite endorsements, this minority can be large enough to determine the outcome of a referendum, especially in a close vote.

VOTER PARTICIPATION

With very few exceptions, such as the autonomy referendum in Galicia, majorities of eligible citizens participate in referendums. Generally speaking, the turnout at a referendum is not as high as in proximate general elections. Nonetheless, over half of all eligible voters cast their ballots in almost every international-issue referendum.

Are citizens adequately educated and informed about the issues? As we have seen, evidence from recent surveys supports diverse answers. On the one hand, many voters (sometimes as many as a third of those queried in a given survey) have admitted not knowing the issues involved in a particular referendum or, when questioned, appear significantly misinformed about the substance of the referendum's proposals. On the other hand, over half of those polled have shown knowledge of some of the central issues posed by a referendum proposal ("central issues" as defined by the designers of the surveys). When questioned after casting their ballots, many voters have demonstrated familiarity with specific aspects of proposals—in particular, the possible economic consequences of a contemplated policy. So on the basis of opinion poll evidence, we can conclude that most voters in referendums are somewhat, even if not fully, informed.

An alternative method of determining voters' ability to think about international issues is to look at either voters' formal education or their relative socioeconomic status, which can be used as an indirect indicator of formal education. It could be argued that poorly educated voters have greater difficulty in analyzing and judging the issues involved in a foreign policy question than do well-educated citizens. The more formal education a voter has, the easier it will be for him or her to assimilate information and to weigh the relative benefits and costs of policy proposals in a prudent, deliberate manner. Plausible counterarguments come quickly to mind, however. For example, in the Vietnam War referendums, it was common for a less formally educated person, subject to a country's draft, to appreciate the costs of military undertakings more vividly and accurately than a highly educated person who was exempt from that draft.

In comparison to the citizenry at large, the people who vote in international-issue referendums are disproportionately from the economically and educationally advantaged strata in society. Conversely, the most economically dispossessed and least-educated strata tend to be statistically underrepresented among the citizens who vote in these referendums. Obviously, almost all voters lack career diplomats' detailed knowledge of foreign history, foreign languages, and foreign leaders. There is little evidence, however, that voters lack the modicum of formal education necessary to think about referendum issues, to listen to experts' opinions, and to balance a polity's competing goals and concerns. In short, available sociological evidence does not justify viewing most voters in referendums as completely uninformed or as educationally unable to become informed. In fact, it is one of the purposes of referendums to add to citizens' civic education.

DETERMINANTS OF VICTORY

Do demagogues, the wealthy, and the politically powerful typically win referendums, as critics of referendums often contend? As discussed in Chapter 6, on regional self-rule, it seems that government officials generally lose referendums unless they first build a broad coalition among major parties and interest groups. Stated differently, the passage of a government-sponsored referendum rests largely on the government first securing support from a broad range of influential political and social organizations. Unless political leaders take into account the viewpoints of powerful institutions, the passage of a given referendum proposal is doubtful.

Even the development of a grand coalition of major political and social forces, however, does not guarantee the passage of a referendum proposal. Norway's EEC vote illustrates that a broad coalition of major political and economic groups can be defeated by a broad alliance of politically and economically marginal groups in a country. The Swiss referendum on joining the UN followed a similar pattern. Thus, although intraelite cooperation can influence a referendum vote, the outcomes of referendum votes are not as easily controlled by government officials and the inordinately wealthy as some critics of referendums contend.

The role of demagoguery also is exaggerated by critics of referendums. Although Trudeau in Quebec, González in Spain, Pompidou in France, and Gorbachev in the Soviet Union sensationalized policy implications, vilified opponents, and utilized personal appeals during campaigns, they were not all successful in securing victories for their positions. Demagoguery, scapegoatism, and mudslinging clearly occur in referendums. But in light of the failures of demagogic tactics, such as González's failure in Andalusia and Gorbachev's questionable victory in the Soviet-unity referendum, claims that most voters are easily manipulated by demagogues are not fully supported by the available evidence.

THE SIGNIFICANCE OF REFERENDUMS

Realists often express fears that referendums signal the disappearance of diplomacy and expertise in foreign policymaking, while other critics warn that referendums will lead to policies that promote the interests of the economically and politically powerful. Defenders of referendums counter that as referendums become more commonplace, foreign policies will become more stable and judicious because everyday people are much more fearful of military adventures and rapid changes in the economic environment than are political leaders.

All these views seem to oversimplify the policy consequences of direct democracy. Consider the realists' dire warnings. While there has been an obvious increase in the use of international-issue referendums in recent decades, there is no evidence that diplomacy and expertise no longer play central roles in policymaking. The vast majority of foreign policy decisions remain exclusively in the hands of diplomatic experts and career politicians. Most of the time, referendums have been used to supplement, not to supplant, elites' policymaking.

Sometimes, referendums have been used to promote the interests of economically advantaged groups in a society, as in the case of the autonomy referendums for the already economically advantaged Basque and Catalan regions of Spain. But referendums also sometimes have been used successfully by economically disadvantaged groups, as was the case in Norway's EEC referendum and Andalusia's autonomy referendums. There are also many cases in which it is far from clear that the interests of the wealthy and the interests of the nonwealthy are incompatible. In the Welsh and Scottish devolution referendums, for example, most big businesses and most beleaguered small businesses tended to oppose the proposals' passage. While it could be argued that the referendums' outcome benefited big businesses, it could equally be plausibly argued that smaller economic interests were victorious.

As for referendums leading to caution and conservatism in foreign policy, as some defenders of referendums contend, the record once again seems mixed. There are some cases in which the results of referendums have supported the status quo: the Quebec sovereignty-association referendum and the British devolution referendums come to mind. But there are many cases in which referendums heralded a radically new direction in international policy—for instance, the referendums on regional self-rule in Spain, the independence referendums for the Baltic republics of the Soviet Union, the antiwar referendums in the United States, and the Danish EEC referendum. So, referendums seem neither first and foremost a conservative policymaking procedure nor an inherently radical one. Referendums can lead to both novel innovation and policy continuity.

ELUSIVE EVIDENCE AND CURRENT DEBATES

Both the heralds and Jeremiahs who celebrate and bemoan the growing use of referendums in foreign policy can cite historical evidence to support their position. The problem for both the advocates and critics is that the historical record is more complex than they care to acknowledge.

Stated somewhat differently, the experience of international-issue referendums has thus far been filled with paradox. Power struggles among elites have been the primary impetus behind the holding of some referendums, but certainly not all. Some voters in some referendums are poorly informed. Yet, in most referendums, many voters are informed and reflective. Elites' endorsements, party loyalties, and press coverage can influence the outcome of referendums but seldom can fully determine the outcome. Participation in referendums is hardly universal, and usually the more formally educated and more affluent members of a society participate. Nonetheless, participation in referendums is almost always over 50 percent of the electorate and sometimes much higher than that, and less affluent and less formally educated voters often participate in significant numbers.

International-issue referendums, in short, are contradictory phenomena. They seem neither unambiguously "good" nor purely "bad." They are far from the institutional panaceas that some observers desire and expect. But they are also far from the disasters that some critics perceive. Like legislative elections and town meetings, they are forms of popular self-rule that have both attractive and unattractive features. They therefore easily give rise to ambivalent feelings among careful observers.

Given the multiple characteristics of international-issue referendums, are their benefits worth their risks? To answer this question, we need to place it within the context of both a changing international political reality and an evolving democratic theory. As we have seen, referendums have played a large role in both.

DEMOCRACY AND THE REAL
PRESENT OF INTERNATIONAL POLITICS

As this book was being written, the world of international politics was being convulsed by change. Though it is difficult to characterize all the remarkable events in 1990 and 1991 that set Eastern Europe and the Soviet Union to boil, it is certainly true that all of them effervesced around the idea of democracy. We may not be experiencing Fukuyama's "end of history," but we are certainly living what for many has been a long-anticipated future. The extension of democratic institutions and the prospect of long-term peace among the superpowers are no longer merely idealistic visions of the past or future; they are the real present of international politics.

In the midst of this rush to democracy, it is important not to lose sight of the fact that events in Europe, China, South Africa, and elsewhere manifest the evolution of democracy, not the triumph of one particular brand of it. Whatever democratic forms mature in what is now the Commonwealth of Independent States will not be the same as those in the West. Democratic institutions can assume many shapes and a variety of procedures, and those best suited to one culture may not serve a society whose traditions are very different. In other words, there are now new laboratories of liberty, and all democratic societies can learn from whatever new experiments are carried out in democratizing nations.

As we have seen in Chapter 6, the Soviet Union employed a democratic device not universally utilized by Western democracies: the national referendum. Furthermore, its advisory independence referendums anticipated a consequence of momentous international import. They signaled the dissolution of the Soviet Union and also, therefore, the beginning of a new international world order.

Thus, both democracy and international politics will experience defining moments in the immediate future, and their redefinitions will be the result of what seemed only a few years ago to be an unlikely symbiosis. As we have seen, in many parts of the world referendums have appeared as a preferred mechanism of the new order, and not only as progenitors of domestic policy, but also as agents of change in foreign affairs as well. As such, they challenge both the meaning of international politics and of democratic practice. These are two developments worth probing as we close our exploration of the place of direct democracy in the relations between states.

International Politics in a New Democratic Order

Events in the Soviet Union and Eastern Europe challenged the realist account of international politics. As we have characterized realism, it makes two fundamental claims. The first is that international and domestic politics are two separate realms defined by two sets of principles in no necessary relation to each other. Thus, the foreign policy of a democratic country and a totalitarian one might not be widely dissimilar, though their domestic policies might well be. Second, whereas domestic politics is the realm of normative principles and deeply held values, both of which might vary greatly across different cultures, the domain of international politics is of power, interest, and necessity, defined similarly by all players on the international scene.

Even if it were not clear before, the failed Soviet coup of August 1991 left little doubt that democracy denies the first tenet of realist politics. Largely motivated by a drive to keep the republics in line, the coup attempt and its aftermath demonstrated that the success of democratic values can merge domestic and international politics into a successful devolution movement. Furthermore, pressure in the United States to recognize the newly independent republics came from citizens with relatives or ethnic histories in the Soviet states. President George Bush acquiesced. In two short weeks, several new actors strode onto the international stage. They are the products of domestic dissent in the Soviet Union and are recognized internationally (including membership in the United Nations) at least in part because of the internal politics of nationalism and ethnicity.

This conflation of domestic and international politics also jeopardizes the second tenet of realist theory. The appeal of democracy as a political form hinges not on the promise of increased national power and international influence. Nor does democracy promise greater security for citizens. Rather, democracy offers us liberty and risk, opportunities to succeed and fail, the freedom to take control of our own lives, and the right of others to ignore us as they pursue their own plans. Democracy is about values and ideals, not power. If democracy as an idea is a major force in the current eruptions in international politics, then international politics is no longer exclusively the domain of power, interest, and necessity.

We should be uneasy as we draw this conclusion. International politics in a new democratic order may make us wistful for the days of realpolitik. Thousands of diplomats have had decades of experience with power politics on the international scene; few citizens have yet had the chance to make foreign policy democratically. Those that have done so have left a mixed record of achievement. In the previous chapters we have seen that referendums have not always been praiseworthy processes by which to make foreign policy. The French referendum concerning membership in the EEC produced a woefully low level of citizen interest, even though the voters may have shown insight in their refusal to participate in President Pompidou's political sideshow. More disconcerting was the peculiar parochialism that British voters brought to the referendums on Welsh and Scottish devolution. With issues of independence and a larger role in the world at stake, many voters were primarily swayed by arguments about taxes and the effect on prices at the local store.

These private interests are legitimate concerns to be sure, and they exhibit the mixing of domestic and international concerns so typical of a nonrealist understanding of international politics. They give new meaning to the old cliché that "all politics is local." But the allure of private interests raises the question of whether ordinary citizens have it within them to "get outside of themselves" sufficiently to consider the effect of their decisions on people living on the other side of the world. By definition, foreign policy affects people unfamiliar to us, whose habits we may not know and whose values we may not understand. If power and self-interest are no longer to be the currency of international politics in a democratic, postrealist world, how are voters to decide issues collectively?

It is possible, presumably, that referendums may not denature international politics at all—that citizens will become realists and adopt the credo of self-interest and power politics in their democratically arrived-at foreign policy decisions. If so, then referendums will not really alter the substance of international politics but only its procedures and the number of players in the policy process. This may be enough for believers in participatory democracy who remain wary of too much citizen involvment, but it would still be too much democracy for realists and too little for strong democrats.

Yet, events of the last two years dispute this most ironic of neorealist interpretations of current foreign policy. The world of international politics *is* different today—the Berlin Wall has been demolished and Lenin's statue toppled. Positive liberty has an undeniable cachet in the East as well as the West, though both cultures are getting acquainted with it again as a real political value. These events have changed international politics by introducing the values of and yearnings for real democracy into the decision process. That citizens throughout the world are embracing new decision mechanisms (like referendums) now open to them should not surprise us. Rather, we should recognize that within the new environment of international politics, democratic practice is also amenable to redefinition.

Democratic Practice in a New International Order

The dramatic stirrings of democracy throughout the world are witness to the appeal of positive liberty as a preeminent political goal. Indeed, in countries like the newly independent republics once within the Soviet Union, the achievement of autonomy is likely to mean somewhat less negative liberty in the form of "freedom from" such things as poverty and instability. The use of referendums in these independence movements, as well as in other countries discussed in previous chapters, illuminates the intrinsic connection between this particular democratic practice and the goal of positive liberty. Demands for that liberty by definition mean that individuals must have a voice in decisions that affect their lives, and those decisions are increasingly international in scope. Thus, the evolution of democracy is in the direction of increased opportunity for all citizens to participate in its practice.

As we have seen, not all observers cheer this evolution. Realists especially fear that international politics decisions will be made cavalierly, by citizens without experience or dispassionate knowledge and motivated by emotion or sentimental moralism. Some strong democrats also fear such developments. They worry that without a wider environment of constant political participation, referendum decisions will reflect potentially harmful, xenophobic responses from citizens insufficiently accustomed to being taken seriously in political decisions. These are legitimate fears that we have taken seriously throughout this chapter and this book. In these final few pages we need to explore how democratic practice must also evolve in order to assuage those fears.

The realists, of course, must begin by acknowledging a new political reality. The political map of the world has changed, certainly, but so has the method of these changes. Not only in Germany and the Soviet Union, but also in the United States' antiwar and nuclear freeze movements, real changes were brought by those untrained in the dispassionate, bloodless sophistication of diplomacy. Also, in at least some of the referendum campaigns we have studied in this book, raucous street-level politics led to significant policy changes.

Furthermore, strong democrats such as Peter Bachrach, wary of too fast a move toward the use of referendums in international politics, should consider that here is a widening of positive liberty especially suited to educating citizens about how to look beyond their parochial, potentially xenophobic attitudes. Bachrach may indeed be correct in his belief that without more experience in decisionmaking, citizens are simply too self-absorbed to render mature, morally responsible decisions. But the education must start somewhere, and where better than in international-issue referendums, where the question is precisely that of how we as citizens should interact with those of other cultures. In light of the events of the past two years, most citizens in the West now realize that people in the East believe in the same political goals as they, have the same democratic yearnings, and experience the same emotional responses to liberty. For the first time in a long time, citizens have seen through the official rhetoric about "evil empires" and "capitalist exploiters" to the common humanity they share with the common citizens of other countries. This is a knowledge born of emotion, it is true, but of a peculiarly democratic sort. There is no better time to allow citizens a voice in the international politics decisions that will affect the lives of their fellow lovers of democracy in other countries.

Still, some voice lessons are clearly indicated by our study of referendums in the previous chapters. The practice of referendums needs refinements. Though these will be provided partly by experience and further research, we can make some suggestions about how the "talk" of democracy might proceed through the referendum device.

First of all, the education of citizens is both a requirement and a goal of well-designed referendums. The same is true for democratic politics as a whole, of course, but referendums pose some special problems. Information about referendum issues needs wide dissemination in as balanced a form as possible. As we have seen, different countries approach this need in various ways, but some do seem more successful than others. The Danish public financing of referendum efforts on both sides of the issue succeeds well in informing the public of its choices and is less susceptible to cynical manipulation of public attitudes evident in referendum campaigns in other countries such as France and the United States. Furthermore, the Danish approach treats referendums more like elections, where public funding is provided for candidates for office, thereby bestowing the same level of importance on both types of ballot.

The Danes also provide a model for the role of money in referendum campaigns. As we saw in our study of the United States' limited experience with large-scale referendum movements, when the Supreme Court removed all spending limits on private contributions to referendum campaigns, the referendums themselves became less meaningful as instruments of democratic decisionmaking. Inexperience may provide an excuse for such a lapse, but the Court's decision needs overturning. Spending limits in U.S. electoral campaigns verify the need for restricting the influence of private money in politics. That need is at least as great in referendum politics.

Finally, the education of citizens in referendums comes not only from campaign literature, but also from discourse in a wider sense. If democracy presumes a public sphere in which discussion takes place, referendums as a democratic device need to find ways to further that discourse. Certainly, political leaders and the media have roles here. Referendum movements are sometimes, as in the case of the freeze, instances of political leadership being provided by citizens rather than by elected officials or by other opinion leaders such as the press. But such cases might indicate the breakdown of electoral leadership rather than its essential nature, and our exploration of referendums in Norway, Ireland, and elsewhere show how political leaders can further the democratic discourse of referendums.

The mechanics of referendums can also be designed to maximize discussion and reflection about the issues at stake. Holding referendums at regular intervals and on preassigned days might help institutionalize them as an essential feature of national politics. Also, holding two votes on any major referendum issue, with an interval of some weeks or even months between them, offers a possibility for discussion framed by preliminary and final moments of decision. This "wave" method of referendums has rarely been employed, though the two Vietnam referendums in Dearborn, Michigan, essentially followed this pattern, and, as we saw in Chapter 7, the second vote was accompanied by a dramatically higher voter approval rate. Other refinements aimed at enhancing public consideration and attention are also possible. For instance, a sophistication on the "wave" would be to submit referendum questions to the public with a set of alternative answers from which to choose. After a sufficient period of time for public discussion and deliberation by citizens, a subsequent ballot would then choose between the top two or three vote-getters on the first ballot.

We should remember that as democratic institutions take root in an ever-growing number of countries, their growth and mature form will be dictated as much by the singular cultures of each country as by any general blueprint about the mechanics of democracy. Thus, our modest proposals are only speculative and are, no doubt, at least partly influenced by the democratic culture of the United States. We have taken a comparative approach in this book expressly to avoid stipulating any one model of democracy or of referendum politics as the best or only legitimate one. Therefore, we conclude it now in democratic fashion by welcoming all proposals for referendum design, no matter their source. Because this is clearly a time for new experiments in democracy in many parts of the world, we await the products of a rejuvenated democratic imagination.

Looking backward a few decades from now, we may decide that these experiments took place during democracy's "Machiavellian Moment." This is the creative time when, J. G. A. Pocock tells us, the world momentarily shrugs off the authority of random fortune over its affairs and submits to the governorship of humans and their institutional creations.[2] If this is one of those rare moments, it is not one controlled by any singular "Prince," but by the collective will of people united in their demands for democracy. That will and those demands cover all aspects of democratic life, domestic and international, and they will be heard directly.

NOTES

1. Todd Gitlin, *The Whole World is Watching: Mass Media and the Making and Unmaking of the New Left* (Berkeley: University of California Press, 1980), pp. 1–18.

2. J. G. A. Pocock, *The Machiavellian Moment* (Princeton: Princeton University Press, 1975).

Bibliography

Aitkin, Don (1978). "Australia." In David Butler and Austin Ranney (eds.), *Referendums: A Comparative Study of Practice and Theory*, Washington D.C.: American Enterprise Institute.

Almond, Gabriel A., and Sidney Verba (1965). *The Civic Culture: Political Attitudes and Democracy in Five Nations*, Boston: Little, Brown.

Arias, Inocencio Félix (1988). "Spanish Media and the Two NATO Campaigns." In Federico G. Gil and Joseph S. Tulchin (eds.), *Spain's Entry into NATO: Conflicting Political and Strategic Perspectives*, Boulder: Lynne Rienner Publishers.

Aubert, Jean-François (1978). "Switzerland." In David Butler and Austin Ranney (eds.), *Referendums: A Comparative Study of Practice and Theory*, Washington D.C.: American Enterprise Institute.

Austen, John, David Butler, and Austin Ranney (1987). "Referendums, 1978-1986," *Electoral Studies*, 6 (August 1987): 139–147.

Balsom, Denis, and Ian McAllister (1979). "The Scottish and Welsh Devolution Referenda of 1979: Constitutional Change and Popular Choice," *Parliamentary Affairs* 32 (Autumn 1979): 394–409.

Barber, Benjamin R. (1984). *Strong Democracy: Participatory Politics in a New Age*, Berkeley: University of California Press.

Bentley, J. (1984). *The Nuclear Freeze Movement*, New York: Franklin Watts.

Berg, Larry L., and C. B. Holman (1989). "The Initiative Process and Its Declining Agenda-setting Value," *Law and Policy* 11 (October 1989): 451–469.

Berlin, Isaiah (1969). *Four Essays on Liberty*, London: Oxford University Press.

Berrington, Hugh (1985). "Centre-Periphery Conflict and British Politics." In Yves Meny and Vincent Wright (eds.), *Centre-Periphery Relations in Western Europe*, London: George Allen & Unwin.

Bjorkland, Tor (1982). "The Demand for Referendum: When Does It Arise and When Does It Succeed," *Scandinavian Political Studies*, 5/3 (1982): 237–260.

Bochel, John, ed. (1981). *The Referendum Experience: Scotland 1979*, Aberdeen: Aberdeen University Press.

Bogdanor, Vernon (1980). "The Forty Percent Rule," *Parliamentary Affairs*, 33 (Summer 1980): 249–263.

Bogdanor, Vernon (1981). *The People and the Party System: The Referendum and Electoral Reform in British Politics*, Cambridge: Cambridge University Press.

Bogdanor, Vernon (1981). "Referendums and Separatism II." In Austin Ranney (ed.), *The Referendum Device*, Washington D.C.: American Enterprise Institute.

Bolt, Ernest C., Jr. (1977). *Ballots Before Bullets: The War Referendum Approach to Peace in America 1914–1941*, Charlottesville: University of Virginia Press.

Borre, Ole (1986). "The Danish Referendum on the EC Common Act," *Electoral*

Studies 5 (August 1986): 189–193.

Boyer, J. Patrick (1982). *Lawmaking by the People: Referendums and Plebiscites in Canada*, Stoneham, Mass.: Butterworth.

Brand, Jack (1986). "Political Parties and the Referendum on National Sovereignty: The 1979 Scottish Referendum on Devolution," *Canadian Review of Studies in Nationalism* 13 (Spring 1986): 31–47.

Brand, Jack (1988). "Andalusia: Nationalism as the Strategy for Autonomy," *Canadian Review of Studies in Nationalism* 15/1–2 (1988): 1–10.

Bristow, Stephen L. (1976). "Partisanship, Participation and Legitimacy in Britain's EEC Referendum," *Journal of Common Market Studies* 14 (June 1976): 297–310.

Budge, Ian, and Dennis J. Farlie (1983). *Explaining and Predicting Elections: Issue Effects and Party Strategies in Twenty-Three Democracies*, London: George Allen & Unwin.

Bulpitt, Jim (1983). *Territory and Power in the United Kingdom: An Interpretation*, Manchester: Manchester University Press.

Burg, Steven L. (1990). "European Republics of the Soviet Union," *Current History* 89 (October 1990): 321–324, 342.

Burns, Richard Dean, and W. Addams Dixon (1965). "Foreign Policy and the 'Democratic Myth': The Debate on the Ludlow Amendment," *Mid-America* 47 (October 1965): 288–306.

Butler, David (1981). "The World Experience." In Austin Ranney (ed.), *The Referendum Device*, Washington D.C.: American Enterprise Institute.

Butler, David, and Austin Ranney (1978). *Referendums: A Comparative Study of Practice and Theory*, Washington D.C.: American Enterprise Institute.

Butler, David, and Uwe Kitzinger (1976). *The 1975 Referendum*, New York: St. Martin's Press.

Caciagli, Mario (1986). *Elecciones y Partidos en la Transición Española*, Madrid: Centro de Investigaciones Sociologicas.

Canadian Unity Information Office (1978). *Understanding Referenda: Six Histories: Australia, Newfoundland, Ireland, Norway, Denmark, United Kingdom*, Ottawa: Minister of Supply and Services.

Chazen, Naomi (1979). "African Voters at the Polls," *Journal of Commonwealth and Comparative Studies* 17 (July 1979): 136–158.

Chunkath, A. (1977). "Referendum: Its Genesis, Growth and Raison d'Etre," *Journal of Constitutional and Parliamentary Studies* 11 (December 1979): 86–100.

Clark, Robert P. (1984). *The Basque Insurgents: ETA, 1952–1980*, Madison: University of Wisconsin Press.

Clark, Robert P. (1987). "The Question of Regional Autonomy in Spain's Democratic Transition." In Robert P. Clark and Michael H. Haltzel (eds.), *Spain in the 1980s: The Democratic Transition and a New International Role*, Cambridge, Mass.: Ballinger.

Clotfelter, James (1986). "Disarmament Movements in the United States," *Journal of Peace Research* 23 (June 1986): 97–102.

Codding, George A., Jr. (1979). "The Swiss Political System and the Management of Diversity." In Howard R. Penniman (ed.), *Switzerland at the Polls: The National Elections of 1979*, Washington D.C.: American Enterprise Institute.

Cohen, Carl (1971). *Democracy*, New York: Free Press.

Coleman, William D. (1984). *The Independence Movement in Quebec, 1945–1980*, Toronto: The University of Toronto Press.

Cuercora Atienza, Javier, and Alberto Pérez Calvo (1979). "En Torno al Referéndum del Estatuto de Autonomía del País Vasco," *Revista de Estudios Políticos* 12 (November-December 1979): 179–196.

Cronin, Thomas E. (1989). *Direct Democracy: The Politics of Initiative, Referendum, and Recall,* Cambridge: Harvard University Press.

Cutler, Susan L., H. Briavel Holcomb, Dianne Shaten, Fred M. Helley, and G. Thomas Murauskas (1988). "From Grass Roots to Partisan Politics: Nuclear Freeze Referenda in New Jersey and North Dakota," *Political Geography Quarterly* 6 (October 1988): 287–300.

Daltrop, Anne (1982). *Politics and the European Community,* Harlow, U.K.: Longman.

Davis, James, Jr., and Kenneth M. Dolbeare (1968). "Selective Service and Military Manpower: Induction and Deferment Policies in the 1960s." In Austin Ranney (ed.), *Political Science and Public Policy,* Chicago: Markham.

Deploige, Simon (1898). *The Referendum in Switzerland,* London: Longman, Green.

Dion, Léon (1988). "The Mystery of Quebec," *Daedalus* 117 (Fall 1988): 283–318.

Donnelly, Harrison (1982). "'Freeze' Success Highlights Ballot Measures," *Congressional Quarterly Weekly Report* 40 (November 6, 1982): 2809–2810.

Dougherty, James E., and Robert L. Pfalzgraff, Jr. (1990). *Contending Theories of International Relations,* 3d. ed., New York: Harper & Row.

Doyle, Michael (1986). "Liberalism and World Politics," *American Political Science Review* 80 (December 1986): 1151–1169.

Eisinger, Peter K., Dennis L. Dresang, Robert Booth Fowler, Joel B. Grossman, Burdett A. Loomis, and Richard M. Merelman (1978). *American Politics: The People and the Policy,* Boston: Little, Brown.

Elklit, Jørgen, and Nikolaj Petersen (1973). "Denmark: Denmark Enters the European Communities," *Scandinavian Political Studies: A Yearbook* 8/73 (1973): 198–213.

Eschet-Schwarz, André (1989). "The Role of Semi-Direct Democracy in Shaping Swiss Federalism: The Behavior of Cantons Regarding Revision of the Constitution, 1966–1981," *Publius* 19 (Winter 1989): 79–106.

Fairlie, Henry (1978). "The Unfiltered Voice: The Dangerous Revival of the Referendum," *New Republic* (June 24, 1978): 16–17.

Falk, Richard (1982). "The Anatomy of Nuclearism." In Robert J. Lifton and Richard Falk (eds.), *Indefensible Weapons,* New York: Basic.

Feigenbaum, Susan, Lynn Karoly, and David Levy (1988). "When Votes Are Words Not Deeds: Some Evidence from the Nuclear Freeze Referendum," *Public Choice* 58 (September 1988): 201–216.

Feshbach, Seymour, and Michael J. White (1986). "Individual Differences in Attitudes Towards Nuclear Arms Policies: Some Psychological and Social Policy Considerations," *Journal of Peace Research* 23 (June 1986): 129–141.

Fitzmaurice, John (1985). *Québec and Canada: Past, Present and Future,* New York: St. Martin's Press.

Foulkes, David, ed. (1983). *The Welsh Veto: The Wales Act 1978 and the Referendum,* Cardiff: University of Wales Press.

Fraser, Graham (1984). *PQ: René Lévésque and the Parti Québécois in Power,* Toronto: Macmillan of Canada.

Fukuyama, Francis (1989). "The End of History?" *National Interest,* No.16 (Summer 1989): 3–19.

Gallagher, Michael (1988). "The Single European Act Referendum," *Irish Political*

Studies 3/1 (1988): 77–82.

Gaventa, John (1980). *Power and Powerlessness: Quiescence and Rebellion in an Appalachian Valley*, Urbana: University of Illinois Press.

Gazey, Penelope J. (1971). "Direct Democracy—A Study of the American Referendum," *Parliamentary Affairs* 29 (Spring 1971): 123–139.

Gil, Federico G., and Joseph S. Tulchin, eds. (1988). *Spain's Entry into NATO: Conflicting Political and Strategic Perspectives*, Boulder: Lynne Rienner Publishers.

Gilbert, Alan (1992). "Must Global Politics Constrain Democracy? Realism, Regimes, and Democratic Internationalism," *Political Theory* 20 (February 1992) 8–37.

Gilpin, Robert (1981). *War and Change in World Politics*, New York: Cambridge University Press.

Gingras, François-Pierre and Neil Nevitte (1983). "Nationalism in Quebec: The Transition of Ideology and Political Support." In Allan Kornberg and Harold D. Clark (eds.), *Political Support in Canada: The Crisis Years*, Durham, N.C.: Duke University Press.

Gitlin, Todd (1980). *The Whole World Is Watching: Mass Media in the Making and Unmaking of the New Left*, Berkeley: University of California Press.

Glazier, Kenneth M. (1977). "Separatism and Quebec," *Current History*, 72 (April 1977): 154–158, 179.

Gold, Gerald (1984). "La revendication de nos droits: The Quebec Referendum and Francophone Minorities in Canada," *Ethnic and Racial Studies* 7 (January 1984): 106–128.

Gooch, Anthony (1986). "A Surrealistic Referendum: Spain and NATO," *Government and Opposition* 31 (Summer 1986): 300–316.

Goodhart, Philip (1976). *Full-Hearted Consent: The Story of the Referendum Campaign—and the Campaign for the Referendum*, London: Davis-Poynter.

Goodhart, Philip (1981). "Referendums and Separatism I." In Austin Ranney (ed.), *The Referendum Device*, Washington D.C.: American Enterprise Institute.

Green, Philip (1985). *Retrieving Democracy: In Search of Civic Equality*, Totowa, N.J.: Rowman & Allanheld.

Gunther, Richard, Giacomo Sani, and Goldie Shabad (1988). *Spain After Franco: The Making of a Competitive Party System*, Berkeley: University of California Press.

Gutmann, Amy (1987). *Democratic Education*, Princeton: Princeton University Press.

Hahn, Harlan (1970). "Correlates of Public Sentiments About War: Local Referenda on the Vietnam Issue," *American Political Science Review* 64 (December 1970): 1186–1199.

Hahn, Harlan, and Sheldon Kamieniecki (1987). *Referendum Voting: Social Status and Policy Preferences*, New York: Greenwood Press.

Hahn, Harlan, and Albert Sugarman (1967). "A Referendum on Vietnam," *War/Peace Report* (May 1967): 14–15.

Hansen, Peter, Melvin Small, and Karen Siune (1976). "The Structure of the Debate in the Danish EEC Campaign: A Study of an Opinion-Policy Relationship," *Journal of Common Market Studies* 15 (December 1976): 93–129.

Hastings, Elizabeth Hann, and Philip K. Hastings (1989). *Index to International Public Opinion, 1988–1989*, Westport, Conn.: Greenwood Press.

Held, David (1991). "Democracy, the Nation-State and the Global System,"

Economy and Society 20 (May 1991): 138–172.

Hellevik, Ottar, Nils Petter Gleditisch, and Kristen Ringdal (1975). "The Common Market Issue in Norway: A Conflict Between Center and Periphery," *Journal of Peace Research* 12 (Winter 1975): 35–53.

Hiskes, Anne L., and Richard P. Hiskes (1986). *Science, Technology, and Policy Decisions*, Boulder: Westview Press.

Holm, Hans-Henrik (1989). "A Democratic Revolt? Stability and Change in Danish Security Policy 1979–1987," *Cooperation and Conflict* 24 (December 1989): 179–197.

Holst, Johan Jorgen (1975). "Norway's EEC Referendum: Lessons and Implications," *World Today* 31 (March 1975): 114–120.

Horton, John E., and Wayne E. Thompson (1962). "Powerlessness and Political Negativism: A Study of Defeated Local Referendums," *American Journal of Sociology* 67 (March 1962): 482–493.

Huntington, Samuel P. (1989). "No Exit: The Errors of Endism," *National Interest* 17 (Fall 1989): 3–10.

Ingberman, Daniel E. (1985). "Running Against the Status Quo: Institutions for Direct Democracy Referenda and Allocations Over Time," *Public Choice* 46/1 (1985): 19–44.

James, Arnold J., and John E. Thomas (1981). *Wales at Westminster: A History of the Parliamentary Representation of Wales, 1800–1979*, Llandysul, U.K.: Gomer Press.

Johnson, Nevil (1981). "Types of Referendum." In Austin Ranney (ed.), *The Referendum Device*, Washington D.C.: American Enterprise Institute.

Jones, J. Barry, and Rick Wilford (1979). "The Welsh Veto: The Politics of the Devolution Campaign in Wales," Working Paper Number 39 of the Centre for the Study of Public Policy, University of Strathclyde.

Jones, J. Barry, and Rick Wilford (1982). "Further Considerations on the Referendum: The Evidence on the Welsh Vote on Devolution," *Political Studies* 30 (March 1982): 16–27.

Keith-Lucas, Bryan (1981). "Summing Up: Referendums for Britain?" In Austin Ranney (ed.), *The Referendum Device*, Washington D.C.: American Enterprise Institute.

Kellas, James G. (1989). "Prospects for a New Scottish Political System," *Parliamentary Affairs* 42 (October 1989): 519–532.

Kellas, James G. (1989). *The Scottish Political System*, 4th ed., Cambridge: Cambridge University Press.

Kerr, Henry H. (1979). "Swiss Electoral Politics." In Howard R. Penniman (ed.), *Switzerland at the Polls: The National Elections of 1979*, Washington D.C.: American Enterprise Institute.

King, Anthony (1977). *Britain Says Yes: The 1975 Referendum on the Common Market*, Washington D.C.: American Enterprise Institute.

King, Anthony (1981). "Referendums and the European Community." In Austin Ranney (ed.), *The Referendum Device*, Washington D.C.: American Enterprise Institute.

Kipnis, Kenneth, and Diana T. Meyers, eds. (1987). *Political Realism and International Morality*, Boulder: Westview Press.

Kirchheimer, Otto (1966). "The Transformation of the Western European Party Systems." In Joseph LaPalombara and Myron Weiner (eds.), *Political Parties and Political Development*, Princeton: Princeton University Press.

Ladd, Everett Carll (1982). "The Freeze Framework," *Public Opinion* 5 (August-

September 1982): 20–41.
Lasch, Christopher (1981). "Mass Culture Reconsidered," *Democracy* 1 (October 1981): 7–22.
Lee, Eugene C. (1981). "The American Experience, 1778–1978." In Austin Ranney (ed.), *The Referendum Device*, Washington D.C.: American Enterprise Institute.
Lee, Eugene C. (1988). "Can the British Vote Be Trusted?" *Public Administration* 66 (Summer 1988): 165–180.
Leigh, Michael (1975). "Linkage Politics: The French Referendum and the Paris Summit of 1972," *Journal of Common Market Studies* 14 (December 1975): 157–170.
Leishman, Rory (1988). "Quebec and the Constitution: Completing the Patriation Process." In R. D. Olling (ed.), *Perspectives on Canadian Federalism*, Scarborough, Ont.: Prentice-Hall Canada.
Leleu, Claude (1976). "The French Referendum of April 23, 1972," *European Journal of Political Research* 4 (March 1976): 25–46.
Lemieux, Vincent, and Jean Crête (1981). "Quebec." In Howard R. Penniman (ed.), *Canada at the Polls, 1979 and 1980: A Study of the General Elections*, Washington D.C.: American Enterprise Institute.
Llera Ramo, Francisco José (1981). "Caracterización Sociopolítica del Sistema de Partidos de la Communidad Autónoma Vasca y Navarra," *Revista de Estudios Políticos* 20 (March-April 1981).
Lowenstein, Daniel Hays, and Robert M. Stern (1989). "The First Amendment and Paid Initiative Petition Circulators: A Dissenting View and a Proposal," paper presented at the American Political Science Association convention, Atlanta, August 1989.
Luke, Paul, and David Johnson (1976). "Devolution by Referendum? A Look at the Welsh Situation," *Parliamentary Affairs* 29 (Summer 1976): 332–339.
MacCallum, Gerald C., Jr. (1967). "Negative and Positive Freedom," *Philosophical Review* 76 (July 1967): 312–334.
McCormick, James M. (1985). "Congressional Voting on the Nuclear Freeze Resolutions," *American Politics Quarterly* 13 (January 1985): 122–134.
McCrea, Frances B., and Gerald E. Markle (1989). *Minutes to Midnight*, Newbury Park, Calif.: Sage.
McGuigan, Patrick B. (1985). *The Politics of Direct Democracy in the 1980s: Case Studies in Popular Decision Making*, Washington D.C.: The Institute for Government and Politics, The Free Congress Research and Education Foundation.
Madison, James (1787). *Notes on the Debates in the Federal Convention of 1787*.
Magleby, David B. (1984). *Direct Legislation: Voting on Ballot Propositions in the United States*, Baltimore: Johns Hopkins University Press.
Manning, Bayless (1977). "The Congress, the Executive, and Intermestic Affairs," *Foreign Affairs* 55 (Spring 1977): 306–324.
Manning, Maurice (1978). "Ireland." In David Butler and Austin Ranney (eds.), *Referendums: A Comparative Study of Practice and Theory*, Washington D.C.: American Enterprise Institute.
Mansbridge, Jane J. (1980). *Beyond Adversary Democracy*, New York: Basic.
Mansbridge, Jane (1986). *Why We Lost the ERA*, Chicago: University of Chicago Press.
Marques, Alvaro, and Thomas B. Smith (1984). "Referendums in the Third World," *Electoral Studies* 4 (April 1984): 85–105.
Martorell, Joaquín (1988). "Spain, A Singular Ally." In Federico G. Gil and Joseph

S. Tulchin (eds.), *Spain's Entry into NATO: Conflicting Political and Strategic Perspectives*, Boulder: Lynne Rienner Publishers.

Meyer, David S. (1990). *A Winter of Discontent: The Nuclear Freeze and American Politics*, Westport, Conn.: Praeger.

Miller, Kenneth (1982). "Policy-Making by Referendum: The Danish Experience," *West European Politics* 5 (January 1982): 54–67.

Miller, William (1981). *The End of British Politics? Scot and English Political Behavior in the Seventies*, Oxford: Clarendon Press.

Moaz, Zeev, and Nasrin Abdulali (1989). "Regime Type and International Conflict, 1816–1976," *Journal of Conflict Resolution* 33 (March 1989): 3–35.

Morgan, Kenneth O. (1981). *Rebirth of a Nation: Wales 1880–1980*, Oxford: Oxford University Press.

Morgan, T. Clifton, and Sally Howard Campbell (1991). "Domestic Structure, Decisional Constraints, and War; So Why Kant Democracies Fight?" *Journal of Conflict Resolution* 35 (June 1991): 187–211.

Moriarty, Janet, and John T. Rourke (1978). "The Spanish Cortes: Democracy Re-established," *Contemporary Review* 232 (May 1978): 234–238.

Mowlan, Marjorie (1979). "Popular Access to the Decision-Making Process in Switzerland: The Role of Direct Democracy," *Government and Opposition* 14 (Spring 1979): 180–197.

Newton, Mike (1983). "The Peoples and Regions of Spain." In David S. Bell (ed.), *Democratic Politics in Spain: Spanish Politics After Franco,* New York: St. Martin's Press.

Nilson, Sten Sparre (1978). "Scandanavia." In David Butler and Austin Ranney (eds.), *Referendums: A Comparative Study of Practice and Theory*, Washington D.C.: American Enterprise Institute.

Nilson, Sten Sparre (1981). "Elections, Referendums, and Public Goals," *Scandinavian Political Studies* 4/1 (1981): 1–18.

Nilson, Sten Sparre, and Tor Bjorkland (1986). "'Ideal Types' of Referendum Behavior," *Scandinavian Political Studies* 9 (September 1986): 265–278.

Noam, Eli M. (1980). "The Efficiency of Direct Democracy," *Journal of Political Economy*, 88 (August 1980): 803–809.

Olcott, Martha Brill (1990). "The Lithuanian Crisis," *Foreign Affairs* 69 (Summer 1990): 30–46.

Ornstein, Michael D., and H. Michael Stevenson (1981). "Elite and Public Opinion Before the Quebec Referendum," *Canadian Journal of Political Science* 14 (December 1981): 745–774.

Overby, L. Marvin (1991). "Assessing Constituency Influence: Congressional Voting on the Nuclear Freeze, 1982–1983," *Legislative Studies Quarterly* 16 (May 1991): 297–315.

Page, Benjamin I., and Richard A. Brody (1972). "Policy Voting and the Electoral Process: The Vietnam War Issue," *American Political Science Review* 66 (September 1972): 979–995.

Paine, Christopher E. (1985). "Lobbying for Arms Control," *Bulletin of the Atomic Scientists* 41 (August 1985): 125–130.

Pammett, Jon H., Harold D. Clarke, Jane Jenson, and Lawrence LeDuc (1983). "Political Support and Voting Behavior in the Quebec Referendum." In Allan Kornberg and Harold D. Clarke (eds.), *Political Support in Canada: The Crisis Years*, Durham, N.C.: Duke University Press.

Parry, Bruce (1983). "Binding Referenda," *Social Policy* 14 (Summer 1983): 33–34.

Pateman, Carole (1970). *Participation and Democratic Theory*, Cambridge: Cambridge University Press.

Payne, Keith B., and Colin S. Gray (1984). *The Nuclear Freeze Controversy*, Boston: University Press of America.

Pelletier, Gérard (1988). "Quebec: Different But in Step with North America," *Daedalus* 117 (Fall 1988): 265–282.

Penniman, Howard R., ed. (1979). *Switzerland at the Polls: The National Elections of 1979*, Washington D.C.: American Enterprise Institute.

Penniman, Howard R., ed. (1981). *Canada at the Polls 1979 and 1980: A Study of the General Elections*, Washington D.C.: American Enterprise Institute.

Pérez Royo, Javier (1988). "Repercussion on the Democratic Process of Spain's Entry into NATO." In Federico G. Gil and Joseph S. Tulchin (eds.), *Spain's Entry into NATO: Conflicting Political and Strategic Perspectives*, Boulder: Lynne Rienner Publishers.

Pierce, Roy, Henry Valen, and Ola Listhaug (1983). "Referendum Voting Behavior: The Norwegian and British Referenda on Membership in the European Community," *American Journal of Political Science* 27 (February 1983): 43–63.

Pocock, J. G. A. (1975). *The Machiavellian Moment*, Princeton: Princeton University Press.

Porras Nadales, Antonio (1980). "El Referéndum de Iniciativa Autonómica del 28 de Febrero en Andalucia," *Revista de Estudios Políticos* 15 (May-June 1980): 175–194.

Prevost, Gary (1986). "Spain's NATO Choice," *World Today* 49 (August-September 1986): 129–132.

Proctor, J. H. (1982). "Lessons from the Scottish Referendum on Devolution," *Journal of Constitutional and Parliamentary Studies* 15 (January-June 1982): 1–20.

Ranney, Austin (1978). "United States of America." In David Butler and Austin Ranney (eds.), *Referendums: A Comparative Study of Practice and Theory*, Washington D.C.: American Enterprise Institute.

Ranney, Austin, ed. (1981). *The Referendum Device*, Washington D.C.: American Enterprise Institute.

Ranney, Austin, and Howard R. Penniman (1983). *Democracy in the Islands: The Micronesian Plebiscites of 1983*, Washington D.C.: American Enterprise Institute.

Rappard, William E. (1912). "The Initiative, Referendum and Recall in Switzerland," *Annals of the American Academy of Political Science* 43 (September 1912): 110–145.

Richmond, Anthony H., ed. (1982). "After the Referenda: The Future of Ethnic Nationalism in Britain and Canada," report of a joint international seminar held at the University College of North Wales, Bangor, November 5–9, 1981, Downsview, Ont.: Behavioral Research Institute, York University.

Robertson, C. L. (1988). "Switzerland Rejects the United Nations," *The Fletcher Forum* 12 (Summer 1988): 311–320.

Rodríguez, Emilio A. (1988). "Atlanticism and Europeanism: NATO and Trends in Spanish Foreign Policy." In Federico G. Gil and Joseph S. Tulchin (eds.), *Spain's Entry into NATO: Conflicting Political and Strategic Perspectives*, Boulder: Lynne Rienner Publishers.

Rosow, Stephen J. (1989). "Nuclear Deterrence, State Legitimation, and Liberal Democracy," *Polity*, 21 (Spring 1989): 346–367.

Rossiter, Clinton, ed. (1951). *The Federalist Papers*, New York: New American

Library.

Rummel, R. J. (1989). "The Politics of Cold Blood," *Society* 26 (November-December 1989): 32–40.

Russett, Bruce M. (1990). *Controlling the Sword*, Cambridge: Harvard University Press.

Sakamato, Yoshikazu (1991). "Introduction: The Global Context of Democratization," *Alternatives* 16 (Spring 1991): 119–128.

Salomon, Kim (1986). "The Peace Movement—An Anti-Establishment Movement," *Journal of Peace Research* 23 (June 1986): 115–128.

Schmidt, David D. (1989). *Citizen Lawmakers: The Ballot Initiative Revolution*, Philadelphia: Temple University Press.

Schumpeter, Joseph (1943). *Capitalism, Socialism, and Democracy*, London: George Allen & Unwin.

Seymour-Ure, Colin (1978). "Press and Referenda: The Case of the British Referendum of 1975," *Canadian Journal of Political Science* 11 (September 1978): 601–616.

Shapiro, Robert T., and Benjamin I. Page (1988). "Foreign Policy and the Rational Public," *Journal of Conflict Resolution* 32 (June 1988): 211–247.

Sherrill, Peter T. (1980). "Separatism and Quebec," *Current History* 79 (November 1980): 134–137, 145.

Small, Melvin (1987). "Influencing Decision Makers: The Vietnam Experience," *Journal of Peace Research* 24 (June 1987): 185–198.

Small, Melvin, and J. David Singer (1976). "The War-Proneness of Democratic Regimes, 1816–1965," *Jerusalem Journal of International Relations* 1/1 (1976): 50–69.

Smith, Gordon (1974). "The Referendum and Political Change," *Government and Opposition* 9 (Fall 1974): 294–305.

Smith, Gordon (1976). "The Functional Properties of Referendums," *European Journal of Political Research* 4 (March 1976): 1–23.

Smith, Joel, and Allan Kornberg (1983). "The Quebec Referendum: National or Provincial Event?" In Allan Kornberg and Harold D. Clark (eds.), *Political Support in Canada: The Crisis Years*, Durham, N.C.: Duke University Press.

Smith, Thomas B. (1986). "Referendum Politics in Asia," *Asian Survey* 26 (July 1986): 793–814.

Solo, Pam (1988). *From Protest to Policy*, Cambridge, Mass.: Ballinger.

Stålberg, Krister (1987). "Public Opinion in Finnish Foreign Policy." In *Yearbook of Finnish Foreign Policy, 1987*, Helsinki: Finnish Political Science Association.

Starr, Harvey (1991). "Democratic Dominoes," *Journal of Conflict Resolution*, 35 (June 1991): 356–381.

Thompson, Kenneth W. (1984). "The Ethical Dimensions of Diplomacy," *Review of Politics* 46 (July 1984): 367–388.

Thucydides (1951). Findley, John H. (ed.), *The History of the Peloponessian War*, New York: Modern Library.

Treverton, Gregory F. (1988). "Spain, the United States, and NATO: Strategic Facts and Political Realities." In Federico G. Gil and Joseph S. Tulchin (eds.), *Spain's Entry into NATO: Conflicting Political and Strategic Perspectives*, Boulder: Lynne Rienner Publishers.

Tusell, Javier (1988). "The Transition to Democracy and Spain's Membership in NATO." In Federico G. Gil and Joseph S. Tulchin (eds.), *Spain's Entry into NATO: Conflicting Political and Strategic Perspectives*, Boulder: Lynne Rienner Publishers.

U.S. Congress, Senate Committee on the Judiciary (1977). *Voter Initiative Constitutional Amendment*, hearings before the Subcommittee on the Constitution on S.J. Res. 67, 95th Cong., 1st Sess.

Valen, Henry (1973). "Norway 'No' to EEC," *Scandinavian Political Studies*, 8 (August 1973): 214–226.

Valen, Henry (1976). "National Conflict Structure and Foreign Politics: The Impact of the EEC Issue on Perceived Cleavages in Norwegian Politics," *European Journal of Political Research* 4/1 (1976): 47–82.

Valen, Henry, and Willy Martinussen (1977). "Electoral Trends and Foreign Policy in Norway: The 1973 Storting Election and the EEC Issue." In Karl Cerny (ed.), *Scandanavia at the Polls: Recent Political Trends in Denmark, Norway, and Sweden*, Washington, D.C.: American Enterprise Institute.

Vallés, Joseph, Francisco Pallarés and Ramón María Canals (1986). "The Referendum of 12 March 1986 on Spain's Remaining in NATO," *Electoral Studies* 5 (December 1986): 305–311.

Waller, Douglas C. (1984). "The Impact of the Nuclear Freeze Movement on Congress." In Steven E. Miller (ed.), *The Nuclear Weapons Freeze and Arms Control*, Cambridge, Mass.: Ballinger.

Waltz, Kenneth N. (1979). *Theory of International Relations*, Reading, Mass.: Addison-Wesley.

Walzer, Michael (1984). "Deterrence and Democracy," *New Republic* (July 2, 1984): 16–21.

Wambaugh, Sarah (1933). *Plebiscites in the World War*, Washington D.C.: Carnegie Endowment for International Peace.

Wasmuht, Ulrike C. (1984). "A Sociological Survey of American Peace Movements," *Alternatives* 9 (Spring 1984): 581–591.

Wiesteltier, Leon (1989). "It's a Small World After All," *New Republic* (September 18–25, 1989): 7–9.

Wilcox, Delos F. (1912). *Government by All the People, or the Initiative, the Referendum, and the Recall as Instruments of Democracy*, New York: Macmillan.

Wildhaber, Von Luzius (1986). "Das Schweizer Nein zu einer Vollmitgliedschaft in den Vereinten Nationen," *Europa-Archiv* 15 (August 10, 1986): 461–467.

Wright, Vincent (1978). "France." In David Butler and Austin Ranney (eds.), *Referendums: A Comparative Study of Practice and Theory*, Washington D.C.: American Enterprise Institute.

Zakheim, Dov S. (1973). "Britain and the EEC—Opinion Poll Data, 1970–1972," *Journal of Common Market Studies* 11 (March 1973): 191–233.

Zirakzadeh, Cyrus Ernesto (1989). "Economic Changes and Surges in Micro-Nationalist Voting in Scotland and the Basque Region of Spain," *Contemporary Studies in Society and History* 31 (April 1989): 318–339.

Zirakzadeh, Cyrus Ernesto (1991). *A Rebellious People: Basques, Protests, and Politics*, Reno: University of Nevada Press.

Zisk, Betty H. (1987). *Money, Media, and the Grass Roots: State Ballot Issues and the Electoral Process*, Newbury Park, Calif.: Sage.

Index

About the Book
and the Authors

Though democratic politics has sprung up where it never before existed, and democracy is now no longer the exception, but the rule, the representative form of democracy that prevails today may not be the ultimate form of democratic governance. The use of the referendum/initiative process, for example, has grown dramatically in Western democracies in the twentieth century. And not only are citizens sometimes deciding domestic policy questions, they also have begun to acquire an authoritative voice on international issues.

This book examines the growth, use, and impact of international-issue referendums and discusses current debates over the promise and perils of direct democracy. Comparing more than twenty international-issue referendums, the authors explore the political contexts that give rise to referendums, the dynamics and rhetoric of referendum campaigns, influences on voters' participation and decisions, and the effect of referendums on national foreign-policy traditions. They offer both empirical and normative conclusions.

The authors' specialties in international relations, comparative government, and political theory result in a book that has an especially broad appeal across the political science discipline.

John T. Rourke is professor of political science at the University of Connecticut and author of numerous articles and books, the most recent of which is *Making Foreign Policy: The United States, the Soviet Union, and China*.

Richard P. Hiskes is associate professor of political science at the University of Connecticut. His most recent book is *Science, Technology, and Policy Decisions*, which he wrote with Anne L. Hiskes.

Cyrus Ernesto Zirakzadeh is associate professor of political science at the University of Connecticut and author of *A Rebellious People: Basques, Protests, and Politics*.